Pop Cult: Religion and Popular Music

r

P

f

Dy

Ple

Also available from Continuum:

Call Me the Seeker, Michael J. Gilmore

The Continuum Companion to Religion and Film, edited by William L. Blizek

Fundamentalisms and the Media, edited by Stewart M. Hoover and Nadia Kaneva

Pop Cult: Religion and Popular Music

Rupert Till

continuum

Continuum International Publishing Group

The Tower Building
11 York Road
London SE1 7NX

80 Maiden Lane
Suite 704
New York NY 10038

www.continuumbooks.com

© Rupert Till, 2010

British Library Cataloguing-in-Publication Data
A catalogue record for this book is available from the British Library.

ISBN: HB: 978-0-8264-4592-6
   PB: 978-0-8264-3236-0

Library of Congress Cataloguing-in-Publication Data
Till, Rupert
  Pop cult : religion in popular music / Rupert Till.
    p. cm.
  Includes bibliographical references.
  ISBN-13: 978-0-8264-4592-6
  ISBN-10: 0-8264-4592-6
  ISBN-13: 978-0-8264-3236-0 (pbk.)
  ISBN-10: 0-8264-3236-0 (pbk.)
  1. Popular music—Religious aspects. 2. Popular music—Social aspects. I. Title.

ML3921.8.P67T55 2010
781.64—dc22

2010007108

Typeset by RefineCatch Limited, Bungay, Suffolk
Printed and bound in India by Replika Press Pvt Ltd

Contents

Acknowledgements

I would like to thank the following:

My wife for putting up with and supporting me as I have written this book; Huddersfield University, for supporting my research; Catherine Wilson for her work on Gorrilaz which provided some useful input; all of those who completed questionnaires or were interviewed.

I would like to thank all those who have contributed to the project by discussing my research with me and encouraging me, including Tom Howat; Hillegonda Rietvelt; Graham St. John; Gordon Lynch; Wolfman Styles and all the members of Ruby Tuesday, Headless, Chillage People and the Abstract Film Orchestra; Graham Cray; Lisa Colton; Bob Davis; the Walkley Posse Bridge Club; all the members of the Deep Crookes Vibe; everyone at Club 60; and various other IASPM-ites.

The chapter on personality cults draws upon material that is to be published in the *Implicit Religion Journal* and the *Journal of Beliefs and Values*. The chapter on trance cults draws on material that has been published in *Exploring Religion and the Sacred in a Media Age*, edited by Chris Deacy.

Introduction

Pleased to Meet You: Pop Cults and the Sacred Popular

This book investigates the cults of popular music that exist within what I term the sacred popular. Although it deals in some detail with the question of whether parts of popular music cultures are religions or new religious movements, this is not at the heart of this book. The main question being addressed is not whether pop cults are religions, but whether functions formerly served within society by religions are now being addressed by cults of popular music. It does suggest that popular music is like, or linked to, religion. It therefore uses language that might more usually be used to describe religion, in order to try to understand what popular music means to those involved, and what roles it serves in society. It explores the effects of postmodernity, or liquid culture, on religions, and the roles of cults of popular music in this process.

This book has been written using a blend of emic (from one's own experience) and etic (aiming for objectivity) perspectives. The idea of an absolutely objective academic opinion is a questionable concept. Even in scientific experiments, the choice of question, the method of investigation, and both context and previous experiences all colour the results. In this kind of book, investigating areas including the arts, music, religion, meaning, belief, philosophy and ethics, it is almost impossible for one's own context to not have an effect on what is written. In addition, there is a need to critically engage with what is being studied. I feel it is useful for the reader to understand the context from which I am writing, and therefore I will outline briefly how I came to write this book.

Much of this work has been participant observation, in which one acknowledges that the writer is closely involved with the subject they are writing about, and that this may interfere with a sense of complete objectivity. I have chosen this approach, as without that level of closeness participation brings, it is difficult to fully understand the subject under scrutiny. Without knowing these pop cults, genres and scenes, it is difficult to understand them. Like any other cult, only those within can best understand what is happening, as much is hidden from the outside, and yet only by stepping outside does one have a chance of describing accurately what is happening within. I have tried to balance these two competing dynamics of engagement and objective distance.

This book stems from a lifelong involvement in popular music. Perhaps it was becoming a teen Adam Ant fan that first gave me an experience of a pop cult. Having collected all of his records, the first concert I went to involved dressing as him, complete with a fake Hussars jacket, skull and crossbones belt buckle and cape. Later in life I took three degrees in music and eventually became a University lecturer specializing in teaching popular music.

In between I have attended, DJed and performed at Electronic Dance Music Culture events, performed in numerous rock bands, crowd surfed at metal concerts, danced to Britpop bands, camped out backstage at Glastonbury, collected records, organized Christian/ecumenical trance events, been promoter of a Sunday chill out club, seen bands perform in unlicensed underground venues before chart success, helped organize free parties or 'raves', been at Live Earth, mixed and lit live bands as a sound and lighting engineer, and spent too much time following music in virtual worlds.

This research has developed from sixteen years of teaching and studying popular music. I first became interested in the relationship between popular music and religion at a concert at Wembley stadium. It was a concert dedicated to the then-jailed African National Congress leader, Nelson Mandela, campaigning for him to be set free. The stadium was full of tens of thousands of music fans, looking forward to seeing a stellar line up of performers. Added to the expectation was the excitement of feeling that this concert had a greater purpose, and was part of the campaign to end the racist Apartheid based regime in South Africa, a campaign in which musicians had played a prominent role.

The first performer on stage was Sting. He walked on with a group of black backing singers, who began to sing one of his hits, beginning as an acapella chorus of voices, singing in a gospel style and harmony the lyrics 'free, free, set them free'. By the end of the first line, the 70,000 or more voices present were all singing as one, sending a message out to the millions watching the television signals that were being broadcast around the world by satellite.

My body reacted instinctively, and I can still remember the moment vividly. My body was filled with excitement, the hairs on my arms stood up, and the ones on the back of my neck prickled. I was washed with a wave of euphoria, my whole body tingled, filled with energy, with excitement, with the moment of Kairos, of time that stood still, that had quantity rather than pace. I experienced joy, elation, exhilaration, as well as passion, political motivation and conviction.

Had I been in a Church, Mosque or Synagogue, I would have regarded this as a religious experience. I had a background of involvement in Christian churches, I had sung in church choirs for years, and I had also attended Pentecostal services which had produced a very similar experience. Later in life I felt the sense of family of being in a band with a small but committed group of fans. I understood the rituals of performing music every night for two weeks. I enjoyed the thrill of leading an audience who applauded my performance. I experienced a sense of rapture achieved by spending hours dancing to indie, disco or house music. No longer actively involved in Christianity, as a DJ, musician, promoter and clubber I came across dynamics and activities I recognized as religious in club culture contexts, or at least that I recognized as partly the same human functions, experiences and feelings.

Armed and enthused by these and other experiences, but older and less caught up or influenced by and involved in them, I have tried to investigate how and why it is that popular music can lead to such experiences. How it inspires devoted and obsessive fans, and why it is that it seems to fulfil some of the same purposes in society as religion.

Within contemporary postmodernity, in liquid times, religion is being deregulated, and belief, meaning, faith and religion are to be found in popular culture as well as in traditional organized religions. An interesting (and potentially legally significant in the UK) example of this is a recent court judgement that effectively equated commitment to ecological views to religion, and granted it equal treatment in law.

The man involved believed he was being treated unfairly as a result of his ecological beliefs, and had appealed to the court to be given permission to submit his case under UK Employment Equality (Religion and Belief) regulations that are phrased to cover any religion, religious belief, or philosophical beliefs.

A solicitor involved in the case, Shah Qureshi, said:

> Essentially what the judgment says is that a belief in man-made climate change and the alleged resulting moral imperative is capable of being a philosophical belief and is therefore protected by the 2003 religion or belief regulations. (BBC 2009, Online)

But the ruling was challenged, by the employer involved, on the grounds that green views were not the same as religious or philosophical beliefs. The court ruling means that belief systems other than mainstream organized religions like Christianity, Islam and Judaism, may be considered equal under the law, and recognizes that in contemporary society what equates to a religion is a complicated issue.

The Guardian newspaper, among others, reported the findings.

> Mr Justice Michael Burton, presiding, decided that 'A belief in man-made climate change, and the alleged resulting moral imperatives, is capable if genuinely held, of being a philosophical belief for the purpose of the 2003 Religion and Belief Regulations.' In his written judgment, Mr Justice Burton outlined five tests to determine whether a philosophical belief could come under employment regulations on religious discrimination
>
> - The belief must be genuinely held.
> - It must be a belief and not an opinion or view based on the present state of information available.

- It must be a belief as to a weighty and substantial aspect of human life.
- It must attain a certain level of cogency, seriousness, cohesion and importance.
- It must be worthy of respect in a democratic society, not incompatible with human dignity and not conflict with the fundamental rights of others.

Humanism was given as an example meeting the criteria, while belief in a political party or the supreme nature of Jedi knights, from the Star Wars movies, were offered as ones that do not. (Guardian 2009, Online)

The question of what constitutes a religion is a complex issue, which will be discussed in Chapter 1. It is an issue that has moved beyond the worlds of priests and theologians, as is at large within popular culture.

The secular theory is becoming increasingly disavowed. We are no longer moving towards a secular world. Christian and Islamic fundamentalism both have experienced an upsurge, and movements and activities that bear many similarities to religions are emerging in unexpected places within society.

Meanwhile, music has become increasingly significant. Many pieces of music are testament to this. The disco song 'Lost in Music' tells us that for the singer, or for the dancer in the disco who is singing along to the lyrics, 'music is my salvation'. The New Radicals 'You only get what you give', proclaims 'you've got the music in you'. Another disco singer claims, 'I've got the music in me'. Numerous other examples will be discussed in more detail during the course of the rest of this book.

We should not perhaps be surprised that music is being linked in a number of ways to religion. Music venues have always been places that are full of meaning, whether it is the group identity formation of the rock concert, or the loss of self on the dancefloor. Religious venues such as temple and cathedrals have often been filled with music, and music and religion are inseparable in many traditional cultures.

In Chapter 1, I introduce the terms 'cult' and 'new religious movement'. I discuss definitions of what constitutes a religion, and discuss why I think it appropriate to discuss elements of popular music as pop cults. I use the word cult as a way to reclaim the term, and in order to harness its more oppositional references. New religious movement is sociological term, and I discuss why cult might here be more a relevant term for artefacts of popular culture. In Chapter 2, I look at sex within popular music. I discuss body–mind duality within religion, and attitudes to sexuality within African American music. I investigate how rock and metal music address sexuality, looking in particular at the video for the song 'Girls, Girls, Girls' by Motley Crue. I go on to focus on Madonna, and in particular what she means by 'Like A Prayer'. Chapter 3 addresses drug cults of popular music, addressing the different music scenes that have featured drug taking. Chapter 4 looks at cults of personality, and the construction of popular icons. It looks in particular at the work of Prince, and at his performance of 'Let's Go Crazy', in the film *Purple Rain*.

Chapter 5 looks at the importance of locality in cults of popular music, investigating in particular the development of Britpop. Chapter 6 Looks at virtual cults, at the artificial construction of popular music bands for consumption by the media or to be sold by the music industry. It looks at the formation of animated band Gorillaz, and at how and why this cartoon group emerged. Chapter 7 discusses the death cults of metal and rock music. It looks at the 27 club of dead popstars, at why risky lifestyle choices are common among musicians, and at the audience/performer dynamics that have led to the death of so many famous musicians. It looks at how this seeming death cult of popular music played out in the Norwegian black metal scene, leading to church burnings, suicide and murder. Chapter 8 investigates the possession trance cults of Electronic Dance Music Culture, and Chapter 9 draws conclusions, and analyses the way pop cults have been constructed and developed.

This book looks largely at British and American cults of popular music, although this is related to music from other cultures. I use the phrase 'pop cults' as a shorthand for 'popular music cults', rather than using pop with a more strict definition, that might define is as relating to chart or commercial elements of popular music. I will discuss Christianity more than other organized religions, partly because it has been a dominant force within Western culture historically, and partly because it is the religion that has had most effect on, and interaction with, Western popular music.

Chapter 1

Lost in Music: Pop Cults and New Religious Movements

Cults and Pop

Music is found in almost all human societies, is a human universal and is almost always linked with meaning and belief, as Nettl (2000) has discussed. In most traditional societies, Western European culture being a notable exception, musical activity is a social or group-based activity, and is associated with the achievement of altered states of consciousness. Aldridge and Fachner (2006) discuss this in detail. Music has the power to exert enormous influence on the human mind, especially when people are gathered in groups, and the euphoric power of group dynamics is brought into play. This chapter discusses cults of popular music, discussing the nature of cults, and how important music is to our belief systems, setting the scene for the following chapters.

The use of the word 'cult' in the title of this book is both provocative and deliberate. It is a term loaded with meaning, which with this book I will try to recontextualize, reconstruct, redefine, redeem and reclaim. It is a term that is often used in a pejorative or negative way. Being a member of a cult is often seen a bad thing, and it is generally someone external who describes an organization as a cult or as cultic, not the group members who describe themselves as such. This book will describe popular music scenes and movements as cults, not in order to suggest they are wrong and bad, but rather as a joyous affirmation of their glorious transgression of all those things that those who would use the word cult negatively hold dear.

Cults have been studied the most by two groups of people. Those who study religion, and in particular those studying the sociology of religion, describe cults as new religious movements (NRMs). They use this term so as not to give power to those who have traditionally used the word cult to attack such groups and support their own beliefs and attitudes, and in order to remain neutral towards the subjects of their study. NRM is the politically correct term for a Cult. NRMs are seen as important signs of significant changes in culture, and of society coming to terms with these changes. They are an artefact of postmodern culture, of liquid times or the post-historical, of the era we are living in. That they are prominent and numerous is perhaps the result of the impact of postmodernity on religion.

The other main body of people who study cults are anti-cult groups. These organizations, such as the Cultic Studies Association (formerly known as the American Family Foundation) and Family Action Information and Resource, oppose cults, sometimes offering deprogramming or intervention in order to 'save' cult members, or more often producing information about cults, warning members of religious (usually Christian) groups about the dangers of cults, and generally doing a good job of inadvertently providing marketing, promotion and advertising for obscure groups with few members to a wider audience, and generating a sense of moral panic or outrage. Anti-cult groups often have fundamentalist or extremist Christian groups at their core, but despite that they might be defined as cults by their own descriptions, they seem to not see the irony in this situation. Cowan and Bromley (2008) and Chryssides and Wilkins (2006) provide a useful introduction to NRMs, and the Catholic Truth Society (1986) has provided other interesting relevant information.

It should also be pointed out that the term cult has also been (and was perhaps originally) used to describe localized traditional religious practices that were specific to a particular tribe or group. This sort of cult, whether linked to ancestor worship, spirit possession, the worship of a local deity or a set of peculiar and/or individual practices, has been demonized in much the same way as NRMs by fundamentalist groups, although again the pentecostal-ist practices of many of these groups are very similar in nature to spirit posses-sion, when analysed objectively. Generally however these will not be the kind of cults that this book will be discussing, although they will become part of the discussion at some points.

A number of religious movements of various ages have been called cults, for example the Church of Scientology, Unification Church ('Moonies'), International Society for Krishna Consciousness, The Family, Rastafariansim, Transcendental Meditation, The Branch Davidians (David Koresh/Waco) and Wiccans. Anti-cult groups have defined cults such as these and others as having particular properties. Although I would in no way suggest these are accurate definitions of what goes on within these groups, investigating these suggested properties will help to explain why it is that I have chosen to use the term cult in this context.

Cults are often described as involving dedication to a single person. They are often thought of as having a charismatic individual human leader (or leaders) who claims to be divine, God-like or have some special link, com-munication with or blessing from divine authority. The long-dead divinised human leaders of older established religions, have at least the advantage over these NRMs that their spiritual authority has outlasted the majority of the innumerable individuals who claim to have a greater religious authority than the general populace, and indeed it is this track record that principally distinguishes established religions (old religious movements or ORMs) from their newer equivalents. The leaders of NRMs are usually alive or recently deceased in comparison to figures such as Jesus, Mohamed or Buddha, usually less than 300 years old.

Membership of a cult is usually thought of as involving a very high level of commitment of time to the group. This level of involvement is sometimes seen as damaging relationships with family members, and as creating an us-versus-them mentality. Cults are sometimes seen as isolationist and secretive, and although many of the groups' activities may relate to gaining new members or converts, it may at first be difficult to gain access to the group or to find out about it. It may be that a level of commitment must be proven in order to become a full member of the group.

Cults are often accused of using unethically manipulative techniques of persuasion or control, although others say that such brain washing is a myth, and that this is merely strong social influence or peer pressure. However cults are often accused of indoctrination, often using repetition or sensory deprivation. Another supposed characteristic of a cult is the use of mind-altering practices to excess. This can relate simply to a substantial focus on meditation, although in some cases the use of psychotropic or psychedelic substances is associated with cult membership, especially in traditional contexts.

Whereas use of psychoactive drugs is seen in some way as 'natural' in traditional cult contexts, the use of drugs in Western culture, especially if their use is illegal, is perceived as transgressive of either mainstream practices, or more particularly, of the normative practices of those describing the religious movement as a cult. Other practices that are considered outside of 'normal' behaviour for those within a religious organization are sometimes described as characteristics of cults. Sexual practices that are linked to religious beliefs, or outside the normal conventions of for example Christianity, are often associated with cults.

Another element described by anti-cult groups as being a typical sign that an organization is a cult, is a preoccupation with making money, or that members are expected to give a large amount of their money to the group. Other suggested cult characteristics relate to particular cultural traditions, such as the wearing of a particular style or type of clothing or haircut. Some cults have become associated with death or suicides. Some have been characterized by reference to new forms of Paganism, such as Witchcraft, Druidry, Wicca and Satanism.

For some, such as the anti-cult groups, cults are the epitome of all that is deviant and dangerous. For others NRMs offer an insight into the way that humans construct meaning within contemporary culture, and into how religions are created and constructed. What may be a cult to one person may be a normal tradition to another, and the term is frequently used, as Cowan and Bromley (2008, p. 14) put it, as 'a 4 letter word for any religion someone doesn't like'. Words like sect and cult are used to describe organizations that do not reflect an individuals own preferences, choices and traditions, using terms like religion, church or denomination, to indicate an organization that an individual considers authentic. Thus religious authenticity in this context is performed by the individual, and dependent on the opinion of the individual performer.

For others NRMs in the west are a result of what that the Christian church is failing to do, is a result of mainstream religions in Western Europe becoming disconnected from, and out of touch with, public opinion following the rapid cultural change that has occurred in the twentieth century. Religions have always had a role in the control of the many by the few, in political and social control and formation. However, in a literate culture with widespread education, where religions have become heavily influenced by accumulated cultural practices rather than their original teachings, if those cultural practices and preferences become out of pace with public opinion, then the religion concerned is in danger of no longer being culturally relevant.

To illustrate this, let us for a moment consider whether a Christian church could be considered a cult. A single living individual usually is given the individual responsibility for having a divine calling to communicate with God. They often have an authority among their followers that cannot easily be challenged. Their original leader, Jesus Christ, was the inspiration for an offshoot heretical organization that sprang up from within Judaism. Christian churches often require a great deal of the time of their members, many describe a church 'family' which replaces an individuals' original family to some extent, and they have their own separate culture, music, festivals, social events. This could be considered to be creating an us-versus-them dynamic. They describe those not with their organizations as 'unbelievers' or 'non-Christians', further creating an us-versus-them mentality. They often focus much of their time on trying to convert others to their cause. They often use mind-control techniques such as repetitive chanting or singing, prayer or meditation, as well manipulating opinions with emotive preaching.

Attitudes to sexuality are very different from mainstream culture within Christianity, with sexual activity generally being repressed without a church-authorized ceremony; homosexuality being persecuted and taboo; and women rarely being treated equally to men. This is often the case even in countries where there are laws against discrimination based on gender or sexuality. Despite these official church attitudes, numerous examples of sexual abuse or manipulation by church officials have come to light, and there are actually many gay and women priests.

As well as spending a large amount of time on the group's activities, members are expected to give their money to provide for the chosen spiritual leaders, and to pay for the opulent lifestyles and lavish accommodation, jewellery and garments of the highest leaders, despite many such groups having huge financial holdings. Church leaders have peculiar clothing to wear, and religious literature often features satanic imagery and references to mythical creatures. It is clear that to some extent Christian anti-cult groups have projected their own characteristics onto cults, and defined them in terms that actually describe their own beliefs, experience and definitions, or that relate to their own beliefs. To some extent, cults are brought into being by the anti-cult groups that attempt to define and pigeonhole them.

Part of the difficulty in the defining of NRMs/cults is the complexity of trying to adequately define religion. Greil and Bromley (2003) provide a useful discussion of this topic. Although religion is a very commonly used word, it is one that is used to mean many different things by different people. Some writers have defined religions as having to involve a belief in a supernatural being. There are a number of religions that do not involve belief in such a supernatural deity however, and so this can perhaps be excluded from a definition of religion.

Many simply describe religion as those things related to religious organizations, either those organizations traditionally regarded and recognized as religions, or those who choose to regard themselves as religions. This is rather a circular argument; it is not particularly helpful to a definition of religion to describe it as that which is religious. For others a religion is a set of beliefs and practices.

Some have described religion as that involving something that is treated with the highest level of seriousness. This must be seen as a personal choice, as one person will regard something as of the utmost importance (for example adherence to a rule regarding eating a particular food), while this is of no relevance for someone else. Combining these elements, perhaps a religion is something that is treated by an individual with the highest level of seriousness, and that involves a set of beliefs and practices. Separate then, or different, from religion and the religious, are spirituality (which usually refers to relationships with other people), mysticism and the transcendental (which relate to experiences), cosmology (which relates to people's relationship with the universe) and other associated terms.

Durkheim (1965) has described religious activity in terms of those things that relate to the sacred and/or profane. One of the ways that some pop stars have achieved fame is by courting notoriety by mixing the sacred and the profane. If Durkheim defines religion as that relating to the sacred and profane, the secular is regarded perhaps as being that existing between these two poles. This book aims to show how popular music mixes, confuses and plays with imagery and traditions that are traditionally regarded as either sacred or profane, transgressing borders and creating a 'Sacred Popular' set of popular cults that lie between the two, in the realm of a popular culture often thought of as secular, but in fact drenched in meaning, belief, faith, worship and ritual, and thus presented here as religious.

For this reason the term 'sacred' is used in this paper to refer to anything relating to religion or meaning, referring to those things that are especially important to an individual, whether within popular music culture or Christian theology, adopting a broad rather than narrow interpretation of the term, and using it to reference Durkheim's definition. In the same way 'profane' is used to point out those things often presented as transgressional, outside of 'normal' behaviour or conventional mainstream morality, or in opposition to religion in general and Christianity in particular. Sacred and profane are terms used in order to illustrate where this polarity is in operation.

The meaning of the term religion has been changed by use within popular culture to include a wide range of activities. Religion and the religious have increasingly become used to describe aspects of what was previously regarded as secular culture. If something is done 'religiously' it must be, has to be done, regularly, it cannot be missed. It is done without questioning, other commitments must be laid aside in order that this activity can continue, and there are often rituals that are associated with the activity. Often the activity would have to occur even if there would be good reasons why it should not, such is the commitment to it, and it has priority above other things. As less people in the West have come to describe themselves as Christians, other activities have begun to replace traditional religions as the focus of their beliefs, hopes, faith and commitments, and a variety of things have been studied as being religious.

The study of such secularized religions has taken a number of forms. Gordon Lynch's book *Understanding Theology and Popular Culture* (2005) is a good introduction to such theories. One approach has been to regard older, traditional mainstream religions as primary institutions, and others as secondary institutions. Secondary institutions are described as having a lesser level of requirement of the individual, less strict rules and freer codes of how to behave. Such distinctions are problematic, as for example Christianity has groups of liberal adherents who interpret its traditions as guidelines rather than rules and focus on that everything is permissible. This smacks of the older established religions being given a higher level of authenticity because they are established, and because it is adherents to them who write much religious literature.

More useful perhaps to this book is the work of writers such as Edward Bailey (2001) and others, who differentiate between implicit and explicit religion. Explicit religion is that identified by the participants as religion. Implicit religions are those that have all the hallmarks of religion, but that may be focused on elements that may be regarded as belonging within the secular realm, or include elements that are not within easily defined boundaries of the sacred and profane. Implicit religions often involve an intense level of commitment and seriousness as well as a set of beliefs and practices. Activities described as being implicit religions have included atheism, vegetarianism, consumerism, sport and various elements of popular music and its associated cultures.

The cultures associated with these activities often require a huge level of commitment, regular participation, extreme seriousness, irrational faith and belief which is instinctive and passionate as much as it is rational and reasoned, ritualized participation and strict codes of practice. This indicates that they are either religious they can be regarded as such, or they are the same as the religious. Whether or not one agrees that these are religions, by defining them as such, a different form of analysis can be applied to them, which can offer new interpretations and insights into popular cultural forms. This kind of analysis indicates that some of the functions of religion within society are so important to human culture, that when traditional religious organizations begin to diminish and recede, they are replaced by other activities that take over these functions.

Large institutionalized religions have historically been integrated into political systems and played a part in social control by elite ruling classes. They have thus integrated the opinions and preferences, as well as reflected the interests, of these elements of society. As popular culture has emerged, and education has spread from the few to the masses, it is perhaps not surprising that older religions that still have such class-ridden moral and social attitudes embedded within them, have ceased to be chosen by the majority of popular culture and society as the centre of commitments, beliefs and codes of practice. And it makes complete sense that popular religions should spring up, not be recognized as religions, in particular by ORMs that cannot compete with their more culturally relevant replacements, and be regarded as implicit rather than explicit religion.

Popular music cultures are a common form of popular or implicit religion. Rather than describing them as NRMs, I have described them as cults for a number of reasons. First, popular music cultures fit many of the typical characteristics of cults already mentioned. They are usually focused around one individual figure or a group of figures who are treated as being special or more important than anyone else and are often worshipped as though they were divine. Their claim to have some kind of special link with the divine, or divine authority, comes through their musical abilities. These are often identified as being a 'gift', some kind of magical ability that they possess or have been given, and that raises them above other people. When asked why they make music, musicians often claim that they want to express their feelings, as though in some way their emotional expression were more important, interesting or powerful than those of others. They become known as icons or rock gods, and when dead, become idealized and their status is often described as legendary and superhuman.

Adherence to a particular musical group or popular music scene can involve large levels of commitment and participation, as will be described in subsequent chapters. Parents are described as becoming alienated from their growing teenage offspring, as the latter choose pop cultures as alien as possible to their parents and families, joining youth cultures that deliberately aim to separate themselves from previous generations. One may have to spend much time becoming part of a scene, getting to know enough to be accepted within this scene as an 'authentic' member, finding out about the often secretive and hard to find detailed insider knowledge and sub-cultural capital available. The term fan, or fanatic, gives an indication of the level of commitment of pop cult members, fanatics can be obsessive, changing their characters and behaviours to copy pop icons, turning bedrooms into temples to stars with posters and photos, reading about their heroes and heroines and obsessively collecting and consuming their paraphernalia.

At the centre of such pop cults are shadowy industry figures who are rarely seen by the public, and who are only known to the high ranking initiates of the pop star world. Managers, promoters, A&R men, record company executives, pluggers, sales forces, DJs, producers, tour managers, agents and others exist in a backstage world closed to the ordinary pop cult fan(atic) membership. These figures work tirelessly to increase the membership of the pop cults they are involved in, obsessed with trying to make the pop icons involved internationally known, and with making as much money as possible.

There is evidence of brainwashing type activities. Fans repeatedly sing along to, or listen to, music that is in itself repetitive. This is a form of repetitive chanting that reinforces the messages contained within the music. Marketing, lighting, sound, strobe, laser, video and other effects are used to enhance the effects of the music, and ultimately manipulate cult members into spending increasing amounts of money on group-related activities. Special venues have ritualized activities, which feature scenes of ecstatic loss of self. Crowd dynamics are artfully used and manipulated to great effect. Illegal and legal drugs of various kinds are often associated with pop cults, as are unusual and transgressional sexual practices. Pop cults have often involved specific clothing that identifies members; suicides by cult members and/or leaders; and references to new forms of paganism including Satanism. Pop music cults fit almost all of the criteria that anti-cults have used as typical indicators of cultic activity, including that they have often been represented by fundamentalist religious groups as being evil and/or immoral.

There are very powerful reasons why musical cultures can be so readily identified as religious, and as cults or cultic. Music is not just a form of entertainment; it has important roles in human culture and society. In all traditional human societies, music is used within rituals, in addressing the supernatural, to change an individual's consciousness or to change or set the ambiance of an event. It is also often associated with dance, or to be more specific, dance is usually accompanied by music of some kind. Dance and music are intimately related, and in fact in some cultures are so intertwined that there are no separate words for music and dance, one single word being used to mean both. As Ehrenreich says,

> In large parts of Africa, for example, the identification between communal dance and music, on the one hand, and what Europeans might call "religion" on the other, was profound. The term the Tswanas of Southern Africa use for dance (*go bina*) also means "to venerate," and in the Bantu language group of southern, central and eastern Africa, the word *ngoma* can mean "ritual," "cult", "song-dance" or simply "drum". (2006, p. 157)

As this quote explains, music and dance are often intimately related to religion and meaning. Much of contemporary western popular music is derived from African American music. Popular music features this link between music, dance, religion and cult, perhaps partly from deep-rooted influences from Africa, but also perhaps because such relationships are a deeply embedded part of human culture and perform important social functions. Dance turns music into motion, synchronizes the body to time, and writes music in terms of space. Indeed music can act to change the way one perceives time. While we have one word for time, the ancient Greeks usefully had two words for different types of time, chronos and kairos. Chronos is the sense of time of everyday experience. It is time that flows, that ticks by second by second, the time that passes minute by minute, hour by hour, day by day and year by year. Kairos is time that has quality, that is that moment in time when the clock seems to have stopped, when one is acutely aware of one's position in time, when one understands at a deeper level what time it is. Kairos is the time of the ecstatic moment, is the way time passes when one has lost track of chronos (time), is the moment that seems to last an eternity, the long period of time that seems to have passed in an instant. Music seems to be a bridge between chronos and kairos, capable of moving a person between the two.

When one experiences music and/or dance, one is no longer synchronized to the pulse of the second, the hour, the day, the year, one's internal clock is linked to the musical time that is passing, whether bars, beats or phrases. It thus helps one to become unlocked from chronos, from a normal perception of time, and for one's state of mind or consciousness to change. It also allows a number of people to synchronize their sense of time, and their bodies, together, which is a powerful communal experience. It seems that music may have developed in humans at the same time as fire, shelter and tools (Freeman 2000, p. 422), as the ritual technology needed to bond large groups together, to pass on knowledge and build long-term settlements, relies so heavily on music. The group-based experiences that are common to many forms of popular music, and the sense of community, identity and belonging they engender are highly significant, and will be discussed in detail in later chapters.

Since the renaissance and enlightenment, intellectual culture has been struggling to understand and control the world it inhabits. At the end of the modern era this resulted in theoretical approaches to music that focused on the intellectual rather than the emotional, the rational rather than the religious, on reason rather than faith. This resulted in art music traditions somewhat disconnected from the body, individualized and intellectualized. This art music was separated by an intellectual superiority complex that placed it above the vernacular, and that had become separated from popular mainstream culture. Postmodernity marked the end of the power of intellectual elites formed from the upper classes to define what is good or worthy culture in general, and music in particular. As Zygmunt Bauman put it, postmodernity ... brings 're-enchantment' of the world after the protracted and earnest, though in the end inconclusive, modern struggle to dis-enchant it ... Dignity has been returned to emotions; legitimacy to the 'inexplicable', nay *irrational*, sympathies and loyalties which cannot 'explain themselves' in terms of their usefulness and purpose ... Fear of the void has been blunted and assuaged ... we learn to learn to live with events and acts that are ... inexplicable. Some of us would even say that it is such events and acts that constitute the hard, irremovable core of the human predicament. (1993, p. 33)

Postmodernity has put popular music on the same footing as art music. It has in a similar way allowed popular religions, or cults, to challenge traditional religions for the allegiance of the populace, to offer alternative pop cults that can provide a focus for commitment, belief and ritualistic practices. While traditional religions avoid cult-like behaviour, the music industry has no such scruples and has moved in to fill the void left by western religions that are still associated with a disenchanted mainstream culture. Pop cults happily accept their implicitly religious roles, practising what Small calls the art of social happiness:

The art of social happiness is the supreme human art, to which all other arts, and the sciences also, must contribute. The arts, and especially that great performance art of music-dance-drama-masking-costume for which we lack a name, are vital means by which human identities and relationships are explored, affirmed and celebrated. (1987, p. 395)

The Catholic Truth Society (1986) has discussed why people join cults. It listed a number of reasons, or needs; the need to belong, feel special and be involved; the need for spiritual guidance and vision; the search for answers, wholeness, cultural identity and transcendence. Tied up in traditions and its socio-political associations, and with a credibility gap in terms of cultural relevance and reference, mainstream religions do not convince mainstream cultures that they can address these issues, despite their best efforts. Pop cults are regarded as far more able to succeed, as we shall see in a series of examples.

Chapter 2

Let's Talk About Sex: Sex Cults of Popular Music

For a number of reasons, popular music has often been associated with sexuality. This chapter investigates popular music as a sex cult, in particular looking at the work of Madonna. Many forms, styles and genres of popular music have traditions of featuring sexually explicit material. This chapter asks why that is, when this began, how it happened, who are the main protagonists and what this involved.

Popular music has often operated in oppositional to mainstream culture. This is part of it being firmly placed within popular culture, as opposed to high society. An oppositional attitude gives subcultural capital, authenticity and authority to popular music forms, and assists participants in developing a sense of individual identity. Within youth culture, a sense of transgression allows a distance from the culture of older generations. This creates an environment in which there is a perceived freedom to create an individual identity. In this context enough space is sought to allow personality and a sense of self to develop. Thus popular music styles that have developed often contain elements that might be regarded as oppositional. One powerful vehicle for transgression of mainstream cultural values is through sexual behaviour that contravenes the norms of 'polite society'.

The break-up of clear boundaries between popular culture and society is one of the characteristics of postmodernity, or liquid times, the era we live in today. In Europe human culture has sought since the enlightenment to find the latest new understandings of the world, and by doing so has hoped to feel able to control it. Since this period, science fought to challenge old assumptions, traditions and superstitions, and to show that the mind and reason had the power to explain the universe. Cosmology, our understanding of the universe, began to be constructed by science rather than religion. Intellect and thought began to be seen as a way to gain power, as opposed to (or in partnership with) physical or religious power being used as the primary route to dominance and control of society. The constant seeking of the latest technology and knowledge became a fight by humanity to control and master its surroundings, a struggle against embodiment and environment. This process has accompanied the efforts of political and ruling elites to control the mass populace. The control of the many by the few has required the control of the body by the mind, something that was achieved as much by religious regulation as by politics and law (although the two are closely related).

Before the ready availability of contraception in the twentieth century, the control of sexual behaviour has been an important part of the control of society. Religious organizations have often been in the forefront of efforts to control the sexual activities of individuals. Within European culture, sexual ethics based on Christian morality have prohibited sexual activity outside marriage, and have espoused a restrained, one might say repressed, attitude to sexuality, especially after the rise of Calvinism and Puritanism during the sixteenth century. This has played a major part in the development of a negative attitude to the physical in general, and to sexuality in particular.

Cartesian duality and dualism are terms used to describe a dualistic attitude to the body, and to the mind. Within a dualistic way of thinking the body and mind are considered to be fundamentally different. The mind is the focus of reason, intellect and control, while the body is seen as the site of instinct, unthinking reflexes and uncontrolled emotional response. Put more simply that which is associated with the mind is presented as good and those things associated with the body are bad. This way of thinking has its roots within Christianity, in as early as the first century AD, in St. Augustine's background as a Manichaean and his interests, via the work of Plotinus, in Plato's ideas.

Augustine's neo-Platonism focused on happiness being beyond the physical. His experience of Manichaeism instilled in him the idea of a separation between good and evil, with the body being associated with evil. After his conversion to Christianity, Augustine reacted against his own previous sexual behaviour, which he now regarded as sinful. He maintained a dualistic approach to the physical that was rooted in his earlier religious interests, rather than any theology specific to Christianity. St. Augustine became an important and influential figure in early Christianity, and became an important influence on Christian theology and traditions. His life and influence is well described in many texts, including that by Marrou (1957). He is perhaps only one example of the religious thinking that led Christianity to have a repressive attitude to sexuality in particular and the body in general; there are of course many other complex influences that developed this philosophy.

This kind of dualistic attitude is problematic, as we have begun to understand that the body is a holistic system, in which there are rarely clear and simple distinctions like mind and body. However, this dualism has been a significant part of Western European philosophy and religion for many years, and it still has a strong influence on contemporary culture. Augustine was a key influence on the Calvinists and puritans. These and other Christian traditions adopted and reinforced a negative attitude to the body, and also to the physical world in general. This meant a repression of sexuality, with bodily activities seen in a negative light. Catholic priests are still barred from sexual relation-ships, sexual activity outside marriage is largely prohibited by the mainstream Christian church, and homosexuality is also regarded as sinful. More than this, sexuality is rarely discussed freely and openly within Christian contexts.

The Christian bible speaks often about adultery, but very little about the sexual activities of the unmarried. The bible was written at a time when attitudes to sexual activity were very different. It was set in a Jewish culture with its own specific traditions of marriage. The conservative sexual tradi-tions adopted by the church, based on negative attitudes to the body, are, in the twenty-first century, substantially out of touch with attitudes within contemporary society. In addition, biblical rules outlawing homosexuality, designed for example to address homosexual activity among temple prosti-tutes in biblical times, sit uncomfortably within a church that has many gay priests, and a Western culture where homosexuality is broadly accepted. Issues relating to sexuality and physicality have dogged the Christian church in recent times, partly because there is a huge gap between normal sexual practice in contemporary culture, and the rules of Christian tradition. In a contempor-ary culture where the equal treatment of women has long been accepted, the adoption of women priests by the Anglican Church, and the selection of female bishops in the USA, has caused deep schisms, although such sexual discrimi-nation would be illegal in most other organizations in England. The difficulty Christianity has with issues of gender and sexuality, has given popular culture leverage to appear counter-cultural, oppositional, taboo and irreverent in rela-tion to Christianity. Popular music has mined this seam, this sociological fault line, in order to take advantage of the reaction of the socially conservative forces it contains.

Much Western popular music has roots in African American tradition, a tradition that has a different relationship to the physical to white European mainstream culture. It is important not to indulge in a kind of orientalism or African essentialism, which might pretend that there are simple ways to describe all African (or African American) culture. However, it is true to say that the sub-Saharan African culture that influenced African American culture, did not generally have the same history of dualistic philosophy as Europe. Plato, Descartes, Plotinus and Augustine have had less influence, and a differ-ent attitude to the body, dancing and the physical is apparent in African tradi-tional cultures, and to a lesser extent African American culture.

This can be seen within a number of African American musical traditions. It may or may not be the case that this is an influence from Africa, this may have its roots in the African diaspora, but it is certainly the case that African American musical forms have a more deeply ingrained, more effusive, more effervescent, more significant physicality than many European musical cul-tures. This physicality is played out in the various dance styles of a number of forms of African American music, which have had a strong influence on Western popular music since the beginning of the twentieth Century.

The African American dance and musical styles of swing, jazz, charlston and ragtime all had an influence on Western music, becoming very popular, especially as developments in technology made recordings of this music more readily available. Blues, rhythm'n'blues, rock'n'roll, soul, funk, disco, ska, reggae, hip hop, rap, and house styles followed, also becoming popular within, and adopted and appropriated by, mainstream white culture in the USA and Europe. Many of these traditions had dance cultures associated with them as well as an openly sexualized context, and this was perceived to be an important part of their appeal.

For example early blues musicians often performed in jook (or juke) joints. These were not just bars or music venues, but often also sometimes acted as dance halls, brothels and casinos. Many early blues musicians such as Jelly Roll Morton and Blind Lemon Jefferson spent time accompanying striptease or performed in brothels, and the Storyville area of New Orleans famous for its early blues and jazz scene was an area of the city in which prostitution was legal. It is perhaps no surprise then that there is a tradition of blues material with sexually explicit lyrical material.

Sexual references are suggestive in blues music such as 'That Black Snake Moan' by Blind Lemon Jefferson, or 'Pig Meat Papa' by Leadbelly, rather than being specific. Within white culture these songs were controversial not only because they made reference to sexual activity, but also because recordings allowed the discussion of sex by black men and women to be heard by white women and men. In other examples sexual references were coded to make them more acceptable. For example references to the kitchen were used to disguise sexual references to a song's true meaning, for example in 'Ain't got nobody to grind my coffee' by Clara Smith, or 'Kitchen Man' by Bessie Smith.

Other songs were overtly sexual. In 'Shave 'Em Dry' by Lucille Bogan, she sings 'I got nipples on my titties as big as the end of your thumb, I got something between my legs can make a dead man come'. It was easier for black female singers to get away with singing songs with sexual content in the lyrics than it was for their male counterparts. Black female blues singers were able to achieve success with mixed black and white audiences far more readily than men, as for a white man to lust after a black woman was more socially acceptable at the time than for a black man to be openly sexual in a mixed audience.

As blues developed into rhythm'n'blues (R'n'B), sex remained a regular topic within its lyrical content. Wynonie Harris is a good example of an R'n'B musician who deliberately sexualized his performances in order to attract audiences. He gyrated his hips, curled his top lip and windmilled his arms around when performing live, successfully appealing to the women in his audiences, having a physical act full of innuendo and sex appeal. R'n'B also had coded terms for having sex, one of which was to 'rock'n'roll'. One of Harris's hit songs 'Good Rockin' Tonight' is a good example of this, as are 'Rock Around the Clock', and 'Shake, Rattle and Roll'. In all of these songs the word rock is a thinly disguised replacement for the word 'fuck' that could not be used on a recording. The R'n'B of Harris, Big Joe Turner and others was renamed Rock'n'Roll, originally by those such as disc jockey Allan Freed who wanted to disguise the fact that it was essentially black music. Given a country flavour by white artists such as Bill Hailey and Elvis Presley, R'n'B was rebranded in order to make it more palatable to a mainstream white audience.

Presley courted controversy just as Black R'n'B artists had before him. He had seen Wynonie Harris performing and copied his performance style, but performed to a white audience. Collins describes the career of Harris, and the extent to which Presley was a Harris fan, copying his musical and physical stylings (Collins 1995, p. 112). The shaking legs and hips, curled lip and waving arms of Presley are imitations of Harris, and his early recordings also include 'Good Rockin' Tonight', which had been a number one hit for Harris in the R'n'B chart, staying on the chart for six months. The song had a gospel handclap backbeat, and this mixture of gospel and R'n'B became an important element of rock'n'roll. Indeed, one could claim that the Harris version of the record was the first rock'n'roll record, as it was certainly influential.

Presley's version was in comparison a commercial failure. However, as a white performer he was able to access national record distribution and television networks not available to black performers in the USA of the 1950s. Despite his version of Harris's performance being toned down, more conservative and tame, Presley's moves were still recognizable as those of a bawdy, sexual, blues performer. For this reason some of his television shows were censored, with Presley being shown from the waist downwards only, as his hip movements were considered too overtly sexual to be shown.

Presley, and Colonel Tom Parker, the media svengali who managed and promoted him, were aware that such sexualized performances could generate controversy within the press and media, could generate publicity, and that although this might by some be regarded as bad publicity, it would be very popular with a young audience. It served to offend parents and give youth culture a music that their parents did not approve of, a culture that was theirs and that transgressed mainstream attitudes. Rock'n'roll music and its associated culture came to play a key role in the development of a youth culture that was separate from that of the older generations.

Other rock'n'roll performers were also controversial because of issues related to sexuality. Little Richard was a bisexual mixed race performer, who developed a controversial performance style influenced by Billy Wright. Wright was gay, and performed in drag in gay venues as well as tent and medicine shows. He filled his work with innuendo, and performed an early version of the song 'Tutti Frutti'. Tutti frutti is a kind of ice cream that is made up of a mixture of flavours, and as fruit was slang for a gay man, the phrase was used to refer to a mixed-race gay man. Little Richard had a hit record with a sanitized version of this song. He describes the song:

I'd been singing 'Tutti Frutti' for years, but it never struck me as a song you'd *record*. I didn't go to New Orleans to record no 'Tutti Frutti'. Sure, it used to crack the crowds up when I sang it in the club, with those risqué lyrics: 'Tutti Fritti, good booty / If it don't fit, don't force it. You can grease it, make it easy …' But I never thought it would be a hit, even with the lyrics cleaned up. (White 2003, p. 55)

'Loose booty' or 'good booty' was replaced in the song with non-sexual nonsense words such as 'aw rootie'. Little Richard sang this and other songs, with a wild performance style, screaming and hammering the piano, and also wearing make-up.

Another rock'n'roll pioneer, Jerry Lee Lewis, caused a sexual scandal when he married his first cousin, who was only 13 years old. Once the press heard of this it ended the singer's career. Chuck Berry was jailed when an ex-employee in this club was arrested as a prostitute. Although Berry maintained he was jailed due to racial discrimination (there is certainly some evidence to support this), it seems that his club was at least not completely free of sexual controversy. The raw, open sexuality of rock'n'roll music, or even the sanitized versions of that sexuality performed by Presley and others, made young people dance and scream, and the moral panic and press outrage that followed only helped to boost the music's success further. Within African American music culture, soul and funk music such as that of James Brown, and 'What'd I Say' by Ray Charles, mixed gospel euphoria and erotic groans, creating a driving mix that also focused on the body and dancing.

These musical forms crossed the Atlantic to re-emerge in the recordings of the Beatles and the Rolling Stones. The Beatles inspired further scenes of screams and ecstasy, being chased by increasingly manic fans, until they eventually ceased performing live. The Rolling Stones wrote sexually charged R'n'B songs like 'Honky Tonk Woman', and 'Brown Sugar' from the *Sticky Fingers* album. The cover of this LP featured a picture of a man's crotch, with a zip that could be undone. They also became associated with unusual sexual behaviour, a hypocryphal urban myth developing that a police raid discovered singer Mick Jagger in the act of performing oral sex on a chocolate bar that had been inserted into his girlfriend. An overt and open sexuality became part of the 1960s music scene as the hippie and psychedelic scene espoused free love. At the same time, the contraceptive pill became widely available, and sexually charged blues and R'n'B became increasingly influential musically.

The electric guitar acted as a central musical focus in this era, and the guitar neck was often presented as a phallic symbol by guitarists. Guitarists would move their left hand suggestively up and down the fret-board of the instrument, and the motion of moving thumb and first finger quickly up and down at the base of the neck has masturbatory connotations.

T-Bone Walker, an early blues pioneer, would jump around while playing, play with the guitar behind his neck or while doing the splits, and sometimes play the strings of the guitar with his lips and teeth instead of his right hand. American singer/guitarist Jimi Hendrix adopted this and other blues guitar performance tricks and presented them to a white audience, initially in the UK. He sexualized his performance, using his mouth on the guitar, playing it with the neck sticking out from between his legs, thrusting it forward while bending the notes he was playing, making the guitar groan with lust. He combined this with sexual references in his lyrics, such as those in 'Crosstown Traffic', and with a reputation for drug taking and sexual promiscuity. These techniques hark back to earlier blues, R'n'B and rock'n'roll artists, Hendrix having toured as a guitar player for many well-known artists including Little Richard, the Isley Brothers, Jackie Wilson and King Curtis. Hendrix was hugely influential, and popularized this image of the guitar hero in the UK, complete with sexual posturing and virtuoso playing. I have described in detail how blues guitarists created a blueprint for rock musicians in the book *Cross the Water Blues* edited by Neil Wynn (Till 2007).

Hendrix inspired many guitarists, the most obviously similar being Prince. The guitar hero became an iconic figure within what Frith and MacRobbie (1990) describe as 'Cock Rock'. They describe how sexuality plays an important role within popular music in general, and rock music in particular. Young people explore their sexual feelings and behaviours within youth culture scenes like that surrounding rock music. Music scenes offer ritualized situations in which they feel safe to learn to understand more about themselves within their peer group.

Cock rock presents itself as dominated by masculinity. Most of the musicians are male, as are many of the fans. Images of men within the genre are often intended to be archetypally male. Musicians often dress in a fashion that is reminiscent of historical heroes and warriors, or cavemen. The band Manowar for example are seen on their album covers wearing fur, and studded leather, holding swords and with long hair, rippling muscles showed off by skimpy costumes. Images of women in comparison often show women as sex objects, scantily clad, buxom, wearing tight clothing or semi naked, with long hair and often in suggestive or submissive positions. This is a fantasy sexuality, influenced by comic books, graphic novels, science fiction and soft porn, where people are caricatured and idealized, images presented that are taken from adolescent fantasies. Sexuality is presented as being wholly heterosexual, uncomplicated and straightforward. In song lyrics dominant, masculine men have sex with willing, feminine women. Concerts are often full of young men dressed like their idols who express and begin to understand their complex whirl of adolescent emotions through the simple, safe sexuality presented within rock music.

Whitesnake are an interesting example. The band began as the solo project of Deep Purple singer David Coverdale. Their music is packed with sexual references. Coverdale was influenced by blues music, and the band's name is a reference to the Blind Lemon Jefferson song 'Black Snake Moan' and the use of snake as a lyrical reference for a penis. The album cover of their album *Lovehunter* features a naked women astride a giant snake. Song lyrics often discuss sex, and lyrical content is indicated by song titles such as 'Ready an' Willing', 'Come and Get it', 'Wine, Women and Song', 'Dancing Girls', 'Slide It In', 'Spit It Out', 'Slow an' Easy' and 'Slow Poke Music'.

In press interviews stars discuss their sexual promiscuity, in particular their having sex with female fans known as groupies while on tour. Numerous books describe the extreme behaviours of rock stars, and fans live vicariously through these activities, imagining what it would be to have that life, and safely experiencing and imagining their fantasies through them. For example the 1985 book *Hammer of the Gods* by Stephen Davis describes the most outrageous of tour stories of the band Led Zeppelin, including that of inserting various things into female groupies, including supposedly the tail of a fish or small shark. The book has been described by band members as largely fictional, and its main source was tour manager Richard Cole, rather than the band itself. However, it portrays a world of freely available sex with a succession of willing participants, and whether true or not, writing of this kind has helped to create a mythical world in which fans could imagine themselves participating.

Rock music culture contains all of these overt expressions of heterosexual sexuality in order to provide a situation where young people can try out expressions of sexuality, sexual identity and sexual behaviour, either in reality or within their imaginations. However, beneath these straightforward representations lie other aspects of sexuality. Beneath the surface lies a strong homoerotic undercurrent. Although rock stars are portrayed as being expressions of idealized masculinity there are many elements of their image that are far more feminine.

Long hair is the most obvious example of this, but hair is not just long, but often elaborately styled with hairspray, and permed and coloured hair is also used to exaggerate hairstyles. Many acts also have worn make-up, including The Sweet, Slade, David Bowie, Kiss, Marilyn Manson, Twisted Sister, Hanoi Rocks, Mötley Crüe, Marc Bolan, Alice Cooper, Manic Street Preachers, Peter Gabriel and Ozzy Osbourne. Although this is partly theatrical make-up which will make the artist look better under stage and television lighting, it often creates an image that is more commonly associated with women than men. Clothing is also often extreme and exaggerated. Scarves and frills, tight trousers and lycra are all feminine clothing styles worn by male rocks stars, but in cock rock one of the most interesting elements is the use of leather.

The wearing of leather jackets in rock music has its roots in the jackets seen in films such as James Dean's *Rebel Without a Cause* and Marlon Brando's *The Wild One*, creating associations with motorbikes, racing cars and outlaws. Leather jackets became standard wear within rock'n'roll and later rock music culture. One rock star, Rob Halford of Judas Priest, took this image somewhat further. Halford was gay and adopted an iconic gay image dressing in head-to-toe leather, like an exaggerated biker, complete with leather cap. He also integrated elements of imagery associated with sado/masochism and bondage or fetishistic sex scenes, including studded leather and whips. This image was adopted by the New Wave of British Heavy Metal that Judas Priest was part of, without an understanding of the roots of the style in gay culture.

In light of this homoerotic element in cock rock, the image of Manowar for example with their bare chests and rippling muscles, seems more likely to appeal to an audience of gay men rather recalling heroic warriors from some past age. This is particularly the case when one considers that it is an audience of young men watching and idolizing, cheering, screaming at or obsessing over these male rock stars with their long hair, make-up, effeminate or gay fetishistic clothing, tight trousers, sexualized lyrics discussing wanting to make love to the listener, and muscular physiques.

Another interesting example is the band Mötley Crüe. The band were formed in Hollywood, and the band spent much time socializing on Hollywood's Sunset Strip, an area full of bars, music venues, strip clubs and prostitutes. The area was a notorious red light district, until English actor Hugh Grant was caught with prostitute Divine Brown in a car on a street corner in 1995, after which authorities made an effort to clean up the area's image.

Mötley Crüe, Van Halen and other bands performed in the area, developing a genre that became known as glam metal, or more interestingly hair rock or hair metal. This music genre is perhaps best known for its image, rather than its music, that is not very different to other forms of (cock) rock music. However bands such as Mötley Crüe had particularly flamboyant haircuts, using backcombing, hairspray, perms, hairdye, and crimping. Infuenced perhaps by both the glam rock of the 1970s and goth/alternative scene exemplified by the Sisters of Mercy, Mötley Crüe also began to wear make-up and sport hairstyles which involved their hair standing up at the front and on top, teased out to look as 'big' as possible, following the 'big hair' traditions of the 1980s. The band seem to have based their image, which included their hair, make-up, torn lace and fishnets, on the strippers and prostitutes they saw on Sunset Strip, modelling their image on women.

The band try to exemplify masculinity in their video for the song 'Girls, Girls, Girls', at first glance succeeding by riding motorcycles, drinking, threatening someone with a flick-knife, watching strippers, wearing 'biker' leather and denim and singing about their sexual exploits with what are described as girls, rather than women. However, on closer inspection the band are not wearing biker leathers, but shiny, thin, 1980s fashion leather jackets. They are also sporting the extreme bondage, fetishistic, studded leather of Rob Halford's leather man image, straight out of gay subculture, and this image is exaggerated further by some of the band being bare-chested beneath their jackets.

There are many parallels between the female strippers who feature in the video for the song, and the band members. One of the female strippers is also wearing a fetishistic leather outfit with a glam metal style studded belt, and leather boots and gloves, dressed in fact similarly to the band. Strippers crawl provocatively across the floor, and a band member does the same at one point. A different woman sits astride a chair in a clichéd pose, the chair placed backwards, her arms on the chair back in front of her, and again a band member adopts the same position. Band and women are shown together backstage, as the women dress and put on their make-up.

One might think that the band are seducing the women, but there is no contact, flirtation or involvement in the dressing room. A band member plays the guitar as women put on make-up and adjust their hair, another helps a woman to dress, the women ignore the band either as if they were not there, or as if both groups are performers, preparing similarly. At one point one of the women is seen wearing one of the band's jackets, and at another the band are seen running their hands suggestively over the head of a male fan. A dancer is shown flicking her head and hair while dancing onstage, the video cuts to a band member flicking his slightly longer hair in the same way. Fast cuts and superimposition show how a guitarist and dancer are alike, swinging their hips and holding poses, the drummer and another dancer are also shown entertaining their respective audiences.

The implication is clear, the band are like strippers, dancing in front of an audience for money, wearing similar clothing, make-up and hairstyles, appearing in videos, pretending to be one thing when the cameras are on them, but presenting a fictional image constructed for the pleasure of the audience. The audience are mostly young men, presented with a mix of imagery presented as male (rock star) and female (stripper), confusing and mingling the two, but presenting them with a surface level narrative that implies a simple heterosexual relationship where the band are presented as archetypal dominant men lusting after submissive women.

During their career, the band developed this image as part of their art, consciously developing a fictionalized background to the band. They performed even when fans might have imagined they were being themselves. They staged arrests, for example, for attempting to carry pornography through customs, and also staged a bomb threat, blurring the boundaries between the real world and their fictional onstage personae.

They frequently discussed their promiscuous sexual activities with female fans, or 'groupies' in interviews, and presented themselves as able and willing to sleep with the many female fans presenting themselves backstage. In doing this the band are not only presenting themselves as prostitutes onstage through their visual image, but are backing this up with (at least stories of) their behavior. Female fans, who had paid to see them onstage, were also allowed to have sex with them. If this were one of the strippers, as presented in their video, performing onstage and then having sex with a customer backstage in the dressing room, one would assume that stripping had moved on into prostitution, and it is only the power dynamics of western society, in which men often (and women rarely) pay to have sex with the opposite sex, that make this situation different.

These parallels are made clear, as in the video the band use their bodies as part of their performance, to generate money, implying that having sex with female fans (or at least discussing doing so) is part of that money-making process.

This complex exploration of the line between reality and fiction was further confused when band member Tommy Lee and his wife Pamela Anderson had a tape of them having sex widely circulated on the internet as celebrity pornography, after reportedly being stolen. Anderson had become famous as a glamour model, appearing in Playboy magazine, and went on to appear in swimwear in the TV show Baywatch. Lee and Anderson sued a video company over the issue of the video tape, but rather than blocking its distribution, after successful legal action the video became commercially available, earning money for the couple. Finally, a member of Mötley Crüe had become a porn star in real life, taking the band's stage profile to its logical conclusion, aided by Anderson's fame for her breast implants and glamour modelling.

Cock rock presents itself as a simple masculinity that allows young men and boys the chance to practice their sexual feelings and behaviour in a safe, 'straight'-forward context in which they are not presented with the complexities of real-life sexuality. In reality it offers a mixture of sexual flavours and colours, gay and straight, extreme and simple, fantasy and real, a sexual world that fans can explore freely without considering the underlying issues they are exploring. Fans are drawn further into this mythical world by the implication that it is real, that unlimited sexual activity is available if one only emulates rock stars, that glamorous, promiscuous sex is freely available to the most naïve and inexperienced young rock fan, if only in a mythical world lived through the lives of these cock rock purveyors of sexual fantasies.

Cock rock is not a bold, challenging or controversial approach to sexuality, at least in the way it is overtly presented, although of course in reality it is far more complex than it seems. It is paralleled, at least in the writing of Frith and MacRobbie (1990), by the world of teen pop. In the 1940s young girls in the USA screamed, rioted, fainted and swooned over a new young singer called Frank Sinatra who had progressed from singing to make films. Sinatra's fans wore bobby socks, white socks that had been worn in the UK because of a lack of nylon for stockings caused by World War II. These were worn in the USA by teenagers, and became a teen fashion that separated young people from older generations, wearing their trousers turned up and showing off the socks. Sinatra became a teen idol, hugely successful, and closely associated with his 'bobby-soxer' fans. In the 1950s Elvis Presley caused similar hysteria and adoration in his female fans. In the 1960s the Beatles inspired Beatlemania, and in the 1970s David Cassidy and Donny Osmond were the teen heart-throbs of the day.

These teen pop stars provided young girls with their own safe place to explore sexual feelings and juvenile emotions. Girls were able to fall in love with these male pop stars, safe in the knowledge that there was no risk of an actual relationship, so that the emotions involved could be practised, explored

and experienced in a safe, virtual world of media and music business constructions. Fans knew these stars from television, radio and film, and from their
recordings, which were perhaps the most important and personal element of
the stars' power over fans, as through recordings the male singer in particular
could develop a personal communication with the fan, while alone with them
in their bedroom.

Bing Crosby had prototyped a crooning singing style made possible by
developments in microphone, loudspeaker and amplification technology. Up
until these technological developments, singers needed to project their voices
powerfully, using technically strong singing technique, in order to be heard
above other instruments and to an audience. This use of the same, particular
technique meant that singers sounded generally similar, it reduced the amount
of the singer's natural speaking voice, what Barthes called the grain of their
voice that could be heard by the audience in their singing. In comparison,
singing close to a microphone, amplified powerfully through speakers, heard
on the radio, film or television, singers could sing quietly and still be heard.
Singers began to sing in a softer tone, singing quietly, 'crooning', as if they were
talking to an individual who was listening, rather than projecting to a crowd or
group. Higher fidelity recording equipment and smaller record players allowed
the detail of these voices to be heard, and developments in film sound and television meant that the voices of stars could be accompanied by their faces, on
screens. Record players became common in teenager's bedrooms.

Sinatra's crooning was different, because of the age of his audience. Bing
Crosby's records were aimed in style and content at adults, who had the spending power to buy them. After 1945, a post-war generation of teenagers had
more disposable income than previous generations, that they were willing to
spend on music, and Sinatra was one of the first music stars whose recordings
were aimed at this younger audience. He was the first American teen pop idol
of the 1940s, aided perhaps by so many other young men being away at war,
and was the blueprint for many other male popular music singers who would
inspire rioting and hysterical legions of female fans, achieving a huge level of
commercial success by exploiting this market.

Such teen pop music has been considered more disposable, less intellectually challenging, more feminine, simpler, and more commercially focused than
other musical forms. The crooning of Sinatra was thought of as more romantic, soft and commercially driven than for example the African American based
jazz of the era. Elvis Presley similarly appealed to young female fans with a
series of romantic lead roles in films, and became progressively more safe and
unchallenging during his career by moving from country and R'n'B music, to
releasing recordings of soft ballads with slow tempi. The Beatles played soul
and R'n'B tunes in an English accent, becoming one of the first manufactured
boy bands as manager Brian Epstein groomed them by changing their proto-
cock rock leather jacketed greaser image, to one that would be more appealing
to young female fans, wearing suits and with modern, co-ordinated haircuts,

taking them from rock'n'roll outsiders to teen heart-throbs. All three took the raw sexuality of African American dance music styles such as jazz, swing, R'n'B and soul, and packaged them within the music of safe, white, mainstream commercial teen pop music, taking bodily orientated black dance music and changing it into intellectualized white listening music.

The music industry found musicians who had developed their skills in working class backgrounds difficult to work with once they became rich, famous and powerful. It became difficult to control stars like Little Richard, Jerry Lee Lewis, Elvis Presley, The Beatles, the Rolling Stones, Chuck Berry and The Beach Boys, whose careers were affected in various ways by drug busts, sexual allegations, or early retirements from performing and/or recording. In order to overcome this, the music industry began to find clean-cut young stars to mould into more easily controlled, safe versions that could be marketed to a mass audience. For example Little Richard and Elvis Presley were replaced by Pat Boone and Cliff Richard, and The Beatles were aped by the Monkees, who were put together to make a television series. These stars had less of the overt sexuality of the artists whose styles they approximated.

In the 1970s singers like Donny Osmond and David Cassidy provided increasingly feminine teen pop singer role models. Singing increasingly saccharine material referring to teen romance, driving African American rhythms were replaced with smooth arrangements, perfect smiles and unthreatening boy-next-door images. Some artists even flirted with the world of cock rock, managing to appeal to both male and female fans.

In the UK, Scottish band the Bay City Rollers were a manufactured boy band who tried a series of different lead singers before finding a team that were commercially successful. Playing their own instruments and singing, in their peak they brought the part of the centre of London near BBC TV centre to a standstill, as fans knew the band were due to perform on UK television chart show Top of the Pops. Stars were presented in a way that would appeal to their crowds of ardent fans, and inevitably this meant that pop stars became increasingly feminized, allowing young female fans to associate with and understand their heroes.

Other stars took this feminization of the pop world further. Glam rock stars like Marc Bolan and David Bowie presented an androgynous image, which could appeal both to the young male cock rock fans and audience, and to the young female teen pop fans. Bowie in particular explored a more complex sexuality. Drawing on his theatre training, he created mythical characters who were larger than life, and increasingly mixed the masculine and feminine. Ziggy Stardust, Alladin Sane and The Thin White Duke were versions of Bowie, characters he played, media constructions that were part real, part fictional. Bowie discussed his bisexuality in public, and presented a media image that was not so much more feminine than other cock rock stars, but that acknowledged the gender bending that he was participating in, unlike many of his rock star peers.

In the 1980s a number of UK musicians mixed the image of David Bowie with the dance beats of gay disco. Following the Stonewall riots in America, gay rights activists had begun to make homosexuality legally and socially more acceptable. The Stonewall riots occurred when police raided a gay bar and club in New York. Following a number of days of rioting by the gay community, over police and legal oppression and abuse, enough pressure was exerted to change the policy of the police in New York towards open expressions of homosexuality, such as dancing together or kissing in public. A number of gay clubs opened up in which DJs played records for people to dance to, and being able to dance together in public became one of the ways in which gay culture was established, developed and expressed. This form of musical expression was at odds with the live performance culture of the (cock) rock music of the time. Gay disco venues became one of the most public expressions of gay sexuality and culture.

One of the first gay discos in New York to become well known was the Sanctuary, a deconsecrated church where DJ Francis Grasso began slip-cueing, now known as beat-matching, mixing the end of one record into the start of the next. Rather than the intellectual sincerity of rock music, disco focused on loss of self in the moment, it was centred on the body, on expressions of physicality, and, within a new-found legality, on the open expression of gay sexuality. This required a constant flow of regular beats; it was music to dance to, not to listen to. As well as being far cheaper than live music, beat matching allowed an extended series of records, a constant thrusting beat that could go on for many hours, driven on by the sexually charged, drug-enhanced atmosphere of underground gay clubs.

Later, The Loft (David Mancuso's events there starting in his attic), the Continental Baths (a bath-house or sauna where Bette Midler and Barry Manilow started their careers together), Studio 54 (which became a favoured haunt of celebrities) and the Paradise Garage (which was the first 'super-club' with an elaborate lighting and sound system) all became famous New York city gay disco venues. Many of these venues had highly sexualized atmospheres, in the Sanctuary people would have sex in the pews, in the baths it was in cubicles, and in Studio 54 it was in the balcony.

The music in these venues began by reflecting the tastes of the African American and Latin American clientele. Later, synthesizers were used to replace real instruments, especially being used for bass and drum sounds, to produce a driving rhythm section. This reached its most extreme in Giorgio Moroder's productions with singer Donna Summer. First, 'Love to Love You Baby' provided a vocal track featuring erotic orgasmic simulation. This was followed by 'I Feel Love', which was accompanied by a purely electronic backing track, using synthesized sounds. Extended into a dance remix, the music's throbbing hypnotic pulse provided the template for electronic dance music for years to come.

In the 1980s, a number of British pop acts blended the image of David Bowie with the electronic dance music grooves of disco and German band Kraftwerk, within the new romantic or synth-pop scenes. These music scenes were far more open about sexual experimentation and difference than those of most mainstream popular music. For example Soft Cell's Marc Almond made no efforts to hide that he was gay, turning northern soul stomper 'Tainted Love' into an electronic torch song with a camp accent. The Human League replaced the phallocentricity of the electric guitar with the androgyny of the synthesizer. Visage's Steve Strange emulated Bowie's image while Tubeway Army's Gary Numan and Japan's David Sylvian emulated Bowie's voice. The images of Culture Club's Boy George, singer Marilyn and Dead or Alive's Pete Burns were as much influenced by drag acts as rock stars, deliberately androgynous.

Many of these stars, as well as the members of bands such as Duran Duran and Spandau Ballet, wore make-up and extravagant, colourful stage costumes. The rhythms of the feminized space of the dance floor combined with a focus on fashion, exaggerated make-up and haircuts. The image of the scene began with the flamboyance of Bowie's Ziggy Stardust and Alladin Sane era, and later moved on to echo his suit-wearing Thin White Duke Image. The focus on image, fashion and dancing was unusual because it embraced the feminine side of teen pop, overtly engaging with an audience of teenage girls and gay men without a veneer of masculinity to satisfy more mainstream tastes.

Adam and the Ants were also part of this 1980s scene. The band was part of the punk scene originally, with a leather and bondage image and song titles like 'Whip in My Valise' and lyrics discussing the size of God's penis. After the rest of the band left with Malcolm McLaren (who was managing the band) to form Bow Wow Wow, Adam Ant returned with a new backing band. He had abandoned the punk image, began wearing make-up, and became a hugely successful teen pop star. Despite being presented as a mainstream star to young female fans, the band's motto was 'ant music for sex people', left over from their punk years, which featured on artwork, and in lyrics. Adam Ant, whose real name was Stuart Goddard, has discussed his career in detail in his autobiography (Ant, 2006).

Adam and the Ants toured with Siouxsie and the Banshees, and was originally integrated as part of the London punk scene. Adam Ant was a close friend of Jordan, who worked in the London clothes shop owned by Vivienne Westwood and Malcolm McLaren, which was called Sex. Jordan's clothing and extreme make-up were an important influence on punk. She had a relationship with Adam Ant and also managed the band at one point, McLaren also later acting as manager. The Sex boutique sold fetish clothing including rubber, PVC and leather clothing, featuring zips, chains and handcuffs, which became part of punk fashion. Punk was another influence on the new romantic scene, and it offered a more complex sexuality, with men wearing make-up and coloured hair, and women presenting unorthodox and aggressive images.

I do not intend to address issues relating to gender and the role of women in the music industry in further depth, this is discussed in detail in books such as *Women and Popular Music: Sexuality, Identity and Subjectivity* by Sheila

Whiteley and *Gender in the Music Industry* by Marion Leonard. Female punk stars like Siouxsie Sioux did not conform to conventional images of femininity, and punk offered male and female images that were less traditional than earlier music scenes. Whereas in cock rock and new romantic scenes men adopted elements of traditionally feminine imagery, in punk women adopted less traditionally feminine imagery, and elements of a more traditionally male image.

The 1980s produced superstars such as the androgynous Michael Jackson and the overtly sexual Prince, who is discussed in a later chapter. Jackson had outgrown his boyhood image, and his image as a solo star involved him grabbing his crotch as a signature dance move, also integrating a robotic asexuality, into his style. Prince deliberately adopted a sexualized image in order to generate publicity and controversy. However, the star who most significantly addressed sex in the 1980s, and possibly caused more sexual controversy than any other musical act, was Madonna.

Numerous books have discussed Madonna and her career. She was a professional dancer before beginning her musical career, and the body and physicality have always been part of her work. Although not her first single, 'Like a Virgin' was her first US number one single, and was the release that established her as a major star. The song's lyrics contain a number of double entendres. It could be a romantic song about feeling a freshness in a new relationship. However, lyrics about feeling good inside, could relate to emotional or sexual pleasure, and other lyrics in the song, such as discussing being 'had', similarly have dual meanings.

The title of the song immediately points out that the singer is not a virgin, she is like a virgin, and the chorus tells us that she is being touched sexually, not for the first time. The vocal of the song features a breathy, gasping, orgasmic quality that confirms the sexuality of what is being sung about. The video made for the song takes this further. Madonna dresses in something that is like a wedding dress, but is not one. The top half is more like a white basque with a light lace or net covering, and is certainly underwear, rather than outerwear, in an act of bricolage that Madonna repeats many times. She recontextualizes and mixes meanings of clothing, in order to confuse whether one is experiencing a highly personal sexual encounter or an ordinary one, bringing sexuality from the realm of the personal into that of the public. The bottom half of the dress features a long train but a very short skirt. She is lain on her bed by her groom, who is symbolized by a male lion, which stalks her through the video, the link between the lion and the man she is singing to being made by a mask worn by her 'groom'. The music itself is produced by Nile Rodgers, famous for his disco productions, and it is both a teen pop record and club dance track, aiming at the young female audience of the former, as well as the feminized space of dance floor.

Madonna performed the song at the 1984 MTV video awards. For this performance she wore a similar outfit to that she wore in the song's original video, but made it more extreme, with a top that was more overtly underwear, and a skirt made of netting that revealed white stockings and suspenders underneath. At the end of the performance she knelt down and moved up and down, simulating having sex (or masturbating), with her in a dominant position, on top. She crawls and rolls, ending in an orgasmic heap on the floor. On her 1990 tour she unequivocally simulated masturbation along to this song, wearing underwear and writhing on a bed.

Madonna discussed the song in an interview in *Songtalk* magazine in August 1989.

Interviewer: Do you remember hearing "Like a Virgin" for the first time?
Madonna: I thought it was sick. I thought it was sick and perverted and that's why I liked it.
Interviewer: And that appealed to you?
Madonna: Yeah! Sick and perverted always appeals to me.
Interviewer: And it sounded like a song you could pull off well?
Madonna: Yeah. Because there were so many innuendos in it. I thought, "This is great. This will really screw with people."
Interviewer: You like that, when people get upset?
Madonna: Yeah, controversy. I thrive on it.

Madonna offered her largely female audience an adult image of a woman, sexually active, in control and with no male backing band. She became known for controlling her own career, and offering an alternative to male-dominated music industry norms. She paved the way for a series of female pop singers with a sexual image, including Britney Spears and Christina Aguilera. These two singers sang the song 'Like a Virgin' at another Brit awards event. They were both dressed in copies of Madonna's wedding dress image, and were then joined by Madonna on the song 'Hollywood'. The performance is full of sexualized moments, before Madonna, dressed in the black and top hat of a bridegroom, gropes each of the other women before sharing an open mouthed kiss with each.

Madonna's lyrics and videos continued to challenge gender stereotypes and the boundaries of acceptable public sexuality. The song 'Like a Prayer' was released as the soundtrack to a Pepsi advert, as part of a multimillion pound advertising deal. Andre Crouch's gospel choir gave the song a layer of religious sentiment, something that had often been present in Madonna's music, rooted in her catholic upbringing. Madonna's image had often featured crosses and crucifixes combined with provocative hemlines and cleavages. Here, in a song she co-wrote, the title plays with sexuality, using gospel lyrics that could imply sexual or religious metaphors. When she sings that 'Like a Prayer' she'll take us there, contextualized by gospel backing vocals, she sounds at first as if she is talking about taking us to religious ecstasy, or to heaven, perhaps referencing the Staples Singers song 'I'll Take You There'. However, the Staples Singers' lyric is preceded by describing the heaven that one is taken to, and the band, known as a gospel group, are suggesting that that it is God who will do the taking, God who is the 'I' in the lyrics.

Madonna's 'I'll Take You There' lyric is preceded by 'Like a Prayer', recalling the sexuality of 'Like a Virgin'. Madonna is known as being overtly sexual rather than a gospel singer, and by suggesting that we are discussing something that is like (and therefore not) a prayer, we must consider what else it is that is being discussed. The least sexual interpretation that we can draw is that sexual and religious ecstasy are being compared. This is suggesting that the feeling that dancing in church to gospel music brings, that a moment of connection to the divine in a religious context can inspire, is similar in nature to what is felt in a moment of sexual pleasure or ecstasy. The song uses another soul lyric, the title of 'In the Midnight Hour', which is a Wilson Pickett song that again mixes gospel and sexual/romantic stylings and imagery. The midnight hour is a biblical reference to revelation, the last moment before the return of Christ, and a gospel music catch phrase. The structure of Pickett's song also bears some relation to gospel music, and Pickett had a background as a gospel singer. However, it was a secular hit, with a romantic relationship between a man and a woman being the focus of the song, replacing a gospel song focus of the relationship between human being and God.

Madonna's music is clearly set in a secular context, and the person she is singing to is clearly a man, although she deliberately infers that she may be either speaking as, or to God. Even this is confused, as the 'I' in her song can feel the power of the person she is singing about, but can also take us there. The beginning of the song is also obviously in the first person, with her discussing how she hears a voice. Thus religious metaphor is secondary to her being the 'I' in this case. We must assume that she is telling us that she can take us 'there', by doing something like (but other than) prayer. This 'other than' could be music. The song discusses music, God, and both sexual and emotional relationships providing ecstatic feelings, and all of these are supposed to be compared and related to one another by the song. However, there is a more explicit sexual message present, which is suggested as much by the video that was made to accompany the song, as the song itself.

Gospel choir leader Andre Crouch refused to participate in the video, and so actors were used to stand in for the group. It is difficult to know which of the many issues involved may have been considered sacrilegious. A religious statue, either a saint or Jesus, comes to life as an African American man; Madonna dances in front of burning crosses; she kisses the man in a church, on the foot recalling the biblical woman caught in sin, and on the mouth more suggestively; she dances vigorously in the church, the straps of her dress dropping to her shoulders exposing her cleavage, discontinuity (the straps are up and then down in subsequent shots) showing this is no accident; and she is pushed to her knees where she bounces around recalling her previously eroticized video and live performances. It also suggests that when Madonna's first verse lyrics discuss being down on her knees, wanting to take someone there, as if praying, feeling their power, at night, that she is referring to performing oral sex, especially when one considers the rest of the context of Madonna's work. It seems indeed that 'Like A Prayer' is at least partly about a kneeling woman performing oral sex on a standing other person.

The 'Like a Prayer' recording and video further established Madonna's reputation. Pepsi had been running a trailer, encouraging people to hear Madonna's new song on their advert, and they had made their own more saccharine video to accompany the song. Pepsi staff had not seen the Madonna version, and although the first showing of the Pepsi advert during the hugely popular Cosby Show was successful, perhaps as many as 250 million people seeing it worldwide, the Pepsi ad was never shown again after Madonna's own video unleashed a storm of controversy. Jack Doyle (1989) describes this controversy.

> Rev. Donald Wildmond of the American Family Association, a Christian group. Wildmond threatened to have his *AFA Journal's* 380,000 subscribers boycott Pepsi until the company bowed to his demands.
> ... A Catholic bishop from Texas, Rene Gracido, added his voice to the fight, calling Madonna's video offensive. He too called for a boycott of Pepsi and its other corporate holdings – including Taco Bell, Pizza Hut, and Kentucky Fried Chicken. The protest began to grow. Some Catholic groups in Italy started to protest. Then came a giant blow: the Pope released a statement by the Vatican that banned Madonna from appearing in Italy. The album *Like a Prayer*, was later censured by the Vatican.

The 'Like a Prayer' single, video and tour had their advertising massively boosted by the controversy, and Madonna learned more about the power of controversial material to bring public attention. The album cover, with its image of Madonna's crotch, rosary, unbuttoned jeans, nimbus (or halo) appearing from her belly button, and religious iconography, barely generated a mention, the image recalling the (like a) Rolling Stones' *Sticky Fingers* album cover, and its sexual lyrical content.

This video has been discussed by both Curry (1990) and Scott (1993). Curry blames the controversy on that,

> Madonna worships a statue of a black male saint in the church, who is thus moved to life, and first blesses and later erotically kisses Madonna as she is sprawled on her back in a pew ... The video's commingling of representation of interracial religious fervour and sexual ecstasy refutes distinctions strenuously maintained by dominant American institutions. (1990, pp. 26–7)

Here it is the kiss and Madonna's dress that are the controversial erotic elements. Scott claims that the 'real problems posed by the video lie in the manner in which Madonna exposes America's negative and unresolved attitudes about race and racial interaction' (1993, p. 63). Based on Curry's analysis, Scott concludes that the stirring to life of a religious statue in the video, a kiss in the church and the way Madonna is dressed, are the three areas that caused controversy. Scott is more interested in the racial issues that are indeed raised by the video, which he discusses well. However Madonna's video is not the original work, the song indeed had two videos made in this case, one for Pepsi, and one for MTV and other promotion.

Naively Scott claims that there is 'no evidence anywhere in the video that anything more than a kiss is involved', and that the straps on Madonna's dress fall down because of her movements. In fact the straps are placed up and down, some up and some down, in subsequent shots, the obvious discontinuity drawing attention to them. Scott seems to think that 'in the context and sacred setting of the video it is difficult to accept any interpretation that alludes to some sort of sexual seduction between the characters.' If this were not the Madonna who liked 'Like a Virgin' as a song because it was dirty, and who has brought sexuality into so much of her work, this might seem less naïve, and again Scott forgets that the song had its own meanings before and without the video. The video enhances the racial issues present in the song, the narrative of an imprisoned black man and black statue is not present in the lyrics or music.

In addition Madonna's own comments about the song are illuminating. The Allaboutmadonna website has an excellent collection of transcriptions of interviews with Madonna, and there are a number from the period after the release of the *Like a Prayer* album. In the May 1989 issue of *Interview Magazine* Madonna discusses the *Like a Prayer* video.

It's probably going to touch a lot of nerves in a lot of people ... I kept imagining this story about a girl who was madly in love with a black man, set in the South, with this forbidden interracial love affair. And the guy she's in love with sings in a choir. So she's obsessed with him and goes to church all the time. And then it turned into a bigger story, which was about racism and bigotry.

Then Mary Lambert got involved as the director, and she came up with a story that incorporated more of the religious symbolism I originally wrote into the song. The whole album has a lot of religious imagery in it.

It is clear that the album is full of erotic and religious references, and also that racial issues are addressed. It is also clear that Madonna's character in the video is supposed to be obsessed with the black male character, and that a relationship between the two is implicit. Madonna also makes it clear that she is interested in addressing the relationship between religious and sexual ecstasy in a *Smash Hits* magazine interview from 11 July 1989, and that she knew this would cause controversy.

The passion ... there's something almost sexual about it really, if you want to get really psychoanalytical about it ... it's a very taboo subject to have an interracial relationship and the idea of that kind of joyousness in a church. It dealt with a lot of taboos it made people afraid. And I think the people who reacted negatively to it were afraid of their feelings that they have about those issues.

She discusses this further some time later in *Esquire Magazine*, 'Mailer on Madonna', in August 1994.

> I do believe religion and eroticism are absolutely related. And I think my original feelings of sexuality and eroticism originated in going to church ... It's very sensual, and it's all about what you're not supposed to do. Everything's forbidden, and everything's behind heavy stuff—the confessional, heavy green drapes and stained-glass windows, the rituals, the kneeling—there's something very erotic about that.

Here she provides a suggestion that the references to kneeling in 'Like a Prayer' are indeed to some extent sexual and referring to oral sex. It is clear that there is no one single explanation of this Madonna song, album and video, that she raises a number of issues, that there are sexual, racial and religious subjects discussed, explored, transgressed and confused.

Madonna's suggestive imagery and lyrical references, dance beats, physicality, sexuality, and powerful female image are still layered in suggestion and inference, and this approach has perhaps more in common with most popular music culture than her later more explicit work. Her song 'Hanky Panky' suggested lyrically that there was nothing like a good spanking, but this was nothing compared to what would follow. The video for 'Justify My Love' featured women kissing, S&M and bondage imagery, and nudity. She released a book containing sexually explicit images, and erotic fantasy writing, an album called *Erotica* and a burlesque-styled tour. Provocative comments on David Letterman's US television show, and rumours of lesbian relationships added reality to the provocative entertainment products. Madonna has continued to mix sexuality and religious imagery in later work. She has shown herself in her *In Bed with Madonna* documentary film, praying with her team before concerts, and made a public feature of her Catholic background.

Madonna is perhaps the most extreme example of how sexuality that is considered taboo or outside of what is acceptable to the mainstream in public, is deeply enmeshed within the fabric of popular music culture and cults. In contrast to most traditional religions, in which individuals are often proscribed from particular behaviours, pop cults offer freedom to the individual to behave as they choose. It is perhaps not the opportunity to carry out the sexual activities and attitudes Madonna and others present that is most attractive, but the freedom to do so. As Fiske puts it,

> The meanings of the Madonna look, as of the Madonna videos, cannot be precisely specified. But that is precisely the point, the pleasure that they give

is not the pleasure of *what* they say, but of their assertion of the right and the power of a severely subordinated subculture to make their own statements, their own meanings. Madonna's invitation to her girl fans to play with the conventions of patriarchy shows them that they are not necessarily subject those conventions but can exercise some control over their relationship to patriarchy, and thus over the sense of their identity. (1988, p. 233)

Madonna is a good example of how a transgressive approach to sexuality is often at the core of popular music.

In Chapter 1, I described typical characteristics usually associated with a cult. In this chapter, I have provided evidence in order to suggest that popular music is much like a form of sex cult. It is interesting to consider to what extent a popular music sex cult might fit these typical characteristics. Like other cults it often involves an extreme level of devotion to one or more single person who is thought of as being charismatic, or having some link to the divine. For example, in the case of Madonna her name alone implies a link to the divine, whether this link is supposed to be real, or simply present to enhance an artist's marketability, is irrelevant. In many cases musicians mix religious/transcendental and sexual metaphors together, blurring the boundaries between the two. This has deep roots within popular music that are related to the integration of gospel and blues music. Music has often provided a release for repressed sexuality or physicality within western cultures. It has also become an important vehicle for the expression of gay sexuality, gay culture often pioneering or influencing new dance forms in particular. Young people's exploration of their sexuality is often contextualized within popular music scenes, which provide a safe space for experimentation and learning about sexuality.

Membership of the sex cult of pop often involves a very high level of commitment, some fans becoming obsessive, and sexually fantasizing about stars, or idealizing them, putting their images on their bedroom walls, young boys putting images of their male cock rock idols on their walls, young female fans romanticizing male pop stars or more complex female role models such as Madonna. The commitment to a pop scene can be seen as damaging relationships with family, causing arguments when fans copy a pop star's image, whether that might be a young boy told to cut his hair by his parents, or a parent worried about a girl wearing skimpy clothing, heavy make-up or emulation of Madonna's sexual behaviour.

Like other cult leaders, pop stars are sometimes accused of using sexuality to manipulate fans into becoming more committed, and into parting with their money. The sex cult of a popular star like Madonna, as well known for her sexuality as for her music, is associated with sexual practices that are linked to religious belief, again something specifically characteristic of a cult. For some, popular music, like any other cult, is considered the epitome of all that is deviant and dangerous because of its attitude to sexuality, acceptance of homosexuality and other sexual practices considered unacceptable to mainstream society or 'traditional family values'. Its mixture of religion and sexuality have led to bans, record burnings and numerous condemnations by conservative Christian groups of popular musics and musicians such as blues, rock'n'roll, Elvis Presley, Little Richard, soul, disco, Boy George and Madonna.

Most of the characteristics used to define a cult are present when one considers popular music as a kind of sex cult. Sexual or physical transgression of mainstream values are at the core of many popular music scenes, and are mixed up with issues of meaning, identity and commitment. Changes in sexual practices in the West have been enabled by the widespread availability of contraception, but the changes in social attitudes which have made sexual activity and living together outside of marriage the accepted norm rather than the exception have often been led by practices in popular music-led youth cultures and scenes rather than mainstream philosophical developments.

The acceptance of the extreme sexual practices of pop and rock stars has made relatively minor variety in sexual conduct seem comparatively unchallenging. The explicit or suggestive discussion of sexual practices in songs has helped to normalize less conservative sexual attitudes. Some music scenes have explicitly encouraged a more liberal attitude to sexual ethics, examples being the eroticism of the blues and soul, the free love of the hippies, the rhythm'n'blues raunch of the Rolling Stones, the fetishism of Punk or the gay culture of disco. Music has played a key role in the changing of mainstream sexual ethics, both reflecting and leading changes in an area that is often a key issue within religious belief. Popular music has thus played an important role in the development of human philosophy and belief in the west as it relates to sexuality. It has changed the belief systems and ways of life of Western culture, and this is a new rather than ancient approach, as with other NRMs.

People in 1970s New York gay discos attended secretive weekend events where men had sex in the pews of a deconsecrated church; the Woodstock inspired hippie movement tried to exist outside of society and set up communes at which so-called 'free love' was a feature; young people were so committed to music scenes that they wore punk bondage clothing and new romantic make-up despite this creating a separation with their families; and underneath all of this, the music scene conspired to make commitment more and more fervent in order to take more money from fans, who were unaware of the power of the marketing techniques used and the profits being made.

Thus it seems reasonable to describe some popular music scenes or elements of popular music as pop sex cults, at least as much as it is reasonable to describe anything as a cult or sex cult. Indeed popular music is sometimes described as having sex, drugs and rock'n'roll at its core, and sex and drugs are often linked. Having investigated sex cults within popular music, it makes sense to move on next to the complex subject of the drug cults of popular music.

Chapter 3

I Want to Take You Higher: Drug Cults of Popular Music

Drugs and Music in Prehistory and Traditional Culture

Many human cultures make use of different substances in order to achieve some kind of altered state of consciousness. This process is often closely linked with musical culture, and many popular music cults and cultures have one or more of these substances intimately associated with them. Alcohol is a legal drug that has particular links to popular music, but it is the wide range of drugs that are currently illegal in much of the western world that will be discussed in some detail in this chapter. Rather than use terms such as psychedelics, psychotropics, narcotics and stimulants, I will use the term drugs to describe this wide range of substances. This is because it is the term commonly used in the music industry, and part of the iconic term 'sex, drugs and rock'n'roll'. I use it in the same way I have used the word cult, to take advantage of its transgressive appeal. Many drugs have powerful effects on the mind and body, and natural substances taken from traditional ritual, religious or cultic practices have been used as have artificial drugs extracted from other substances or developed from scratch by scientists.

Humans have consumed a variety of different drugs since prehistory, whether acting as stimulants, psychedelics or narcotics. Terence McKenna (1993) suggests that it was the taking of mushrooms that were capable of causing psychotropic effects in humans, that kick-started human evolution. Although this is far from being a widely accepted idea, it is true that there is plenty of evidence of drug taking in early human culture. For example cave drawings found on the Tassili Plateau of Northern Algeria, thought to be from around 5000 BC, show human figures decorated with mushrooms, pictured morphing into other shapes, presumably under the effects of the mushroom.

Western culture separates religious experience from day to day 'secular' life, but this is often not the case in other cultures, especially within traditional cultures. Gods, ancestral spirits, superstitions and rituals are often woven intricately into daily living, they are ever present rather than being contained within a compartmentalized part of existence. Drug taking is often contained within ritualized or cultural settings, with particular religious meanings or cultural activities closely associated with the experiences associated with the drugs. Drugs have been used to cause what are often described as altered states of consciousness.

Aldridge and Fachner tell us that our consciousness is something that

> is a mutual activity; it is performed ... Making music together is an active way of changing consciousness that is embodied, which is why dance has been such a powerful medium for cultural and personal expression. (2006, pp. 10–11)

They usefully describe ordinary consciousness as but one of many types of consciousness that we experience. Drugs are one way of achieving what is perceived by the drug taker as some kind of extended consciousness. The same book tells us that between 80 percent (Meditteranean) and 97 percent (North American) of societies feature altered states of consciousness, and that these are universal human phenomena (p. 43). They also state that according to Kleinman, 'only the modern, secular West seems to have blocked individuals' access to these otherwise pan-human dimensions of the self' (1988, p. 50). Kleinman describes how the West not only does not use altered states of consciousness, but also denies it is of any value. Western consciousness is described as dissociated, not able to become totally absorbed in the moment, in lived experience, something that is the very essence of highly focused altered states of consciousness. This disconnection, and how it has led to the homeless self, is further discussed in the chapter on trance cults of popular music.

Some religious practice aims to achieve altered (or 'higher') states of consciousness through various techniques, including the use of chanting, meditation, breathing control, music and dancing. Drug taking is a short cut that allows those within Western culture who have few skills in this area to achieve such states, in a society that has moved away from rehearsing these practices. Drug taking is popular because mainstream western religions have often abandoned such practice, and yet it is a universal and perhaps essential part of human culture.

Lewis-Williams and Pearce (2005, pp. 44–55) discuss how altered states of consciousness caused by hallucinogenic drugs have characteristic effects in different cultures, and are often linked to music. They also point out that it is odd and remarkable that this is the case despite the different substances involved in different cultures and their effects. People commonly experience bright geometric patterns, floating or flying, passage through a tunnel, transformations into one thing or another, transformations into an animal, and enhanced, vivid sight. They also list other ways as well as drug taking that these effects can be achieved, many of which are present in popular music contexts, including intense rhythmic dancing, auditory driving by clapping or other rhythmic participation, and flickering light (i.e. flashing lights and strobes). They characterize the successive three stages of altered consciousness.

This begins with geometric mental images, such as grids, parallel lines, dots, zig-zags, spirals and other patterns. In the deeper, second stage people 'try to make sense of the entoptic forms they are seeing by construing them as objects with emotional and religious significance ... As subjects move towards Stage 3, a more profound altered state of consciousness, they often experience a vortex or tunnel, at the end of which is a bright light' (Lewis-Williams and Pearce 2005, pp. 50–1). Sometimes this involves travelling under, across or through water. In the final stage hallucinations may be experienced, with more patterns, and sometimes featuring transformation into an animal. The fact that these stages appear in numerous forms of drug-induced or shamanic hallucinogenic journey shows that these stages are universal and therefore likely to be a result of the nature and structure of human brains.

Of course in popular music cults it is not always drugs that cause visual hallucinations but most drugs, and most music, act to some extent to change or affect the consciousness of participants and listeners. Different states of consciousness are not restricted to extremes such as normal or some kind of possession trance with no consciousness present. 'Human beings are not either conscious or unconscious, as may be popularly supposed. Normal, everyday consciousness should rather be thought of as a spectrum' (ibid., p. 56). At one end of this spectrum is a busy, active, socially engaged, active person. In the centre are relaxed states of mind, absent daydreaming, half-asleep hypnogogic states and dreaming sleep. At the far end of the spectrum are hallucinations and trances. Both drugs and music, and especially the two combined together, are technologies used by humans that allow the individual to adjust their consciousness while staying awake, manipulating the level of dominance of those parts of the human character that relate to the ego and id, conscious and unconscious, waking and sleeping, adjusting the placement of the consciousness within this spectrum.

Drugs with effects on behaviour and on the mind are of course routinely prescribed by doctors in contemporary Western society, in the same way as drugs that have predominantly physical effects. The brain is physical and is part of the body, and the health of a person is affected by the condition of their body, mind, lifestyle, culture and psyche. Whereas many traditional cultures have carefully controlled methodologies for the use of drugs that have powerful emotional or psychological effects, modern Western cultures have largely ruled out the taking of drugs as taboo. Western political systems have done much to wage a so-called war on drugs, but have achieved little success.

Drug taking is widespread in most countries, and illegality or fear of prosecution has not stopped it. Whereas in some traditional cultures drug taking is controlled within set cultural or religious contexts, in Western European culture it has become an illegal, underground activity, with drugs supplied by criminal networks, with restricted information about the nature of what drug users are taking, or about their short- and long-term effects. There have been few detailed and reliable medical studies of illegal drug taking because of their illegality, and government policy is sometimes driven by political decisions rather than science or sociological study. The level of health risk involved in the use of the illegal drugs most commonly taken varies considerably, some may well be mostly harmless, others lethal in large doses, and others likely to cause long-term damage.

In any case, drug taking is commonly associated with popular music cults, and in this context, the illegality that is intended to put young people off from taking drugs seems to act to give them power and authenticity as a way of rebelling against parental values, and to provide the excitement and thrill of law breaking. As religions and governments have removed themselves from moulding the setting of drug taking within popular culture, new rituals and culture surrounding drug taking have developed, with some of these specifically associated with popular music scenes. Music and drug taking are both human technologies that can have profound effects on a person's state of mind and their emotions, as well as directly affecting them physically. Each seems to enhance the experience of the other, and particular musical forms have been developed by musicians who take particular forms of drugs, with musical characteristics designed to interact with the effects of specific drugs.

It seems likely that the illegality of drug taking has contributed to popular music becoming positioned as oppositional to mainstream culture, at least in its presentation. In addition, it would seem that the oppositional nature of youth culture has led to it adopting drug culture. There are also more functional reasons why popular musicians have taken drugs. Drug taking is something that musicians seem to adopt in order to sustain them through the late nights and long hours involved in the music industry. Drugs are also consumed to alleviate the boredom of travelling while touring. They are also taken to console musicians who have left their homes and families behind, and who have become nomads, travelling from venue to venue to perform. In addition, the psychic and emotional high of performing music to an audience is very different to the flat and tedious experience of travelling between and preparing for performances, and drugs are taken to soften the contrast between these experiences.

Playing music is itself a trance-like or transcendental experience, one where musicians often feel like they are somewhere else, have an altered state of consciousness or perceive an enhanced level of connection with their emotions, their fellow musicians and their audience in comparison to when not playing music. Being a musician is generally not a job that provides security or regular income, and it seems that musicians are perhaps those whose nature allows them to live with uncertainty, as well as participation in the music business allowing this side of their character to develop. Thus it may be that practical considerations of being a musician may mean that musicians are more likely to experiment, to take chances, to break the law, to seek ecstatic experiences, and thus to consider taking drugs. It may also be that those with such characteristics are more likely to become musicians, or that both dynamics apply.

A simplistic approach may suggest that fans take drugs because the pop stars they worship do so. There is little statistical evidence to support this, but it seems possible that this is true to some extent. However, professional popular musicians are often engaged with a pop drug cult as fans or ordinary participants, before becoming leaders of such a cult if they achieve wider success. Pop drug cults are being defined in this case as popular music scenes that involve drug taking by musicians or fans as common behaviour. Popular music fans take drugs for a number of reasons that are similar to musicians' reasons, the seeking of ecstatic or mystical experiences, pleasure, experimentation, peer pressure or trance, or due to boredom or disconnection with their culture. It is important however to appreciate the significance of drug taking within popular music culture.

Pop Drug Cults

Harry Shapiro (1999) gives a useful overview of drug taking associated with popular music culture in his book *Waiting for the Man: The Story of Drugs and Popular Music*. Jazz and Blues for example are shown to have numerous links with drug taking. Many early blues musicians performed at travelling medicine shows, which used music to sell pick-me-up cure-all medicines, which contained substances we would now regard as drugs, such as cocaine and morphine. Juke (or jook) joints would not simply be music venues, they would also act as illegal drinking venues (in the years of prohibition), and were home to illegal drug taking, prostitution and gambling. Oliver (1984, pp. 45–7) for example has discussed this. Blues clubs in cities were also associated with drug taking, gambling and prostitution, such as those on Beale Street in Memphis, where musicians such as Louis Armstrong, Muddy Waters, Albert King, Memphis Minnie, B. B. King and Rufus Thomas performed early in their careers.

When blues and jazz were developing, the USA had a powerful temperance movement, driven by religious groups, and within which women in particular had a powerful voice, unhappy with their husbands spending money on gambling, alcohol, drug taking and prostitution. This movement gained momentum in particular during the First World War, as women took up some typically male roles, and were granted equal rights to vote in 1919. It was therefore no co-incidence that alcohol was banned in the USA from 1919 to 1933, although little was done to enforce the ban nationally. Illegal drinking venues proliferated, as did the criminal organizations that managed them. These speakeasies were at the centre of jazz music during this period, and their illegality meant that they became associated with gambling, prostitution and drug taking as well. Nightclubs in cities were often still run by criminals or associated with criminality long after prohibition was abandoned, and jazz musicians became particularly associated with drug taking. Thus both blues and jazz musicians were often working in venues associated with illegality.

Cocaine use was common among black labourers in the Mississippi delta where blues first emerged, and was sold in various forms in cities such as Beale Street in Memphis, one of the key urban sites where blues developed. A number of blues songs discuss cocaine. Cocaine Blues, by T. J. 'Red' Arnall, was covered by many musicians, most famously by Johnny Cash at his Fulsom Prison concert. 'Cocaine Blues (Coco Blues)' was a traditional song associated with Rev. Gary Davis, and was covered most famously by Bob Dylan. 'Cocaine Habit Blues (Take a Whiff on Me)', also known as 'Tell it to Me', is usually associated with Leadbelly, as Sanders (2009) has discussed.

Numerous other blues and jazz musicians have been associated with drugs. Jelly Roll Morton started work as a pianist in a brothel, and reportedly sold drugs. Once marijuana was made illegal, references to it often were encoded, for example by calling it teal or one of a range of other terms. Examples of songs about cannabis include 'Muggles' by Louis Armstrong, 'Reefer Man' by Cab Calloway, 'A Viper's Drag' by Fats Waller, 'Viper Mad' by Sidney Bechet, 'Gimme a Reefer' by Bessie Smith, 'When I Get Low I Get High' by Ella Fitzgerald, 'Ol' Man River (Smoke a Little Tea)' by Duke Ellington, 'Texas Tea Party' by Benny Goodman, 'Smoking Reefers' by Larry Adler and 'I'm Feeling High and Happy' by Gene Krupa.

Marijuana was a little known drug in the 1920s, but was common among musicians, jazz musicians in particular often claiming it helped their playing. Hoagy Carmichael and Louis Armstrong were marijuana users, Armstrong being one of the first famous popular musicians to be arrested for drug use. Anti-drug law enforcement officers in the USA focused on arresting musicians to make examples of them, aiming to prevent others from taking drugs. Drug use was particularly prevalent among musicians, but this link was made more explicit by these prosecutions. Drug taking was therefore increasingly associated specifically with popular music and musicians.

In the 1950s and early 1960s, a large number of the most prestigious jazz musicians were arrested for drug use. This included Gerry Mulligan, Stan Getz, Billie Holiday, Art Pepper, Lester Young, Hampton Hawes, Chet Baker, Thelonius Monk, Miles Davis and Art Blakey. In addition Charlie Parker had a serious heroin addiction, and although he avoided arrest, like Monk he lost his cabaret card, stopping him from performing in New York, an important centre for jazz performers. Jazz clubs in the USA became foci of drug taking and associated culture, and links to organized crime that had developed during prohibition were maintained through drug dealers and suppliers. Drug taking became a normal activity for musicians, and musicians who were not drug takers were introduced to marijuana, cocaine and heroin by musicians who often claimed they helped musical performance.

Different drugs seem to have either inspired, or become associated with, particular types of popular music. Specific musical techniques have developed in music associated with particular drugs, in response to the effects of the drugs, or in order to enhance or interact with such effects. For example, marijuana has become particularly associated with music that originated in the Caribbean. Ska, rocksteady, reggae and dub are all musical genres that have been influenced by the common marijuana use on the island, particularly that of the Rastafarians in the population, who regard smoking the drug as a spiritual practice.

Dub music for example has a slow tempo, reflecting the way that marijuana can cause lethargy and relaxation. It also contains fractured vocal snippets and echo effects, which interact with the auditory hallucinations that marijuana can cause. King Tubby and Lee Scratch Perry's music provide good examples of dub. Marijuana is also often presented as stimulating laughter and confusion, and as inspiring a rambling but euphoric sense of understanding, of making new connections and seeing new ways of relating different concepts. The use of humour, as well as such hippie philosophizing, reflecting marijuana smoking, can be seen in music such as that of Gong, who make music that contains confused and confusing structures, as well as lyrical in-jokes, and rambling ideas.

Reggae music also became associated in particular with marijuana. Therefore many reggae musicians, including Bob Marley, are associated with marijuana. One of Marley's albums, *Kaya*, is a Jamaican slang term for the drug, for example, and there is an image of a marijuana cigarette on the back of the album's sleeve.

Amphetamine, known as speed, has inspired very different musical characteristics. One of the musicians best known for taking speed is Ian 'Lemmy' Kilminster. He was originally a member of Hawkwind, reputedly leaving the band at least in part due to his taking speed rather than the (different) preferred drugs of the rest of the band. On leaving Hawkwind, Lemmy formed Motorhead, whose music was known for being fast (full of speed) and loud, focusing on power and aggression, reflecting the increased heart rate, sense of everything happening with speed and aggression that are characteristics associated with and enhanced by amphetamines. This is another example of music having enhanced the effects of drug taking, and the effects of the drug inspiring the music, or causing it to develop further in a particular direction.

Amphetamines were taken by 1950s rock'n'roll musicians to keep them awake, along with a mix of other legal and illegal drugs that were taken to boost energy levels during late night performances. Jerry Lee Lewis in the USA had a long-term addiction to the drug for example, and Johnny Cash and Elvis Presley were both known to take amphetamines, Presley first taking them in the US army, where they were commonly given to troops to keep them awake, for example on sentry duty. The Beatles took large quantities of a similar drug called Preludin, during their years performing in clubs in Hamburg. In the UK, amphetamines were very commonly used within the mod scene, driving all night dancing at late-night clubs in swinging London. As Shapiro states,

For the mods, amphetamines were symbolically enshrined at the heart of their subculture, fitting into a discrete universe, a system of magical correspondence in which all objects – clothes, music, scooters and drugs – had a precise relationship with one another. Each item was taken from the straight world and redefined within a homogenous cosmos; amphetamines were the subcultural adhesive which joined lifestyles and values, the functional springboard for the frantic activity of staying up, buying clothes, riding and fixing mopeds, and dancing. (1999, p. 88)

Amphetamines went on to be a popular drug with rock musicians and fans. It also became the drug of choice for UK punks, whereas in the USA the bands who had inspired punk, such as the Velvet Underground and New York Dolls, were more associated with Heroin, The Velvet Underground for example writing 'Waiting for the Man' and 'Heroin' about their drug taking. In UK punk music one can readily see the influence of the speed that musicians took. Tempi were sped up; lyrics often had aggressive attitudes; the grain of voice of the singing was aggressive as was the distorted timbre of the guitar playing. In addition clothing was intended to be aggressive or offensive, dancing styles like pogo-ing full of energy and even haircuts spiked and coloured.

In the 1960s and 1970s hippie culture had drug culture closely associated with it, in particular marijuana smoking and LSD taking being prevalent. LSD had a mysticism associated with it due to its hallucinatory effects. The drug was initially used by psychiatrists to treat their patients. Hollywood actor Cary Grant, for example, was treated with LSD, stating afterwards,

All my life I've been searching for peace of mind. I'd explored yoga and hypnotism and made several attempts at mysticism. Nothing seemed to give me what I wanted until this treatment. (Lee and Schlain 1985, p. 57)

Shapiro discusses Timothy Leary's promotion of LSD, as being as if 'a religious fervour had gripped him; religious imagery informed all he felt about LSD. He was a priest of the God Acid; there was a message to preach, souls to be saved, bibles and tracts to be written' (Shapiro 1999, p. 107). Leary did indeed do much to publicize acid, and 'for acid veterans like Leary and Alpert, LSD was the psychic transporter for the journey into inner space and had to be treated with due reverence' (ibid., p. 108).

Jazz musicians such as John Coltrane, Dizzy Gillespie and Thelonius Monk took LSD before the drug became popular with other musicians. In London the Beatles, Eric Clapton, Donovan, Pink Floyd, Jimi Hendrix and the Rolling Stones all took LSD, and in the USA the Greatful Dead, Jefferson Airplane, The 13th Floor Elevators and Janis Joplin all became part of a developing San Francisco scene that featured psychedelic music and drugs, and that spread across the country.

LSD causes hallucinations involving complex and labyrinthine visual patterns and structures, confusion, an elongated or confused sense of time, odd perception, light trails or visual echoes as well as other effects. The music that became associated with it became similarly complex and labyrinthine, with meandering complex structures involving improvisation and repetition. Time structures were confused by the use of unusual time signatures and polyrhythms, and music was elongated to often fill whole sides of albums with one piece of music. Echo units were used to reflect the visual echoes of LSD-caused light trails. Phasers and flangers were used to simulate the changes in perception caused, to create different, altered sounds. Reversed tape loops and techniques drawn from avant-garde music were also used to create a sense of confusion. The early music of Pink Floyd has for example many of these features. Musicians like the Greatful Dead filled their performances with improvised sections, which could wander musically alongside the minds of musicians and audiences. Lyrics reflected the strange visions seen during LSD induced hallucinations. Performances sometimes took place at happenings, with psychedelic light shows, decorations and performance art all enhancing the experience. The happenings, be-ins and love-ins of the 1960s created safe contexts for fans to take drugs, away from their normal lives.

The Beatles' drug taking became particularly public through a series of drugs arrests of members of the band. Like many bands their music made reference to drug taking, drug experiences and the culture surrounding it. 'Lucy and the Sky with Diamonds' was much discussed because the main words in the title spelt LSD; 'A Day in the Life' features McCartney saying that he would love to turn you on and also discussing having a smoke and going into a dream, both drug references which led to the BBC banning the song; 'Day Tripper' is also an LSD reference; and there is also the lyric that says I get high 'With a Little Help From My Friends'.

Cocaine became associated with a number of music scenes. With links originally to early blues musicians, cocaine became the drug of choice for the rich and famous in the 1970s. Rock stars and music industry professionals mixed with the rich and celebrities from other areas, and cocaine consumption became a status symbol for many due to its expense. It was well known that rock stars such as Elton John, Freddie Mercury, Status Quo, Aerosmith and Oasis took cocaine, discussing it in interviews. One might typify music made by musicians taking cocaine as reflecting the way the drug is often described as providing self-confidence or arrogance to the user, and a sense of power and authority. Thus music associated with cocaine, such as some of the rock music of the 1970s, is characterized (especially in live performance) as having long, self-indulgent guitar and drum solos, operatic vocal parts, and involving musicians showing off their technical abilities. It also features power chords, and loud, brash, distorted guitars.

The New York gay disco scene involved various drugs, but in the 1970s cocaine was the drug most associated with clubs like Studio 54, the Loft and the Paradise Garage. Cocaine was taken to sustain and enhance the evening, providing clubbers with the energy to dance all night. While speed and other stimulants would also have been taken in clubs, the famous and glamorous crowd at clubs like Studio 54 were often associated with cocaine, which became increasingly associated with fame and celebrity. Cocaine was also taken to enhance the sexual experiences that often took place in the clubs, with a soundtrack of the pulsing beats of disco music a reflection of the sexualized content of disco music and culture.

Another dance scene that featured heavy drug use was the UK northern soul scene, where dancing all night was facilitated by drug taking much like within mod culture. Northern soul involved dancing to a particular type of obscure soul and Motown records from the USA. The less well known and more obscure the choice of records within the Northern Soul scene, the more popular they were likely to be. DJs competed to find obscure releases, avoiding mainstream material, and targeting the music at a dedicated group of fans. The scene developed its own dance style and iconic fashion sense, the most famous venue being the Wigan Casino, which was the centre of the scene.

Electronic dance music culture (EDMC), or club culture, which is discussed in more detail in another chapter, is also closely associated with drug taking. Ecstasy, amphetamines, LSD, ketamine, marijuana and cocaine are regularly taken by clubbers. Ecstasy was particularly popular when the scene developed in the UK in the late 1980s, the drug becoming well known at the same time as the music, the two growing in popularity and notoriety simultaneously. This was so much the case that EDMC dominated the music scene, and young people at the time became known as 'the chemical generation', with other related cultural forms developing, for example within film and literature.

Sanders discusses the use of drugs in clubs in detail. He describes the rise of club drugs and dance drugs, and that 'drug use remains a *defining* aspect of rave and club cultures' (2006, p. 7). He describes club drugs in three categories,

> Drugs whose use first became popular within club and rave settings (ecstasy, GHB, ketamine); drugs which enjoyed a kind of renaissance within such settings (LSD, psilocybin mushrooms); and drugs with a long history of abuse that also became common in raves and clubs (cocaine, crystal methamphetamine). (ibid., p. 6)

This is an American book, and it should be noted that crystal meth (or Tina as Sanders often refers to it) is not a common dance drug in the UK. Sanders points out that some studies have shown that those who have not taken drugs within EDMC are in the minority in their age group, and that cannabis use in particular has become normalized. It suggests that this is also the case for ecstasy among clubbers. They are aware of the risks involved, and

> Research from various countries generally suggests that young people who use drugs and attend raves and clubs are by and large law abiding. Drug use does not consume their lives, but is rather a contemporary and occasional component of their recreational behaviours. (ibid., p. 11)

This analysis questions whether drug taking can be seen as a marginal activity, either as an escapist activity or as a subcultural practice. The evidence shows that EDMC drug takers function quite successfully in their everyday lives, taking drugs at the weekends, but returning to their normal working lives in between. These are not drug addicts whose lives revolve entirely around drug taking, but people taking a nonaddictive, nonlethal illegal drug fully aware of its side effects. They are not part of a subculture, because they are still connected with mainstream culture. They exist in an electronic dance music scene, based around the clubs and other events they choose to attend.

Pop drug cults are perhaps the easiest section of popular music culture to align with descriptions of typical characteristics of cults. Popular music drug cults feature pop stars as iconic positive representations of drug taking. The pop star is able to achieve all the fan would want in life even though they take drugs (or appear to do so), sometimes in spectacular quantities, and do not seem to suffer any debilitating effects. The drug dealer in the background supplies the drugs, the magical substances that are able to change people's states of mind. They are shadowy figures, like witches or magicians, administering spells and potions that will change people radically, whether these are love/sex potions, or there to provide energy, confidence or mystical visions.

There is no scientific evidence that fans take drugs because pop stars do, although this has been suggested by many different sources. It may just be that pop stars take the drugs that are common in the musical scenes that surround them. To some extent, and in some cases, the stars take the drugs for the fans, so that the fans do not have to, fans living their fantasies out vicariously through iconic stars (as discussed in detail in the chapter on personality cults of popular music). High levels of drug taking often inevitably leads to death, and the star is then raised to a position of legendary icon, frozen in time (see the chapter on death cults of popular music).

Many popular music cults involve drug taking, and audiences may be as likely to take drugs as stars. The drug taking leads to a separation of the person's activities within the popular music cult, from the activities in their everyday life. It is important the two remain largely separate, not wanting their work colleagues to think their work life is affected by their drug taking, also not perhaps wanting their families to know they are drug takers.

This can lead to a secretiveness, which is also enhanced by the processes of finding, collecting, purchasing and taking drugs, all of which have to be secretive to some extent due to the illegality of drugs in most countries. Pop drug cults often use a secretive language to codify and disguise drug taking, creating further an insider us-versus-them dynamic typical of cults. Amphetamines are known as whizz, ecstasy tablets are known as doves or mitsis, marijuana is known as weed or spliff, and numerous song titles reference drug taking with disguised (or not so disguised in some cases) references.

Drug taking is perhaps the most convincing evidence of brain washing in any form of cult, as many drugs actually change the make-up or behaviour of the brain, sometimes with permanent effect. Drugs can change who a person is and how they behave in a substantial long-term fashion, as well as changing their mood temporarily. Many traditional cults have drug taking as part of their ritual ceremonies.

Cults are often accused of presenting themselves as benign, but of actually serving to make money for those behind the cult, and this could certainly be said to be true of pop drug cults. Drug supplies and suppliers often have links to organized crime, and profits are always raised on the black economy. Huge quantities of money are made from illegal drug sales, and the money often finds its way to gangsters and criminal gangs. In the countries of manufacture of these drugs, the drugs themselves often cause social problems, while being an important cash crop for some of the poorer inhabitants of the relevant country.

Individuals meanwhile spend money on something that may be causing them serious harm, with the potential to become addicted to the drug, and be in need of an intervention (again a piece of terminology relevant to cultic practices), and a form of deprogramming or rehabilitation to stop them from relapsing. Drugs may be supplied to bands for free, or by music business representatives, but fans have to spend their money on them, with no guarantee that they are getting the product they are asking for, or that they are not being ripped off. If someone becomes addicted then the cost of the addiction can spiral out of control, and lead the user into criminality in order to feed their habit.

It seems indeed from the ritualized habits of the drug cults of the sacred popular that certain musical scenes and subgenres act as a kind of drug cult. For example, the visions and altered perception caused by LSD meant that it was to be associated with spirituality and mysticism. In his novel *The Doors of Perception*, Huxley had suggested that LSD and Mescaline were able to offer experiences of the ecstasies of mystical revelation, and predicted a world-wide religious revival should such drugs become freely available. Since most of the larger organized religions proscribe the use of drugs, large numbers of people are instead having direct experiences of transendentalism outside of these mainstream faiths. Drugs are now widely available in the west, especially within a number of popular music cults, and it is within these drug cults within the sacred popular that Huxley's predicted religious revival has taken place.

Chapter 4

We Could Be Heroes: Personality Cults of the Sacred Popular*

Introduction

Popular music began in the 1950s to take over from film as the principal site where one would find icons of popular culture. Musicians such as Frank Sinatra, Elvis Presley, the Beatles, David Bowie, Madonna and Prince have become known as popular icons or pop gods and have also all starred in films, although they were first known for their music. The personality cults surrounding them are perhaps more powerful and dramatic than those surrounding film stars, as one knows that film stars are acting, and that their on-screen performances are not real. In contrast, pop stars' performances are assumed to be real, the emotions they portray, the lyrics they sing, the answers they give in interviews are supposed to portray the real lives of these liquid stars, no matter how plastic their public facades, how well constructed their media-friendly masks are. In their films all of these stars have not strayed far from their popular music personae, performing their authenticity within the role, bringing the grain of their pop character, as well as that of their voice, to the diegesis. In their films Presley and Sinatra mostly played romantic leads, reflecting their positions as teen pop heart-throbs, as well as often singing on screen or playing the part of a musician. The Beatles play themselves in their films. Bowie's film parts have reflected the androgynous spaceman of Ziggy Stardust, or smart suit-wearing Britishness of the Thin White Duke. Madonna's roles have often played on images of the sexual temptress, Italian American or powerful individual woman. Prince's films have been vehicles designed around his public pop star personality, *Purple Rain* being semi-autobiographical.

Television provides an even more appropriate platform for such stars than films, this newer screen medium providing what seems like a live feed of

---

* Material from this chapter appears in a different form in Till, R. (forthcoming), 'Pop stars and idolatry: An investigation of the worship of popular music icons, and the music and cult of Prince', *Journal of Beliefs & Values*.

musical performances, even when it is in fact recorded in advance. In the 1950s, the new medium of television transferred the excitement of the moment, of the now, of what was happening today in the world of music, across the planet from exciting metropolitan centres such as New York and London, Seattle and Liverpool, to the smallest village or town. The development and popularization of television went hand-in-glove with the development and spread of popular music youth culture, and its associated star system.

The Star System

A celebrity is someone who is well known for being famous, and whose name alone is recognizable, associated with their image, and is capable of generating money. Stars have various ways of becoming famous. Before the twentieth century, the fame was often achieved through actions, by becoming for example an icon of production, one of those who made the world what it is, or who had particular abilities. In contemporary consumer society stars are icons of consumption, not necessarily having achieved anything substantial other than fame itself, in order to be famous. A number of stars are famous for being famous, for their ability to manipulate the star system. Richard Dyer describes in some detail the star system, and its workings among actors, in his book *Stars*, as does Edgar Morin in his own book *Les Etoiles*. Although film stars dominated the star system in the first half of the twentieth century, and despite film stars still being both popular and famous, the popular music star has perhaps become the dominant form of popular star in Western Europe in more recent years.

For a star to progress to a point where they are described as a popular icon requires their achievement of a level of fame at which they are treated with the sort of respect traditionally reserved for religious figures. In order to be described as a popular icon, a star has to become a religious figure, to develop their own personality cult and recruit followers. Such popular icons have generally had critical success, have gained financial independence, have achieved a high level of fame, receive unconditional audience adulation, and crucially they are usually known by only one name. Many religious figures are recognizable from only one name, including Jesus, Moses, Mary, Judas, Buddha and the Pope. Political figures such as Che, Churchill, Kennedy, Nixon, Stalin, Hitler, Nelson and Lenin are known by one name, as are the most iconic sports stars, scientists and artists including Pele, Ali, Maradona, Einstein, Da Vinci and Shakespeare. A second name defines one's family, so for example there are many people called Mary, for example Mary Tudor, Mary Shelley, Mary Smith, Mary Jones, Mary Brown. However if the name Mary were used with no other descriptor, the name would have to refer to someone who is the most famous example of this name, and with whom the name is so powerfully associated that if one sees the name alone one knows who is being referred to. The Mary referred to in such a case would no doubt be the mother of Jesus.

For example, Nelson (in the UK) would be thought of as the English naval leader at the battle of Trafalgar, whereas Nelson Mandela is known iconically by his surname, one knows if one discusses 'Mandela' it is him one is talking of, any other Mandela (such as Winnie) or Nelson (such as Nelson Riddle) have to have their surname or forename added in order to explain. These relationships can of course change and be different in varying geographical contexts. It is possible for example that in the USA the British Admiral Lord Nelson's fame is being challenged by the use of the name within the cartoon series *The Simpsons*, and that someone may be an icon only in one or more countries, and to one of more generations. The greatest popular icons are known and recognized internationally, by their names and by the image associated with that name, most usually a face. This is a branding that is very similar to the association of a product with a logo.

In the past one's actions had to carry substantial significance for a level of fame high enough to be known by only one name. However, global communications networks and international marketing have enabled successful film stars such as Cagney, Brando, Chaplin, Laurel, Hardy, Monroe and De Nero to achieve a similar level of fame. Directors such as Spielberg and Tarantino have achieved iconic status partly because they have been interviewed or seen performing in films often enough for their faces to be associated with their names. Scorsese and Kubrick are household names, but are less iconic directors, perhaps because their faces are not as well known as their names. Kubrick's name recalls his films *2001: A Space Odyssey* or *A Clockwork Orange*. The projection of the faces of stars onto television and film screens has associated their faces with a single name in a powerful way, allowing a person to become a personified icon. This process is boosted by the fact that this face is shown, even on the 'small' screen of television, larger than their face really exists, the giant face deifying itself rather like the effect of a massive statue of a religious figure such as Buddha. It is our gods that are presented as giants, larger than life, floating in the air on screens, on posters on walls in the street or in our homes. It is this combination of the image and single name description that characterizes the icon and differentiates it from a star. A radio star, for example, rarely now becomes an icon, no matter how famous, as Trevor Horn and The Buggles explained when they sung that 'Video Killed the Radio Star', the video for this song being the first to be shown on MTV in the UK.

The development of the use of icons by the entertainment industry for branding and other marketing purposes has been similar to that in the manufacturing industry. As Longhurst puts it, 'Stars function as trademarks which generate sales for the music business and the culture industries more widely' (1995, p. 185). Marketing and public relations campaigns work to promote products in the same fashion in popular music and other contexts. Nike, Budweiser and Coke all use a single word/name in association with visual branding using artwork, colour and graphics to create an iconic product which can transfer quickly through media channels and be recognizable to a world-wide audience. Thus Coca Cola and Pepsi Cola have become known simply as Coke and Pepsi. Pop stars such as Elvis, Lennon, McCartney, Sinatra, Britney, Madonna, Prince, Bono, Jagger, Hendrix, Kylie and Bowie have been marketed in this way, all achieving iconic (single name) status. This has often been the result of a skilful marketing campaign. A series of managers such as Colonel Tom Parker (Elvis Presley), Brian Epstein (the Beatles), Simon Fuller (Spice Girls, S Club 7, Pop Idol) and Simon Cowell (X Factor) have themselves become famous by marketing the stars they have managed.

Some stars have consciously recognized the power of being known by only one name, notably including Madonna and Prince, choosing to be referred to by single names with grandiose connotations. Others, such as Elvis Presley, came to be known by one name by their fans and the media. Elvis, the King, or Presley are interchangeable, such is his power as the first true pop icon, Sinatra belonging to the earlier jazz and swing era rather than that of the post-1955 rock'n'roll revolution. The importance of image in this process has meant that an artist's image has become as important to success within popular music as the quality of their music. Indeed, it has meant that for some artists the careful handling of branding, marketing and image has been the dominant factor in, and feature of, their success. However, most musical artists who have sustained iconic status also have gained recognition at some point for the quality of their music. To identify a popular music star as having achieved iconic status, one would look for identification by a single name, critical success, financial success, international audience recognition and fame, as well as a musical career that is successful in the long term.

Another way of describing this process is as the creation of a mediapheme. Mediaphemes are quick encapsulations. Once a story, person or event is translated into mediapheme form, it ricochets through the channels of mass mediation with ease, as Baty (1995) tells us. This often makes use of cultural archetypes such as the first of a kind, a great rivalry, someone who risks all, outrageous behaviour, a young dramatic death, a hero or villain, saint or sinner. Fred Johnson (2004) has used the idea of mediaphemes to discuss the work of U2, and it works equally well in the case of Prince. There are many similarities between an icon and a mediapheme, a mediapheme is perhaps a postmodern form of, or term for, an icon. A mediapheme is the media construction that enables a star to achieve the status of popular icon.

Idols and Icons, Idolatry and Iconography

To fully understand popular iconography, it is useful to understand the history of the icon. Christianity has much to say about images and their use when related to the divine, as do Judaism and Islam. The first and second commandments of Christian doctrine state,

7 You shall have no other gods before me. 8 You shall not make for yourself an idol in the form of anything in heaven above or on the earth beneath or in the waters below. 9 You shall not bow down to them or worship them; for I, the LORD your God, am a jealous God. Deut. (5: 7–9).

These commandments are primary tenets of belief for Jewish, Christian and Islamic religions. As this paper is looking specifically at the work of Prince, and Prince's background is Christian, I will focus principally on Christianity's approach to idols and icons. The old testament of the bible here illustrates a historical struggle between the Jewish culture of the time and other middle-eastern traditions, by condemning as idolatry the worship of idols within other local religious traditions. The worship and offering of prayers and sacrifices to religious statues and images of numerous deities was a common part of many non-Jewish local religious traditions at the time, and this is a religious practice that is still common worldwide.

Idolatry is defined in religious traditions such as Christianity as the worship of an idol, image, person or figure, the worship of any illustration of the divine, rather than the divine itself. Judaism and Islam have taken commandments against idolatry literally, and no images of God or the divine are permitted. However paintings of Jesus began to circulate early in the history of Christianity, although a major controversy arose over their use. Many Christian denominations came to the conclusion it was acceptable to use images to direct the mind of the worshipper towards the divine. These images, both two-dimensional paintings and three-dimensional statues, are regarded as hollow vessels which are filled by God. Thus, the worshipper is not worshipping the image, the signifier, but worship is being directed at what is represented by the image, the signified. Orthodox, Catholic, Anglican and Methodist Christianity accept religious images, although some Christian denominations, including those linked to Calvinism or fundamentalism, condemn any use of images of God.

Images of religious scenes, as well as figures in churches, became known as icons. Iconography originally related to the identification, description and interpretation of the content of images, and began by referring to religious images. It can also involve the painting of images, and the semiotic study of images or signs. An icon is an object that portrays something else, and iconography is literally icon writing. The creation of icons developed into an important part of Christian worship. It developed its own symbolic language, with its own codes and networks of meanings. For example a nimbus or halo behind a head was used to indicate the holiness of a figure portrayed in an icon, and colour had specific meanings, for example red representing divine life, blue for human life, purple as a combination of red and blue representing both the human and the divine, or perhaps a mixture of the two. Many authors discuss the history of icons, including Hallick (2001) and Besancon (2001).

Popular Icons

The techniques for constructing popular icons are rooted in, or similar to, these earlier religious traditions, and these techniques are used by the music industry in order to enhance the success of a popular musician. This contemporary popular iconography uses every aspect of twenty-first century multimedia techniques. Videos, websites, photographs, ringtones, clothing, fan clubs, films, concerts and a huge range of other merchandise allow the icon to be a three-dimensional, moving, multimedia creation, based on the character of the performer, but weaving myth and fantasy into a hyper-real legend using public relations companies, press releases and media manipulation.

Popular icons have an entire world that surrounds them, in which the pop star appears to live, and this world is a curious mixture of fantasy and reality. The setting of popular music within a performing arts tradition, in which the body is the main instrument of performance, has made the creation of a semi-fictional pop star character a key part of the art form of the pop musician. 'Pop' is used here to indicate mainstream chart music traditions, pop music being traditionally associated with a younger audience and commercially driven successful current music, whereas 'popular' music includes folk music, underground music subcultures, historical traditions and a broader range of less commercial forms. The star attempts to convince the audience that what they are performing is their own authentic emotions and their 'true' self, while actually enhancing, exaggerating, inventing or selectively revealing material within this presentation to make it interesting to the public. This is not so much deceit as story telling, it is theatre, and in this case quite literally all the world's a stage.

Consumer culture uses popular icons as exemplars of idealized consumers, the music industry in particular presenting them as seemingly perfect, aspirational models of consumption. Their images are used to sell products with little functional value, to add enhanced value, encouraging the purchase of the products associated with these icons. Consumer culture requires consumption to exceed need, in order to ensure that as much is consumed as is produced, with the aim of sustaining never-ending growth (Dyer 1979, pp. 38–43). Popular music icons have what appear to be infinite needs. They sell objects that are not essential, that are not food, shelter, clothing or education, for example. They project an imaginary (or semi-fictional) extravagant life style featuring such things as limousines, designer clothes, huge houses and a large entourage. They sell objects with little inherent value outside of association with their cult, including t-shirts, badges, recordings, DVDs, posters, magazines and perfumes, providing products that the consumer can buy in order to be more like, or feel closer to, their favourite icon, to allow consumption of the icon.

Since the objects in this market sector are non-essential, the potential size of this market is almost infinite. Since there is no physical need for these things that can be satisfied by a certain quantity of them, there is no obvious physical limit to the size of the market. At no point will a dedicated fan call a halt to purchases by choice, they would be likely to consume until they are limited by lack of funds, or the failure of the product to continue to attract their loyalty. Thus as long as the fans' devotion can be maintained, products can be continually created, marketed, sold and consumed. This makes the maintenance of an obsessive devotion to the popular icon by the fan, a key relationship within popular music. If this relationship can be established and sustained, then the popular music icon's career will continue. The quality of the musical product therefore becomes only a small part of that relationship, and not necessarily the most important element in the success of a popular music star. These dynamics drive popular music scenes to become much like a personality cult, where the iconic star, as well as the recording industry lurking behind them, work to maintain the obsessive fanaticism of commitment of the fan to the cult of the star, and where the multi-million pound marketing machines of the entertainment industry use every manipulative technique available to them to enhance and sustain this commitment. This often amounts to a far more sophisticated and subtle process than that present within most other religious cults, which are often small and comparatively poorly funded and resourced.

Traditional religious icons were in the past regarded as hollow vessels inhabited by God. The popular icon is similarly hollow, to be filled or inhabited by the viewer, by the consumer or fan. This means that the fans inhabit the place traditionally filled by a god, deifying themselves. As Bing Crosby puts it 'Every man who likes me sees in me the image of himself' (Buxton 1985, pp. 187–9). In a similar vein George Michael has stated 'It's not the something extra that makes the star – it's the something that's missing' (Goodwin 1993, p. 117). As Chion (1994, p. 50) puts it 'How are legends born? Out of a lack, a void that needs filling'.

The representation can never equal the represented as the signifier is never equal to the signified, and thus it can appear that the more hollow, vacuous and lacking in content the star is, the more successful they can become. Identification with or rejection of these signifiers is used to tell the observers' own stories. Holding back information about a star leaves space for observers to fill in the gaps with their selves, and thus many stars have carefully controlled media identities. Stars like Elvis, Madonna and Prince did few interviews, and kept a sense of mystery surrounding their personal lives. Other stars, such as Britney Spears, whose lives have been widely reported in the press, have lost control of their public identities, and become all too human and well known to their fans. A popular icon whose faults are revealed and who the audience can see is more normal than special is likely to struggle to maintain their iconic status, and as a result to maintain the interest of their fans.

For the performer this process is a mystical one, addressing the void, stillness and space, allowing exploration of the self, and for the divine to indwell the empty vessel. The worshipper seeks a direct experience of the worshipped icon, mysticism being used here to describe involving 'a religious tendency and desire of the human soul towards an intimate union with the divinity' (Sauvage 1911). This is preceded by katharsis or purification, the emptying out of self, addressing the void, stillness and space, so that the divine, in this case the fans' projection of self, can indwell the empty vessel of the popular icon. The process is also similar to the concept of theosis in Christian theology. This is the transformation of believers into the likeness of God, including transforming the mind, character and self, as well as the imitation of, or union with God (Finlan and Kharlamov 2006).

In a similar process, fans are transformed to be like the popular icon, involving imitation and, by projection, union between fan and star. The performer is filled, inspired and sustained by the projected adulation of the fans, the worshipper creating the popular icon, without an audience a star is merely another member of the public. As members of the audience imagine themselves being or possessing a popular icon, they are then embodied as larger than life characters, godlike beings, possessing the star as they consume them and become possessed themselves by the character of the star. Thus the personality cult of the star also becomes much like a contemporary form of possession cult, as stars and audience possess one another (I have discussed possession trances in more detail in the chapter on trance cults). As Morin puts it, 'the worshipper always desires to consume his god ... The faithful want to know everything: possess, manipulate, and mentally digest the total image of the idol' (1960, pp. 90). 'Worshipped as heroes, divinized, the stars are more than objects of admiration. They are also subjects of a cult. A religion in embryo has formed around them' (ibid., p. 71).

As Longhurst describes it, 'Stars appeal because the audience wants to understand or fill in the knowledge that is missing' (1995, p. 186). When the fan is listening to the singing of the star in the privacy of their bedroom, or within the exclusivity of the earphones of their MP3 player, this can seem a very intimate relationship. The insertion of the fan inside the star (or vice-versa) can be a very personal process, with obvious sexual analogies, which many icons exploit with a sexualized style of performance, as has been seen in a previous chapter. Each fan imagines they are like the star, and that the star is like them. Dyer (drawing on Tudor 1975, p. 80) defines four different ways that audiences relate to film stars, namely emotional affinity, self-identification, imitation and finally projection. Projection happens when imitation goes beyond image and affects the person's life in a more substantial fashion (Dyer 1979, p. 18).

Film stars promote their films only periodically, and they play different characters in different situations. Popular music stars usually play only one part, themselves, although those like Bowie and Madonna who have acting experience, have managed to successfully create a series of successful pop star characters. Their appearances onstage add credence and authenticity to their constructed reality, as it is otherwise perceived through songs and interviews. Far more information is available about music stars than screen stars, with fanzines, fan websites, interviews in numerous music magazines, promotion for a series of singles and albums, books, videos, TV appearances, interviews and other material giving detailed information about their behaviour and opinions. This material is not always factual, but it is not clearly fictional. Fans assume that popular singers are singing about their real experiences and feelings, although this is often not the case. Pop stars carefully mix fact and fiction to create a hyper-real personality that is more interesting, and extravagant, than any real person. They draw upon cultural myths and archetypes for their media constructions, upon histories of other icons, and on numerous other media sources.

Unlike film culture, where the audience usually leaves the star behind in the cinema, the artefacts of popular music are designed to penetrate deeply into the life of a fan. Recordings and videos are kept in their homes and carried around in ipods. Images are displayed both on t-shirts on chests and posters on walls. Only the most obsessive fan of a film star quotes or acts out their scenes from a film, whereas pop fans will routinely sing along with a singer, memorizing their words. It is quite normal for popular music fans to feel a deep level of involvement with a star, imitating their dress, hair or image, thus imitation and projection are both common. Karaoke allows fans to imitate their heroes, as do computer games that allow fans to play the part of a popular guitar hero (as in the game Guitar Hero), singer (as in Singstar) or band member (as in Rock Band). Fan clubs, often set up or run by the management of the musician, allow the audience to feel more intimately involved with the star, allowing the musician to market directly to the most interested and obsessive members of the audience, building a personality cult. In recent years, myspace, facebook, twitter and blog websites allow popular icons to offer controlled fans' access to them, offering the fans a carefully moderated insight into the lives of their heroes.

Prince and Mediaphemes

Prince is one such star who has managed to progress to the status of popular icon, using an overt strategy which has proven very successful. Born Prince Rogers Nelson, he launched himself as a solo artist, shortening his name to Prince, creating a mediapheme drawn from his various influences, using a number of themes and traditions. He was born of mixed race parentage in Minneapolis, a US city that had no large black community or separate black music tradition to inspire him (as in for example New York, Chicago, New Orleans, Memphis or Detroit). Prince has therefore drawn from both black and white American musical cultures. He has integrated funk and blues guitar music from black musical culture, along with the most popular white derivatives of the day of black musical forms, new romantic music and cock rock guitar music. He plays with and uses the black and white traditions of the guitar hero, and presents himself as a virtuoso performer and auteur producer. He draws themes of sexuality from the homoerotic yet heterosexual preening of heavy metal, the raw eroticism of early blues and funk, and the gender ambiguity of the new romantics. He plays the part of a pop god, enhanced by an exploration of spirituality and divinity. Neither black nor white, he presents himself as purple. He eventually reduced himself to a symbol, both contesting and enhancing his treatment as a product within the music industry.

Sexuality

Prince consciously adopted an overt sexuality as a deliberate marketing ploy, while working with lyricist Chris Moon. Moon claims focusing on 'naughty, sexual innuendo', as well as the use of the one word name Prince, were his ideas (Hill 1989, pp. 31–2). Whoever was responsible, Prince's early work is full of innuendo and less than subtle sexual references, and it becomes clear that this is a deliberate theme that runs through much of his work. Prince's song 'Soft and Wet', lyrics co-written with Moon, is an early example of this style, with lyrics:

Hey lover I got a sugarcane
That I wanna lose in you …
Soft and wet, you are soft and wet,
Your love is soft and wet.

The lyrics on his album *Purple Rain* continue this theme, and in the song 'Darling Nikki' the lyrics describe a young woman 'in a hotel lobby masturbating with a magazine'. When the wife of American senator Al Gore, Tipper Gore, heard her daughter listening to this song, in response she set up the Parents Music Resource Centre to campaign for parental advisory warning stickers to be attached to recordings with adult themes. This acted to further enhance Prince's reputation and fame, the PRMC inadvertently advertising his music across the USA with the aid of governmental authority and a whirlwind of controversy (Chastagner 1999).

An excellent illustration of the construction and performance of Prince's popular iconic character or mediapheme is the performance of the song 'Let's Go Crazy' from the film *Purple Rain* released in 1984. A vehicle written to feature Prince as its star, the film is styled as an extended rock video, with a loose plot gathered around musical set pieces both live and recorded. 'Let's Go Crazy' begins the film, which blurs reality and fiction, using a mixture of autobiographical and fictional elements, creating a mythical Prince. Some of the music featured (not including 'Let's Go Crazy') was recorded live in concert and this adds to the confusion of how much within the film is real and how much is fictional. This film helped to create the perception of a legendary Prince that no longer had to be bound by reality and could rise to iconic status. It was a critical and commercial success and along with the associated soundtrack album it established Prince as an international musical superstar. It allowed Prince to create and present his iconic construction in detail.

There are many examples of sexual references during 'Let's Go Crazy'. Prince simulates masturbation by crouching down on the floor with the guitar sticking out from between his legs, running his hand up and down the neck. This move is characteristic of Jimi Hendrix who was an important influence on Prince. He thrusts his pelvis, while at the same time gasping twice into the microphone. The grain (Frith 1981, p. 165) of his voice is breathy and full of gasps, using audio compression with a low threshold to enhance these sounds. This works by reducing the volume levels of the most loud sounds and boosting the overall level, meaning that quieter sounds become comparatively louder. One member of the audience is even pictured licking the face of another.

As well using overtly sexual content in his work, Prince presents an ambiguous sexuality. Rather than adopt the clothing of black funk musicians or white rock musicians, guitarist Dez Dickerson brought a mixture of glam rock and new romantic clothing with him when he joined Prince's band. Dickerson claims responsibility for beginning the feminized style consciousness that came to characterize the visual image of much of Prince's work (Hill 1989, p. 54). This included items such as dandy-like ruffs and frills, lace, waistcoats, frock-coats, jackets, suits, silk scarves, colourful and extreme make-up and permed or crimped, extravagantly styled long hair.

Both the new romantic and glam rock music scenes were heavily influenced by David Bowie's asexuality/bisexuality, and his use of costume and make-up. Bowie's creation of semi-fictional characters such as Ziggy Stardust, Alladin Sane and The Thin White Duke (as discussed in the chapter on popular music sex cults) has clear parallels in Prince's work, as does his feminized approach to the role of the guitar hero. Much like Prince, Ziggy Stardust, Bowie's most famous creation, was a guitar hero and singer, looked androgynous, wore make-up and was the star of a film based on live music performances. Bowie said in 1971 that,

> I'm going to play a character called Ziggy Stardust. We're going to do it as a stage show. We may even do it in the West End. When I'm tired of playing Ziggy I can step out and someone else can take over for me. (Auslander 2006, p. 73)

In 1992 he told NME music paper that he would spend 'another few months getting [Ziggy] entirely out of my system, and then we'll don another mask' (ibid.). A film was made of Bowie's last gig as Ziggy, called *Ziggy Stardust and the Spiders from Mars: The Motion Picture*, a concert film and documentary.

Bowie went on to be involved in a number of films, as an actor, often playing parts that overlapped with his onstage persona. His music had also integrated rock guitar and dance rhythms, and his live shows integrated performance art and theatricality with his music. Bowie crossed boundaries, acted transgressionally and paved the way for artists like Prince to make the creation of semi-fictional, semi-autobiographical onstage characters part of the art form of popular music performance. Prince adopts the approach of David Bowie, who has stated 'I have never been convinced by the importance of authenticity … I have always engaged in the idea of an entertainer who performs authenticity. Yes I think one cannot be authentic' (Von Appen and Doehring 2006, p. 38). Prince can also be seen to perform authenticity, and has much in common with Bowie.

Prince crosses traditional lines of gender much as Bowie had done before him. Baitz discusses Prince bridging boundaries of cock rock (male) and pop (female) forms adopting a transgressional approach to gender (2007). Dance music forms and African American music (Prince can be described as both) are not always gendered in as clear and simple fashion as cock rock, are not predominantly associated with the masculine or feminine. Prince's work clearly aims to market itself to both cock rock and pop audiences, to both men and women. It does so by crossing these boundaries and drawing upon other forms such as blues, rhythm'n'blues (R'n'B) and disco. Prince wears feminine clothes and make-up, sings in a high falsetto voice and presents a feminized image. Women are often prominent in his work, presented as the objects of his affections, as well as the inspiration for much of his appearance. He has regularly employed women as musicians, notably including keyboard player Lisa Coleman, guitar player Wendy Melvoin and drummer Sheila E. It was most unusual within popular music at the time for a male solo artist like Prince to have so many female musicians as part of his band. His approach to sexuality is very different from the titillation of pop heart-throbs or of testosterone driven cock rock, dealing lyrically as it does with issues such as incest, masturbation, oral sex and threesomes, adopting a complex approach to sexuality that generated a huge level of media interest. He also understood the power of mixing sexuality and religious references, and that this would help to guarantee controversy and even greater media coverage.

The Sacred and the Profane

Prince had a Christian upbringing, and had adopted many ideas from James Brown's onstage persona, which itself was based on African American gospel preachers. Prince went to a live concert by 'James Brown when he was 10 and he went straight home to practice the moves' (Sutcliffe 1992). Prince uses many of the techniques that are used by such preachers to generate excitement among their congregations. He uses numerous references taken from this tradition to conjure up an atmosphere charged with a feeling of powerful emotions and transcendence. 'Let's Go Crazy' in *Purple Rain* uses many of these techniques and references.

The film begins in darkness with a simple church-like organ chord the only sound heard. From the darkness comes Prince's voice. He speaks as if he is officiating at a church service. His first phrase is 'Dearly beloved we are gathered here today', a reference to the first lines of the Christian marriage service, which begins 'Dear beloved we are gathered here' (Church of England 1978). The marriage service goes on to describe marriage as 'signifying the mystical union that is betwixt Christ and his Church'. In this case Prince is presiding over a joining of himself with his church, his congregation, his audience of fans. This places him in the position of Christ or deity, marrying, possessing and becoming one flesh with his worshippers, carrying obvious sexual overtones. The rest of Prince's opening address is an odd mix of references, but what is notable is the organ accompaniment and spoken style that sets up a religious context not only for the concert, but also for the relationship of the audience with Prince, and for the film in general as well. It makes the audience aware that they are here to worship their idol, not just watch a concert, preparing the way for a film which features numerous opportunities for Prince to be presented as an icon.

Prince is often backlit during 'Let's Go Crazy', the stage lighting from the front replaced by powerful rear white lights that leave the band silhouetted. Backlighting is used much in the way that a halo, a circle of light also known as a nimbus, is placed behind the head of a divine being in religious (iconographic) artwork in Christian, Hindu, Roman and Greek contexts. Within Christianity this symbol is used to indicate the logos or divinity of Christ, Mary or other holy figures. Here it is Prince who is presented as divine.

Beams of light come down from above, surrounded by clouds of smoke from a smoke machine, as if the band, raised up on the stage, were in heaven, set above and beyond the audience. This structuring of music concerts enhances the perception of musicians on stage as being above and superior to the audience. They are brightly lit, raised on a platform and separated by security guards and fences from the audience. The crowd is encouraged to project their appreciation towards the stage by clapping, holding their hands aloft, singing along with, screaming at or imitating the group.

At one point in this performance, the audience mimics Prince's hand movements, joining in with their hero and feeling for a moment connected to him. The audience applauds the musicians onstage, faces looking up in adulation, reaching out towards Prince to touch him. The song finishes with Prince ascending into the light. He climbs up onto the piano, and, with a light carefully placed behind his head to create another nimbus like image, plays a solo guitar cadenza, spotlighting his guitar virtuosity, his extraordinary musical ability. Virtuosity is another sign that a musician has superior powers and abilities than the audience, that they are special, gifted, chosen, close to the divine. At this moment he is alone. He is physically alone on top of the piano, raised up literally and metaphorically above the rest of the band as well as the audience, and musically he is alone, not accompanied by anyone else. He is alone in the light, the one and only Prince, above everybody else and presented for the worship of those below him, deified and ascended, taken up among the stage lights, as if taken up into the heavens among the stars. It is no surprise that the famous are described as stars, glittering brightly up above, placed in the heavens as deities often are, and shining light upon those below.

Black and White

The mixing of sacred and secular traditions is well established within African American music. Blues, rhythm and blues, soul, funk and disco are all African American secular music genres that have included elements that came from gospel music. Prince's work explores and transgresses the boundaries between the sacred and secular, much as he adopts a transgressional approach to traditional sexual boundaries. It is no surprise then that he also explores the boundaries of black and white culture. Mixing colours is part of his transgressive mediapheme, part of that which makes him transgressional and iconic.

Prince was influenced by a number of black musicians. Sly and the Family Stone were a major influence musically on Prince, as were their flower power messages, outrageous clothes and the image of Sly Stone himself. As well as his onstage twirls and preacher-like onstage persona, Prince copied many elements of his musical style from James Brown, including funky drumming (Stewart 2000) and bass lines, keyboard parts, rhythm guitar playing, and arrangements, with a number of interlocking parts based around a central groove. Vincent (1996) provides a good description of groove in funk.

As discussed earlier, Prince modelled his guitar playing in particular on Jimi Hendrix as well as earlier blues guitarists. Hendrix had played in the backing band of rock'n'roll pioneer Little Richard, whose influence is clearly evident in both Hendrix and Prince's work. Little Richard was feminine, looked androgynous, was of mixed race, wore make-up, used a falsetto voice and was a dramatic and extravagant performer. He alternated between religious fundamentalism and promiscuous homosexuality. Hamilton (1998) and White (2003) both describe Little Richard's career in some detail.

> It is almost impossible to overestimate the importance of Little Richard as a formative experience on Jimi Hendrix. On his arrival in England, Hendrix told interviewers, 'I want to do with my guitar what Little Richard does with his voice.' Richard himself told Charles White that Hendrix 'Just loved the way I wore those headbands round my hair and how wild I dressed', 'He began to dress like me and he even grew a little moustache like mine'. (Shaar Murry 1989, pp. 39–40)

Hendrix imitated Little Richard, and Prince would in turn emulate both of them. His work also emulates Stevie Wonder who is like Prince and

James Brown in that he played many of the instrumental parts on his recordings, was a virtuoso player of a number of instruments, and also produced his music himself.

Prince wanted to move beyond the racially segmented audience other black musicians principally performed to, in order to sell to a larger, mainstream, white audience. Following Sly Stone's example Prince employed black and white band members and influences, and integrated musical influences from Led Zeppelin, the Beatles, the Rolling Stones and other white bands. Prince's father was Italian/Philipino while his mother was black, and he has said 'I don't necessarily think of myself as a member of the black race – more a member of the human race' (Salewicz 1981). From white European new romantic musical culture he adopts characteristic electronic sounds.

As already discussed, a dress sense and hairstyles influenced by Bowie and new romantic musical groups had also been adopted from white musical culture. The audience featured in *Let's Go Crazy* in the scenes set in a nightclub, are archetypal 1980s new romantics. The men and women have 'big' hair; excessive, sparkling, colourful make-up; sunglasses that are worn inside the venue; wear lace and ripped fishnet stockings; and have long, extravagant, non-symmetrical, haircuts. They are also largely a white audience. At a time when MTV showed little or no music by black artists, Prince presented an image that mixed and combined elements of black and white culture, and was able to escape the racial stereotyping of the US dance and R'n'B charts.

To further avoid being pigeonholed as either primarily black or white, Prince presents himself as purple. He became well known for being associated with purple, using the colour as a pervasive theme in his work, in packaging, merchandising, lyrics, clothing and videos. Within traditional religious icon design, red represents divine life, while blue represents human life, purple is a mixture of the two, and is a colour that has been used in many situations to signify the regal or transcendental. Purple dye in ancient Rome was worn by senators and emperors in their togas and went on to become associated more broadly with aristocracy (Vout 1996). It is also associated with psychedelia and 1960s culture, referencing the ultraviolet or black light used in hippie lighting effects. An example of this is Jimi Hendrix titling perhaps his most famous song 'Purple Haze' which lyrically references drug-taking. Influenced by the psychedelia of The Beatles and Hendrix, Prince makes the colour purple part of his mediapheme, his film *Purple Rain* prominently featuring a purple jacket, purple motorcycle and purple guitar.

Performance

Prince defines himself as a slick and skilful performer and entertainer. He shows this in the last seconds of 'Let's Go Crazy', as he jumps off the piano, and joins the band in a clichéd end of song blues chord sequence, a good example of his use of performance skills to validate his authenticity. Prince sings, plays the guitar and plays the piano in this section of the film. This is performance art, just as Bowie's most theatrical performances were, but it also echoes the Motown reviews of the 1960s. Motown acts were well known for their dance choreography, members of the backing band performing carefully choreographed dance routines. Prince's band also performs carefully choreographed dance moves, jumping up in the air on cue in time to the music. Prince jumps off the piano at the end of this song, performing a flying leg splits. At another point in the song he spins to stand next to the guitarist and they coordinate their choreography. The band members hold a sequence of static poses, every moment part of a slickly rehearsed show. One is left in no doubt that the band is musically skilled, and that the performance is well rehearsed. Prince's skills are showcased in particular, in order to illustrate that he is a highly talented, virtuoso performer, leader of the band and also a stylish dancer.

Musically 'Let's Go Crazy' is quite simple. Baitz points out in her analysis the clear similarities between the bridge section of the song and that of 'Fire' by Jimi Hendrix. Baitz also claims that the main chord sequence is the same as that of 'Louis Louis' by The Kingsmen, describing it as having a I IV V IV chord progression, and it does indeed have a number of similarities to that song. The Kingsmen's song was the subject of a notorious legal case after there were suggestions that the slurred lyrics contained overtly sexual material. Given Prince's regular sexual references, it would not be surprising that Prince would reference the song.

However I would characterize 'Let's Go Crazy' instead as having a I IV bVII IV progression. This is what is played by the second guitar part, and also is evident in what Baitz calls the turnaround figure, when the band plays on every crotchet. The two harmonic descriptions are not incompatible, a bVII chord being a gospel or blues alternative for the more conventional V chord. This reading shows the chord sequence to also be similar to 'Everybody Needs Somebody to Love', a Solomon Burke soul/gospel track that has been performed by the Rolling Stones and in the film *The Blues Brothers*. Both 'Let's Go Crazy' and 'Everybody Needs Somebody to Love' have a similar drum beat, similar tempi, a rhythmic riff based on a quaver upbeat followed by two crotchets, a similar slightly swung rhythm as well as echoing male-female lead-backing vocal parts.

They also have similar rhythms in the vocal melodies. The line 'Let's Go Crazy' has a similar rhythm to 'Everybody', a similar melodic shape and the same number of syllables, with everybody being shortened to e-v'ry-bo-dy in the Burke song. Both songs feature a breakdown section where the vocals are sung almost acapella, with a much reduced accompanying texture. Both songs also feature at the end a similar double time section (Baitz's turnaround). In Prince's song the keyboard introduces a straight rhythm with a note/chord/beat on every crotchet, with the bass and guitars also playing this driving rhythm. A turnaround is a term taken from jazz and blues harmony, where an extra chord, usually a V7 chord, is placed just before the start of a new sequence, launching the chord sequence back to the beginning and maintaining a sense of harmonic pace and movement. Everybody has a similar double-time section at the end of it, also featuring a turnaround, the bass doubling its tempo and adding the third of the V7 chord on the upbeat, changing the chord from bVII to V7b. Both songs end with a long sustained chord, over which the musicians improvise, creating a typical gospel/blues sound.

Both songs also contain a gospel preacher style vocal introduction. Burke provides an inspirational lyric, with gospel sentiments, but a universal rather than specifically Christian sentiment. Prince takes a similar, if slightly odder, approach. Burke's musical style is generally characterized by the mixing of the driving rhythms of R'n'B with Gospel lyrics and sentiments. By drawing upon this song as an influence Prince references the long history of black artists who have explored the line between sacred and secular music in African American popular music. These include Blind Willie Johnson who switched several times between blues and gospel; Little Richard who abandoned his musical career to become a preacher; Al Green who is a singer and a pastor; Sam Cooke who left gospel group the Soul Stirrers to launch a secular career and Aretha Franklin who was the daughter of a famous gospel preacher and singer. The musical foundation of 'Let's Go Crazy' is therefore rather derivative and simple, but this reliance on earlier musical sources as influences is deliberate and carefully constructed, just part of the musical collage that Prince skilfully creates.

Publicity

Onstage Prince is extrovert, dominant, outrageous, transgressional and is always at the centre of his work. In contrast, in the press, he is not seemingly comfortable promoting his work and has made his reluctance to do interviews part of his mediapheme, and part of his marketing technique. As one journalist who had an interview with Prince arranged has said, 'The thing to bear in mind is that Prince does not do interviews. He certainly didn't do this one, nor any of a dozen others when tabloids and magazines were dangling cover stories as bait' (Cooper 1983). Like David Bowie before him, he has avoided the press.

This has helped him to operate as a hollow icon, to ensure that there is something missing for the audience to complete. As information about him is not readily available, his outer shell can be filled in and fleshed out by the imagination of the audience. Without too much detail being known about him, he remains as an empty space to be filled, a blank screen onto which fans can project themselves, an empty vessel to be inhabited. For the media, the lack of information available means that any information Prince releases is eagerly consumed and regurgitated. All we know about Prince is what we see in his public output, as he keenly maintains the privacy of his personal life. This allows Prince to maintain control over how he is perceived and understood, and how his mediapheme is defined, as he artfully manipulates the press.

The Symbol

Prince has tried to control every aspect of his work. One aspect of his career he could not control was the way he was presented and represented by his record company, Warner Brothers. Despite having carefully packaged himself as part of his art form, in 1993 Prince changed his name to a symbol as a complaint against being treated as a commodity. In a press release that was widely published, Prince stated:

> The first step I have taken towards the ultimate goal of emancipation from the chains that bind me to Warner Bros. was to change my name from Prince to (symbol). Prince is the name that my Mother gave me at birth. Warner Bros. took the name, trademarked it, and used it as the main marketing tool to promote all of the music that I wrote. The company owns the name Prince and all related music marketed under Prince. I became merely a pawn used to produce more money for Warner Bros … I was born Prince and did not want to adopt another conventional name. The only acceptable replacement for my name, and my identity, was a symbol with no pronunciation, that is a representation of me and what my music is about. This symbol is present in my work over the years; it is a concept that has evolved from my frustration; it is who I am. It is my name.

The symbol simplifies his mediapheme to one visual object, to an icon. Prince's description of it evokes the Hebrew approach to God as 'I am who I am', as having a name that cannot be pronounced.

The image Prince chose as his symbol is based on the alchemical symbol for soapstone (Figure 4.1). This is turned 120 degrees clockwise so that the arrow is pointing downwards. A circle is then added to the top. The result is similar to a combination of the planetary symbols for Mars (Figure 4.2) and Venus (Figure 4.3), representing male and female genders, and Prince's androgyny. It

Figure 4.1 The alchemical symbol for soapstone

Figure 4.2 The planetary symbol for Mars

Figure 4.3 The planetary symbol for Venus

Figure 4.4 The symbol guitarist Jimmy Page selected to represent himself on the cover artwork of Led Zeppelin's fourth album

also appears similar to an Egyptian Ankh, and to a cross. This is another way that Prince integrates religion, or perhaps in this case mysticism, into his work. Just as Jesus is represented by a cross, Prince has his own symbol.

Prince had developed his iconography so well that he could be defined by and recognized from a graphical icon. This is something rock band Led Zeppelin had also experimented with. Figure 4.4 is an icon used to represent Jimmy Page, the guitarist who formed Led Zeppelin out of the ashes of The Yardbirds. The band's fourth album had no title on it, referred to only as four symbols, one for each member of the band, as well as one for guest vocalist Sandy Denny. The symbol has been the subject of much study, but it seems to be an alchemical symbol or magical sigil representing Saturn, which represents Page's star sign of Capricorn. The symbol can be seen in the *Dictionary of Occult, Hermetic and Alchemical Sigils* by Fred Gettings (1982, p. 201), and is discussed in detail on the inthelight.co.nz website.

Prince has since reverted to using his name, and the symbol is not reproduced here as Prince has restricted its use. He adopted an icon to represent him much as other products are marketed by a symbol, whether the twin arches of McDonalds or the white tick of Nike. This marks his full-blown adoption of iconography as part of his work. Once free of the contract that caused him to adopt the symbol, Prince continued to use it, playing a guitar with a body made in its image, wearing symbol jewellery and branding his website, publicity and most of his products with the symbol. Despite protesting that his record company had turned him into a commodity, he has continued this commodification for his own benefit.

Prince and Implicit Religion

One way of understanding how it is that popular music cults are religious, is to consider them as implicit rather than explicit religion. In his 1997 book, Edward Bailey defines implicit religion as being focused on those areas often regarded as being outside of what Durkheim might refer to as the sacred or the profane. Implicit religion is a field that allows one to discuss every day activities that lie within these two polar extremes, with the language ordinarily used to discuss religion. For us to consider the cult of Prince to be implicit religion, Bailey tells us that we should expect the cult and culture surrounding him and his music to show evidence in terms firstly of having axes of commitments, secondly of having integrating foci and finally of featuring intensive concerns with extensive effects (Bailey 1977). The cult of Prince does indeed have all of these features.

Fans show commitments, with a sometimes-obsessive fascination with Prince. Fans spend their money on Prince related material, they buy recordings based on their fandom, rather than based on some kind of purely musical judgements. They queue for the best place at concerts or to buy tickets, wait outside his hotel to catch a glimpse of their idol, read his interviews, watch him on television, and would only be regarded as a 'true' fan if they remained committed whatever the quality of his musical output, and no matter how odd his statements. There are of course different levels of initiation into the cult of Prince, from casual fan and occasional record buyer, to the obsessive fan, who might have a level of commitment one might describe as fundamentalist, that is with an unquestioning approval of and belief in both him and his work.

Prince's fans have a variety of integrating foci, of things that bring them together in a form of community. These foci may involve being members of fan clubs, part of a group in a concert audience, or being active on fan-based websites and online discussion groups. Dressing like Prince or wearing Prince merchandise can also be an integrating focus, marking a fan out in public and to other fans. Prince's fans often wear the Prince symbol (that he used to replace his name), as a piece of jewellery, identifying them to other Prince fans (and showing an integrating focus). To an observer the fan is branded as a Prince fan, they understand that it is Prince that is signified (showing to non-Prince fans a level of commitment), in much same way that evangelical Christians today use fish symbols as a mark of belonging.

Intensive concerns with extensive effects (that is a level of intense emotional and intellectual concerns that impact in a wide and/or substantial manner on the person's life) are seen perhaps only in the more extreme fans, who put images of Prince on their walls, dress like him, and even behave or 'act' like him. They may explore sexuality in a way inspired by Prince, express themselves emotionally like Prince, or behave like him in other ways. Posts on a forum of a Prince website provide evidence of all three of these characteristics of implicit religion, showing how his fans sometimes discuss him and think of him. They show in particular the more extreme level of commitment present in fanatical fans that show the last of the three implicit religion characteristics, intensive concerns.

One fan posting on a Prince website (available at www.Prince.org, accessed 24 October 2008) suggests that he thinks Prince's fans can somehow communicate with him telepathically, or instinctively.

I've noticed that several of you seem to have an incredible spiritual connection with Prince that is very rare between musicians and their fans. A lot of you can tell what he's feeling by his photographs, know his intentions before he releases an album, and even know when his soul is on fire with the boundless love of the universe or when it is overcast with doubt from existing in a cruel cruel world. In short, many of you have a direct connection to his soul.

Do you feel you have a spiritual connection with Prince? On what levels have you experienced this? When you cry, do you feel he is crying at the same time?

This fan states that there is a spiritual connection between these fans and Prince, that fans can know him from images of him, reinforcing the idea that his image presents a hollow icon that Prince's spirit can indwell, and that somehow Prince's spirit can reach out through the media to touch fans. Other fans responding to this post confirm this belief.

Yes, I feel a Spiritual connection with Prince. Prince offering his heart through music is definitely how the connection has grown over the years. The way we receive that kind of love is our engagement with that person.

An inexplicable mysticism ... I think that his sadness or happiness can affect me but I don't understand how or why the feeling arises, if indeed there is some spiritual level that allows these kinds of connections between people, in this case an artist and their fans.

With years and learning ... my heart grew fonder 4 Prince. Prince has always been in my heart. And my love 4 God was also deepened by Prince sharing his spiritual heart within music. It has been an intricate weave that I believe is destiny.

In the last case the fan speaks of being committed for a number of years, and of learning, developing and reinforcing their commitment. The fan website and this discussion are both in themselves examples of integrating foci. Another integrating focus is the use of a specific way of writing, that Prince uses on his marketing materials, where for example the word 'for' is replaced by '4' and 'you' is replaced by 'u'.

During the same online discussion, two fans show how being a fan of Prince started to affect the rest of their lives, demonstrating the intensity of the effect Prince had on them, and also the extensive nature of that effect.

Prince was everywhere and I was lapping it up. He started to crop up in all my conversations and I could feel that it was turning a bit obsessive. Prince was starting to be my new Idol!!!

Is it really uncool to admit that, after the release of Purple Rain, I had my bedroom painted purple, wore only purple clothing (including nail polish) and even had a purple hairbrush?

This brings us back to Dyer's four types of relationship between stars and fans, discussed earlier. These fans have certainly moved to the level of projection, when imitation goes beyond image and affects the person's life in a more substantial fashion (Dyer 1979, p. 18).

Prince's work explores the sacred and the profane, and one might conclude that his cult is explicit religion, were it not that it is clearly regarded as part of a secular music industry, and not described as religion either by Prince, or his audience. It is presented as part of day-to-day life, and indeed it is important for Prince that the techniques he uses, taken as they are from religious traditions, are largely unrecognized by his audience, in order to prevent a sense of manipulation surrounding him, which could lead to a collapse of authenticity. The record companies certainly present Prince as part of the music industry, no more or less sacred than any other product. Indeed Prince is acting to expand the boundaries of the secular to include elements of the sacred and the profane, and in doing so is clearly creating a cult that can be seen as implicit religion.

Dell de Chant (2009) discusses how the economy is the sacred ground of postmodern western culture, and that consumption is the dominant focus of mediation, ritual and myth in contemporary western society.

As a recently popular American TV commercial affirmed: "If I could be like Mike [Michael Jordan]," I would consume a particular commodity. So, to be like Mike, I acquire, consume, and dispose of the product. Then, I acquire another. In this way, I am like Mike, the hero of the myth. I hear the narrative of what the mythic heroes acquire, consume, dispose of – houses, cars, boats; I see the clothes they wear and/or advertise; I learn about the foods and beverages they consume. They are consumers too, and the grandest consumers of all. To be like them, to be close to the sacred world they have mastered, I too consume – as often as I can, in as many ways as I can, and preferably I consume products that are like those that they consume. In this way, citizens of postmodern culture are ritually integrated with the sacred order.

There is little space to comment in detail here on the religiosity of consumer culture, something De Chant discusses in some detail in another publication (2002). The sacralization of mediaphemes, such as that of Prince, is part of a sacred popular musical culture that provides forever expanding opportunities for consumption, in a culture where meaning is constructed largely by processes of acquisition, consumption and discarding.

Some popular icons are aware of and have discussed their popular iconic religiosity, and discuss it within their music. For example, in his song 'Bodies' Robbie Williams' lyrics tell us that he loves living like a deity. Others are aware of the construction of their mediapheme. When interviewed on the Jonathon Ross show on his BBC1 television show in 2009, Annie Lennox discussed the way she used and developed her onstage persona, and interviewer Ross, who is well known for his extravagant dress sense and larger-than-life personality, confirms that he participates in the same process.

> Jonathan Ross: I look back on some of your outfits and I love the way you were pretty far out there. Maybe its not so bold for a woman once again as a man to do that, you know Bowie did stuff like that, but it was really quite extreme, you really kind of looked …
>
> Annie Lennox: Sometimes it was a little bit extreme, but I took the opportunity to embrace that because I just loved experimenting and pushing the boundaries, and because if you are a performer there are no boundaries. You can actually take charge, you can do what you like. You get into this persona, which as a normal person, an average person walking down the street, that's not appropriate. So I've enjoyed embodying all those different personas and characteristics.
>
> Jonathan Ross: Well you say it's not appropriate but I still give it a try.

Lennox discusses how she created a different onstage persona to her own real self, and Ross shows that he is influenced by such pop star mediaphemes, as a non-musician and fan trying to emulate stars such as Bowie who he clearly admires.

Personality Cults

Prince's mediapheme was designed to be broad to reach the widest possible market. This included the use of sources taken from throughout popular music history, including blues, R'n'B, Motown, soul, gospel, psychedelia, Stax, rock, funk, disco and the new romantics. He included much that was transgressional, in order to court controversy and media attention. This included elements of black and white culture, as well as the transgression of traditional genre definitions and classifications. He adopted an overtly sexual physicality that mixed the traditionally masculine and feminine, as well as using heterosexual and homosexual references. He mixes this sexuality with religion, and uses techniques traditionally used by religions to create an onstage character that is godlike in that it engenders worship from his fans.

Durkheim's polarized perspectives of the sacred and the profane are often used to simplistically define and separate the religious from the secular, but what is considered sacred or profane is a highly individual, personal and political choice, often equating to what each person likes or considers important to them. Despite this, the separation of the sacred and the profane is often used to define the religious (Durkheim 1965). Clear boundaries between the two are necessary for this definition, but the boundaries between the sacred and the profane are no longer clear in a liquid postmodern world. Prince is part of, and also a result of, a spiritual revolution resulting from the emergence of postmodernity, in which popular cultural artefacts are fulfilling the roles traditionally associated with religions. This is part of the impact of postmodernity (or liquidity, re-enchantment, the posthistorical or postenlightenment) on religion. Postmodernity is characterized partly by the blurring of and tearing down of boundaries, especially those between high and popular artforms.

Prince uses techniques and methods from traditional religions, within a youth culture in which such traditional religions are largely devalued. He and those like him fulfil some of the roles formerly played by mainstream religions. He uses these techniques to create a form of cult based around his personality, drawing fans into the semi-fictional world he creates and increasing his commercial success in the process. Through his music Prince's cult promotes an interest in spirituality (rather than religion), reflecting the growing interest within contemporary popular culture in unconventional expressions of spirituality rather than traditional religious organizations, as discussed by Heelas et al. (2005) and Lynch (2007a). His is a spirituality that mixes and confuses religion, spirituality, physicality, sexuality, dance, music, identity, ethnicity and commerce. By mixing dance music and pop/rock traditions, he merges the sacred and secular, and white and black into a single hybrid in a format that is attractive, easily accessible and sellable.

He plays with and manipulates his public identity and uses iconography and the media as part of his art. He challenges his fans to understand and decode his secretive world and invites them to project themselves into his hollow iconographic shell, revealing their own projections of self as they try to understand him, empowering, deifying and enriching him through the process. Prince offers salvation though a temporary escape from normality into the myth he has created around himself. It is not a world driven by morality or intellect, but by pleasure and the body. When a fan places or projects their self into the shell Prince offers, rather than living in their everyday existence, for a moment they are instead a sexual, spiritual, beautiful demi-god, attractive to men and women, dancing on a stage under concert lights, a star in his sacred popular constellation.

Whether in the audience at a concert or listening to his music at home, the fan feels they are part of Prince's world, that they understand him, that they are the same as Prince. Filling in the spaces he leaves in his character, they create a Prince in their own image who is like them, allowing them to feel close to and part of him, to associate with him and feel reflected glory. The audience is able to live vicariously through Prince, and indeed he is like a vicar to his own congregation, representing or indeed replacing God as the object of worship, and as a representation of who and how the fan would like to be. Prince uses transgression to generate excitement and a sense of transcendence of the ordinary. By addressing and combining both the sacred and the profane he avoids the mundanity of the everyday and exists in the liminal world of the nightclub and rock star lifestyle. 'That's what Prince is about – the twin sides of human nature. "Sin and Salvation," says the man who dedicates to God (the album) Dirty Mind' (Salewicz 1981).

An analysis of Madonna, U2 or many other famous popular music stars or bands could also illustrate how pop stars are worshipped by their fans. Whether one considers these groups of worshippers as constituting cults, new religious movements or implicit religion, or not, it is clear that their behaviour is similar in many ways to that of religious worshippers. It offers the homeless self of contemporary culture (Heelas and Woodhead 2001, p. 53) a place of belonging within Prince's world.

That pop stars are set at the centre of the sacred within contemporary youth culture shows how the focus of religion, belief and meaning in western culture has moved away from the traditional primary institutions of mainstream faiths like Christianity. An icon that flirts with promiscuous sexual practices, incest and objectification of the body provides an unconventional role model for the fans that worship him. Prince is no philosopher or religious leader, his exploration of sexuality and belief is not some carefully thought through development of modes of sexuality within postmodernity, but a development of a marketing ploy designed to make him and others more wealthy.

Popstar lifestyles are semi-fictional, but not presented as such, their realism and authenticity is important to their power. As discussed in other chapters, many of the stars who tried to live out this lifestyle in reality have suffered because of it, Jimi Hendrix, Brian Jones, Janis Joplin, Keith Moon, Sid Vicious, John Bonham and Kurt Cobain all dying young, while numerous others have suffered drug and alcohol addiction or mental illness. A lifestyle of excess is effective as an element of a publicity campaign, is advantageous to a music industry focused on sales at any cost, but raises complicated issues of ethics and morality when becoming the replacement for wisdom traditions that have been designed and developed over hundreds or thousands of years.

The marketing of music as a commodity, using the faces and characters of stars, has individualized musical experience during the twentieth century. This has been a successful process in marketing terms, but has also been something that has been disruptive for communities that rely on music as the centre of communal ritual practices. The music industry has not been able to direct this process exactly as it would have wished. Rather than the clean cut images of many pop stars which the music industry would perhaps find easier to market to a mass audience, and therefore prefer, the cults of icons such as Prince or Madonna have more in common with those of Pan, Bacchus and Dionysus, pointing popular musical communities away from control and towards loss, and pointing them away from the individual and towards collective experiences and the transcendental.

The electronic dance music club culture revolution that dominated the UK music scene from the end of the 1980s and through the 1990s, and more recently the effects of i-tunes, downloads, social networking websites and independent production, has led popular music away from the earlier dominance of the iconic individual pop star as its focus. The musical personality cults of the sacred popular seem to have reached a peak in the 1980s with those such as Prince,

Madonna and Michael Jackson. DJs acting as curators, librarians or ritual leaders took the place of guitar heroes. Pop icons such as Prince or Madonna have not since been replaced by successful younger models, and rock gods like Led Zeppelin have been replaced by a series of lesser stars and sequences of microgenres, as such great unchanging structures have become unsustainable in the fractured geology of postmodernity or the fluid motion of liquidity.

The term pop idol was used as the title of a highly successful talent show, a glorified form of karaoke in a reality TV format, the winners often only having brief careers, judges such as Simon Cowell becoming the biggest stars of the process. As the winners of the first few series of this show failed to rise to the level of pop idols, the programmes titles have been downgraded to reduce the level of expectation, winners now described merely as having an X-Factor, or as providing evidence that Britain's Got Talent. Driven by postmodernity, the singular meta-narrative of the popular icon, and the culture of musical heroes, icons, idols and gods, seem to be slowly diminishing, to be replaced by a multiplicity of lesser stars, of less deified individuals and groups, within a sacred popular pantheism of smaller localized cults and traditions. However, in the last 100 years pop icons have played a key role in developing a popular cultural landscape full of musical festivals, carnival, clubs, cultures and communities.

The cult of Prince is a form of implicit religion in which a popular icon is worshipped religiously. Cult members have images of Prince covering their walls, and they try to behave and be like him. Every would-be pop star sets out to be worshipped by adoring fans, using the power of the media to aid them to develop their cult. Perhaps Bacchus and Pan were originally music stars who have been deified with the passage of time, not so different to Prince. The age of the 1980s superstar pop icon seems to have passed, but as long as musicians and music act at the centre of a heady mixture of communal celebrations, youthful rebellion and behaviour designed to transgress the mainstream, it seems likely that fans will continue to idolize and worship pop stars, and that such personality cults will continue to rise and fall from time to time, much like any other religion, whether implicit or not.

Is there a cult of Prince? Are there those who worship him religiously? There are certainly those who have an image of him on their wall and who try to behave like him. Prince is selling pleasure, selling a hollow shell that makes no pretensions that anything will be found inside. His is a material and materialist religion that is rooted in the sale and use of musical artefacts. While many religions offer a spirit that will come into a person to live inside, Prince offers a shell to wear on the outside, a style. He is a triumph of postmodernity, of style as content, rejecting the concept of external content in a celebration of the individual. The imaginary world he has created began as a complex form of packaging for his music to try to ensure its success, but has evolved and become interweaved into his work as a vital part of a multimedia whole.

It is useful to compare the cult of Prince to the typical characteristics of cults described in Chapter 1, and in doing so evaluate other pop star personality cults. Like many other cults, the cult of Prince is built around devotion to a single, living, character. Prince describes himself as having a divine musical gift, and surrounds himself with religious symbolism, references and iconography. Prince himself has been highly secretive, secrecy being another typical characteristic of cults. As we have seen, some of his fans are obsessive and highly committed. A level of knowledge and commitment is required before someone is considered a true fan and initiate of Prince's cult. His cult and his mediapheme are designed to attract as many members as possible, by integrating white and black, pop and rock musical cultures. It is focused upon gaining as many members as possible, assuring their fanatical commitment and encouraging them to give their money to the cult leader and his associates, again reflecting typical cult characteristics.

The music business uses its enormous marketing machine to brainwash fans into parting with their money for an unending stream of merchandise, hoping to engender a fanatical commitment that will allow a long-term commitment to the cause, again behaviour which is often described as being typically cultic. Indeed the cult of any pop star pretends to be mainly about music, but is really focused around making money. Members of Prince's cult wear particular clothing, make-up and other objects, and have particular images associated with them. He is associated with deviant sexual practices and with new age spirituality, altering traditional liturgies and doctrines to suit him, and preaching them to fans. Prince has been opposed by traditional religious groups who have described him as immoral, profane and blasphemous. Thus, Prince's music and its surrounding culture have most of the characteristics we are told we should expect to see in a cult.

Pop stars acting as twenty-first-century popular icons have played a significant part in generating artificial needs and sustaining and developing consumer capitalism, by creating idealized consumers and training young people in brand loyalty, transforming traditions of religious observance, worship, ritual and devotion into consumer behaviours, by creating gods who have products to sell such as compact discs, posters and t-shirts. In western culture, Prince and his peers in the world of music are fulfilling roles traditionally played by religious figures, such as Moses, Jesus, Mohamed and Buddha, as traditional religions rapidly decline, and consumer capitalism controls the structure and development of society and culture. Like many other pop stars, once he gained fame and commercial success and was raised to the status of popular icon using a carefully constructed mediapheme, Prince struggled with his commodification by the music industry. By adopting a symbol as a name, and playing with iconography using his onstage persona, colour, graphics, imagery, music and religious references, he both adopted and challenged the use of popular icons as idealized exemplars of consumer culture in a creative and entertaining fashion.

Prince initially created an onstage character and developed a myth to surround him, to aid in the marketing of his music, and help overcome his shy personality. This has developed so that the semi-fictional character of Prince is now the main focus of his artwork. Prince's self, or that perceived as such by the public, is his primary text, his body is the principal instrument he uses, his guitar playing and singing subsumed as a part of the cult that surrounds him, represented by a graphic symbol, moving his form from musical artwork to performance art. More than within theatre, film, opera, television or any other multimedia form of performance art, popular icons like Prince are able to confuse the boundaries between the real and the imaginary, the concrete and the mythical. This has enabled him to involve, engage and interact with his audience by stepping off the screen or stage into the real world and validate his artwork as being part of reality rather than fiction. This in turn has allowed him to adopt techniques usually seen within religions as part of his work. It is as if he were creating a new religious movement as an artwork, with himself as the central author, text and performer. The audience takes part in the performance by consuming Prince and the artefacts he sells, projecting into his shell and allowing themselves to be possessed as members of his cult.

The adventures of Prince in hyperreality continue, and it is hard to tell if any news about him is fact or fiction. He recently performed a record-breaking 21 nights at the 23,000 capacity O2 arena in London. He has also apparently become a Jehovah's Witness and surprised fans by knocking on their doors.

It is perhaps unsurprising that, like many pioneering black artists before him, Prince has sought solace in the church. Though he was brought up as a practising Seventh Day Adventist he has recently, like Michael Jackson before him, become a Jehovah's Witness. The story of his conversion broke in typically surreal fashion last October, when a newspaper in his home-town reported how a married couple had answered their door to find Prince proffering a copy of the Watchtower. Though they were orthodox Jews, and it was Yom Kippur, they were also Prince fans. They welcomed him into the house where, with his friend Larry Graham, erstwhile member of Sly & the Family Stone, one of Prince's core influences, he spread the word of Jehovah for 20 minutes before moving on to the next house. (O'Hagan 2004)

It is unclear whether this is fact or fiction, which is of course entirely appropriate.

Chapter 5

In My Beautiful Neighbourhood: Local Cults of Popular Music

Locality and Scenes

Many early studies of popular music featured a study of music subcultures. Dick Hebdige's book *Subculture: The Meaning of Style* (1979) came out of developments in sociology in Birmingham. It discussed the subcultures surrounding elements of popular music culture such as mods, rockers and punks. Subcultures imply that an overarching meta-narrative of some kind existed in some music scenes that defined them. This suggested that punks, for example, were all in some way the same, were all bonded together by a separate culture that they shared, and that this was a subculture, different in a number of ways to mainstream culture. This also implies that there is some kind of coherent mainstream culture from which subcultures are different.

Sarah Thornton (1995) described how individuals developed subcultural capital within a music-based group, looking in this case at club cultures. Mainstream consumer culture was described as being focused around the acquisition of capital by earning money or buying objects such as houses, cars, clothing, washing machines, televisions and the like, and further to this cultural capital could also be gained by knowing about high culture elite arts. Roger Scruton for example describes in his book *An Intelligent Person's Guide to Modern Culture* (2000), and in some of his other books, the works he regards as important. He sets out a canon of what art one should know and appreciate, what literature is important, what music is of value, as if he and his like are the keepers and arbitrators of culture, and other people should aspire to not just his level of knowledge, but his choice of knowledge as well as his taste. This assumes that his view of the world is correct, and that other perceptions or choices are wrong or of less validity.

Subcultural study supports this position, in that it suggests that a music culture such as punk is less, 'sub' or under, mainstream culture. It suggests that there is a coherent mainstream culture that can be defined, by those such as Scruton, by the self-appointed keepers of cultural standards who choose what is desirable culturally. Politically this approach prioritizes the rich and powerful, who are able to sustain a ruling class by passing on cultural as well as financial capital to their descendants, or to those that they choose. It also implies that punk exists as some kind of underground scene that has less value than the mainstream, and perhaps that is critical of the mainstream, is subversive in some way.

In the 1960s and 1970s this political reading of popular music had some validity. The modern era was drawing to a close, an era when meta-narratives, the great stories that aimed to explain or express culture, were appearing and disappearing increasingly quickly. The long periods of slow cultural change such as prehistory and the dark ages had been replaced by the faster speed of development of the enlightenment, as humanity tried to drive forwards the pace of human learning. Classical and Romantic eras gave way as the industrial revolution increased again the pace of technological development and ushered in the twentieth century. Cultural change accelerated to keep up with new technology, futurism, cubism, surrealism, dada, impressionism, expressionism and other cultural movements striving to replace each other as the newest, latest cultural development. Each new cultural form could be understood and acquired as cultural capital, just as new consumer goods were acquired by an increasingly aspirational society in the consumption-based society that replaced the production-based industrial age. Punk, for example, was part of this process, driven by situationist and anarchist politics, an undercurrent of Marxism struggling to get this working class music accepted in the mainstream.

Punk was designed to be deliberately offensive or other to the dominant musical culture of the day, designed to shock, a music culture associated with swearing, spitting, torn clothing, fetishist sexuality, coloured and spiked hair, piercings, and music that is shouted and aggressive, performing iconic songs such as 'My Way' and 'Something Else' with provocatively altered lyrics. Driven by the situationism of Malcolm McLaren and the working class political sensibilities of bands like The Clash and Crass, this was a subculture that was deliberately set up to be offensive to a mainstream audience, to challenge mainstream values, to be oppositional and to be underground, below culture, subverting it from underneath. In this way it was challenging modernity, challenging the idea that Scruton and others could establish what was good art or music, what was acceptable or desirable, by offering cultural capital within working class youth culture that was seemingly the opposite of everything that high society and high art valorized.

Punk had emerged with the New York art scene that had featured Warhol turning popular cultural figures such as Monroe and Presley into artworks, as well as presenting commercial products such as tins of Campbells soup and Coca Cola bottles as art. His work had suggested that popular culture had as much value as traditional 'high' art, and that choices of one over the other within intellectual circles were based on personal choice and the identifiers of the traditional ruling classes rather than underlying value. Or that what constituted value was a subjective choice that in the past was dominated by elite classes, but that the expression of the cultural choices of the masses by popular culture would change what was thought to have value.

Within postmodernity this process has developed further, there is no one meta-narrative that defines what has value, what is of importance and who chooses and builds canon. The boundaries between popular culture and high art are eroded. Thus, the idea of a subculture begins to fall away. The idea of there being a mainstream culture that is challenged by a subculture, is one that makes less sense as modernity is replaced by postmodernity. The histories of a sequence of stories, narratives that define the latest cultural thinking, the latest cultural capital to be acquired, become blurred and confused. Also known as the post-historical, in this era time flows in many directions, and cultural capital can be gained from retrospective movements, whether from the 1960s, from before the enlightenment, from another part of the globe or another tradition, it does not have to come from the latest new western theory.

Zygmunt Baumann (1993) has named the same era liquid culture, as cultures no longer develop in a simple stream, from past to future, rooted in a single simple national identity. The mainstream is understood within postmodernity as a fractured collection of micro-cultures, as a liquid pool of cultural objects that mix and flow, more like an ocean than a series of paths or rivers. Within modernity cultural development flowed in one direction like a river, from the past to the present, with the old discarded, and to struggle upstream seen as negative. Within postmodern liquid culture, with many cultural and national boundaries broken down by global telecommunications and the internet, we are living a more oceanic experience, in which culture flows backwards and forwards, mixes freely, creates new fusion forms, takes from the past and the present, the local and the international, moving around like water in an ocean.

Thus rather than focus on subcultures, the study of popular music has more recently begun to focus on scenes. Scenes are regarded as localized cultural forms, in which particular conditions of one kind or another lead to something that is characteristic and has peculiar individual qualities. These are often, although not always, geographically local. This recognizes that overarching analyses often treat large swathes of cultural production as the same, and thus miss out upon important details. This sort of work often draws upon the experiences or practices of ethnomusicologists or ethnographers, carrying out fieldwork in order to study a scene in detail and understand it from the inside.

This approach values a scene as equally important to any other, whether based in high art or popular culture. Andrew Bennett (2000) has written about scenes such as a hip hop scene in North Eastern England. This scene has similarities to other hip hop scenes, but to simply include it within US hip hop would ignore many of the most important and interesting of its features, and only tell part of the story. There are now so many micro-genres within popular music, that a scene based approach offers a useful approach within a postmodern culture. This can help to understand differences such as those between punk in New York and in London. Although these have superficial similarities, and are seen as part of the same genre or subculture, they were in fact very different in numerous ways, despite the links and interactions between them, and this can be readily understood from an understanding of the differences between the two local scenes.

This focus on the scene illustrates the importance of the local within popular music. A cult of popular music will often be a local one. Many scenes are based in a particular place, and many music genres have their roots in a small local scene, from which they developed to become more popular once they were more widely known. This places scenes as expressions of locality, of local culture, something that has become increasingly important as national borders and identities become eroded within liquid cultures. Music has always played an important role in human culture in providing a sense of local identity. In many traditional cultures, music identifies one community as different from another. Musical participation in traditional cultures bonds the community together, and again the shared cultural capital of common knowledge and experience identifies an individual as feeling and being part of a specific group.

Great Britain is a country that focused for hundreds of years on developing an empire, expanding its boundaries to include countries across the world. As a result it has absorbed elements of the culture of many of those countries into British culture, just as it exported its own culture abroad. This has made Britishness a complex issue, much as national identity within postmodernity is complicated in most countries. The relationships between British and USA culture are particularly intertwined and complex. In terms of musical culture, a series of African American musical dance music genres have been popular in Britain. Blues, jazz, swing, rhythm and blues, rock'n'roll and soul have all been popular, and iconic British pop stars often found fame by having copied these musical styles as accurately as possible. These styles involved elements of European music, which had migrated to the USA, but the culture that they were set within was specifically African American. The influx of US music and musicians to Britain had such a powerful effect, that in order to protect the jobs of British musicians, the British Musicians' Union were successful in banning all American musicians from performing in Britain between 1936 and 1956.

Many British musicians performed American music, rather than composing their own original material. Whereas African American music featured artists who composed their own songs, this was rare in British popular music. Folk musicians focused on traditional songs, and pop musicians sang songs written by professional songwriters, or by American musicians. The conveyor belt production of popular music song, described as a musical product by writers such as Adorno (1990), left no space for local music scenes to develop that reflected their local culture.

The Beatles are a good example of a British band who began their career in this way, performing other people's music. They started out as a group of entertainers working in a red light district in Hamburg, playing endless covers of American rock'n'roll songs. It was when they began to sing in their own accents and to write their own songs that they began to develop their own identity, and one that reflected their locality, both as Liverpudlians and as being British. This difference from other musicians, this connection with their local culture, helped them to develop a cult local following. A hardcore local group of fans in their home town of Liverpool were able to feel that this band was 'theirs', that it represented them in some way.

Just as a solo artist's iconic personality construction can create a star that an individual fan can associate with and project themself into, a band's association with a local culture allows this small group of individuals to represent a place. It allows them to be a group of people with a coherent local identity, with which fans can identify. In this case the fans perceive the musicians to be like them, of them, for the group to be their own. This kind of identification is enormously powerful. If a band can maintain their local identity in some way when they go on to more widespread fame and success, they can take their identity with them, building a scene around them. This local identity adds authenticity to their cult and culture, something that can be enhanced and developed performatively. To be local, to be from somewhere identifiable, and ideally to be from a working class background, adds to a popular audience a sense of rootedness, a perception of truth and believeability, of honesty and of 'keeping it real'.

The Beatles developed their local cult in a number of simple ways. The most obvious element was that they sang in their own local accents. Whereas many earlier popular music artists would sing in American accents or polite received pronunciation accents, with as little local accent as possible perceivable, one could hear when they sang that the Beatles were from Liverpool. Whereas most music in Britain seemed to come from and revolve around London, with the majority of record companies, publishers and music institutions based there, this provided something new and different.

In addition to this, the Beatles played their own instruments. They were not singers with faceless backing musicians playing in the darkness behind them; they played all the music that was heard. In addition they wrote their own songs, providing further evidence that what they said was 'real', and not fictional. This truth, this believeability was vital to the Beatles' success. Later in their career this process would be further enhanced by the band also becoming involved in the production of their records. The development of the Beatles local cult was aided by a Merseybeat scene that was developing around Liverpool. Other bands appeared who were also local to the same area, such as Gerry and the Pacemakers, The Searchers and The Swinging Blue Jeans. Any Liverpool act associated with this scene had immediate appeal, and other Merseyside musicians such as Cilla Black later managed to launch their careers on the back of the Beatles' success. Liverpool gained the impression of being the site of a musical explosion, that there was a scene there where musical talent was being developed. The Beatles were able to ride a wave of musical success, associated with the whole city, and its cool reputation.

As their career developed, the Beatles also began to make specific references to Liverpool, and also to being British. This included singing songs that described the lives of British people. Whether this was having a barrow in a marketplace, being a meter maid, barber, Vicar, or reading Lear, these were references to people who were specifically British. On top of this the band made specific references to particular places in Liverpool and in Britain. Penny lane and Strawberry Fields were places in Liverpool as well as being titles of songs. Abbey Road was the name, but also address, of their recording studio. The Beatles named an album after Abbey Road, and on the cover showed themselves walking across a zebra crossing, a particularly British image. The Beatles identified themselves again and again as being specifically British.

The Beatles provided an archetype for a British popular music band, or Britpop band. They sang in a local regional working class accent, and played their own instruments, which were a traditional rhythm and blues set up of drum kit, bass guitar, electric guitar and keyboards including piano and organ. They referred to their locality in their lyrics, by describing the lives of local people and situations. They also referred to their local identity through publicity materials and artwork, such as record sleeves, posters, photographs and promotional films. In addition this was a band. Although there were lead singers, all of the band participated in the group, rather than being a lead singer with a backing group of musicians.

This local identity was so strong that it was able to reverse the flow of musical culture across the Atlantic, and inspire the so-called 'British Invasion'. A number of British musical acts became enormously popular in the USA, the novelty of a different local, alien culture appealing strongly. The advantage of British culture to an American audience was that it seemed very similar to their own. It was by white musicians, singing in English, and was from a culture that had obvious historical links to that of the USA. On top of this it was British people playing American music, playing rock'n'roll, but in different accents.

The music the Beatles were playing was in many ways highly derivative. The Beatles began by playing many covers, such as 'Twist and Shout'. When they began to write their own material, they would often take a rock'n'roll or soul song they knew, such as 'Watch Your Step' by Bobby Parker, and add new lyrics and a new melody, thus this song became both 'Day Tripper' and 'I Feel Fine'. However Parker had himself been influenced by Dizzy Gillespie's 'Manteca' in writing the song, so the question of influence is not a simple one. There was even a threat of legal action taken against the band in one case, over the use of material from a Chuck Berry Song 'You Can't Catch Me' in the Beatles' song 'Come Together'. Lennon agreed to record material belonging to Berry's publisher as repayment, and ended up releasing an album called *Rock'n'Roll* that was full of R'n'B and soul covers.

The Beatles' backbeat drum sound was taken from rhythm'n'blues and Motown soul music. The harmonica playing on 'Love Me Do' was based on that on Bruce Chanel's hit 'Hey Baby', the harmonica playing being influenced by blues players like Sonny Boy Williamson. The 'Wooh!' that can be heard on 'I Saw Her Standing There', 'Help!' and 'She Loves You' was taken from The Isley Brothers' 'Twist and Shout' and from Little Richard, who himself took the idea from gospel singer Alex Bradford. These elements were all taken and presented as original Liverpudlian Beatles style. I have discussed this in more detail in a chapter of Neill Wynn's book *Cross the Water Blues* (Till 2007).

The Beatles were able to become hugely successful selling rock'n'roll and soul music to the American public, because they were white, and their British identity disguised the fact that this was black dance music. They soon began to outsell the black soul artists whose style they were emulating. The music was still perceived as being from Liverpool, and as being British, as it was wrapped in the Beatles, the containers of the music, the people who made it were clearly from Liverpool, and so despite them initially singing whitened versions of African American songs, they were convincing and authentic. The roots of the music became Liverpool rather than the USA.

This is a pattern that was repeated many times. In London The Kinks represented London and Cockney culture. 'Dedicated Follower of Fashion' mentions Leicester Square, Carnaby Street and Regent Street and the London mod fashion scene. Both 'Waterloo Sunset' and their *The Kinks are the Village Green Preservation Society* album reinforced their Britishness by numerous references. The band joined the British Invasion of the USA, again adopting the Britpop formula of a local cult, with a conventional band instrumental line-up, writing original songs that are sung in a British accent and describe typically British culture.

Other 1960s bands followed this trend. The Who discussed Soho and Brighton in 'Pinball Wizard', guitarist and art college graduate Pete Townshend introducing Union Jacks and British Royal Air Force military roundels into the visual identity of the band, adding colour to the image of mods, but also reinforcing the Britishness of guitar orientated pop music. They also provided the music for the film *Quadrophenia*, which was based on the British mod music scene. The Small Faces were another band that represented Britishness, their jokey single 'Lazy Sunday Afternoon' being sung in a Cockney accent, and the band again being associated with the very British mod scene.

The 1960s established the idea of the guitar-based rock band with an overtly British dimension. Much later a phenomenon called Britpop appeared as if out of nowhere, harking back to the 1960s and announced as a new movement. One could label Britpop as simply a term for a late twentieth century mod revival. However, there were a series of musical scenes that developed in between that show that there is a clear tradition of this kind of music that runs through British popular music culture. The early 1970s saw glitter rock/glitter pop appear, another peculiarly British music scene, which influenced Britpop.

Glitter stars Marc Bolan and David Bowie (and of course Ziggy Stardust) sang in English accents, and the Bay City Rollers proudly displayed their Scottish heritage by wearing tartan costumes, copied by their hordes of fans.

The hard rock scene that developed out of the London blues explosion produced Led Zeppelin, Deep Purple and Black Sabbath who again sang in English accents. Led Zeppelin is an interesting example. Their early music consisted of covers of African American blues music, which were not always properly credited, and the band was sued several times by blues artists. Their third album took a different direction, and has many tracks that are influenced by the British folk music revival, mixing African American and British traditional musical influences together, again sung with an English accent.

Progressive rock music developed in the 1970s in Britain, with lyrical influences from English literary sources. Pink Floyd, Genesis and Yes all integrated influences from Western European Art Music (WEAM) with the lyricism of romantic British poets and British rock music culture. This intellectualist approach failed to dominate for long however, and was swept away by punk towards the end of the decade.

Punk began in the USA, in the music of the Ramones, Television, the New York Dolls and the Velvet Underground. This was based around a local New York scene, of Andy Warhol's heroin soaked Warehouse. Punk in Britain was somewhat different. A small group of young musicians in London, hanging around in a particular set of music venues and clothes shops formed bands, and were associated with the American punk scene largely because Malcolm McLaren had been to America and managed the New York Dolls. He saw potential in the kids who were hanging around the 'Sex' clothes boutique he ran with his partner Vivienne Westwood. A situationist who had been to art college, McLaren saw how the right promotion could take this local scene and spread its cult across the nation. The New York punk scene was based around music clubs like CBGBs, and McLaren set out to promote a similar scene in London.

McLaren managed a London band, who were looking for a new singer. They chose Johnny Rotten (later Lydon), a regular customer in McLaren's shop, who was not much of a singer technically, but had the style and attitude McLaren was after. He wanted to make his band, renamed the Sex Pistols, deliberately offensive, and to build a scene around the band and his (similarly named) shop. McLaren had seen the potential in Rotten as a band front man. Visually Rotten was influenced by Westwood's clothing as well as by Sex shop assistant Jordan's image, and he had short green hair. The band adopted an aggressive attitude, trying to create chaos and confrontation wherever they went. Hebdige (1979) describes this as the creation of a subculture, and that punk was a cultural alternative, that adopted swearing or offense as its key identity. However, this was too small a movement in the beginning to be a cultural alternative. It was a small group of individuals who may never have achieved any level of fame without the unique promotional approach taken by McLaren.

McLaren's situationism led him to feed anarchism, fetishistic clothing, aggression, violence, torn clothing and coloured hair into the equation. The Sex Pistols soon became both notorious and successful, because of the energy, excitement and danger of the events they were at the centre of, as much as the fast, wild musical style. These events included riotous, violent concerts and television appearances featuring Nazi imagery and swearing. In addition a boat trip and performance on the river Thames during the Queen's silver jubilee celebrations was ended by police, and the Sex Pistols' single 'God Save the Queen' rose to the top of the UK singles charts despite being banned by the BBC. The band inspired many of those who saw them to form new bands. The Clash developed after Joe Strummer saw them perform, and Siouxsie and the Banshees, the Damned, Adam and the Ants and the Pretenders were all bands that grew out of that early London scene.

This scene reflected British culture as it developed. The Sex Pistols positioned themselves as anti-establishment, but again made specific references to Britain in their lyrics, and sang in English accents. Two of their most famous singles were 'Anarchy in the UK' and 'God Save the Queen', both attacking mainstream British culture, and yet firmly identifying the band as British at the same time. The latter used artwork depicting a defaced image of the Queen and the British flag, courting controversy in a peculiarly British fashion.

Another important early UK punk band were the Clash, whose first album features one of the band wearing a Union Jack flag on his shirt, and the songs 'London's Burning' and 'I'm So Bored With the USA', placing the band in London, and setting them in opposition to American culture. The band were influenced by American music, and continued to mix US musical influences with an overtly British outlook, their third album featuring a cover that was styled after Elvis Presley's first album, but containing songs such as 'London Calling' and 'Guns of Brixton' that referenced their home lyrically.

UK Punk developed an overtly British sound. Sham 69 were influenced by football (or soccer as it is known in the USA) fans, their name coming from a local football club and the village of Hersham where the band was formed. Their song 'Hersham Boys' describes cockney cowboys, and in 'Hurry Up Harry' the lyrics tell us the band are 'going down the pub'. Splodgenessabounds' first single 'Two Pints of Lager and a Packet of Crisps Please' was also all about British pub culture; the Cockney Rejects' name declared their background; The Stranglers' first album featured a track called 'London Lady'; and there were early punk bands called London and Chelsea.

The Sex Pistols played a small number of gigs in Manchester that inspired audience members to form bands including The Buzzcocks, The Smiths, The Fall and Joy Division. These bands also sang in British accents and made references to British and local culture. The Smiths referenced British culture in many ways, including the cover artwork of their singles. 'What Difference Does it Make' and 'How Soon is Now', both feature an image from a British film; 'Heaven Knows I'm Miserable Now' features a typical northern British terraced street and 'Shakespeare's Sister' features a star of Lancashire-based British soap opera Coronation Street. Singer Morrisey makes numerous lyrical references to British culture. Also the Salford Lads Club in Greater Manchester is featured in the cover artwork of The Smiths' album *The Queen is Dead*, and in the video for the song 'Stop Me If You Think You've Heard This One Before'.

Joy Division, and subsequently New Order, were at the heart of the local scene that developed in Manchester, signed to local record label Factory records. Factory opened a nightclub called The Hacienda, which Joy Division bass player Peter Hook has said was intended to provide a place for the punks in the Manchester to go. Factory records created a Manchester music scene by signing, promoting and supporting local musicians and bands, organizing concerts and establishing what was to become the most famous British night-club of its day in northern England. The Hacienda was built to reproduce the large gay nightclubs in New York, such as the Paradise Garage, in which electronic dance music cultures, such as house, garage and techno, were developing (Hook 2009).

There were other local guitar band based music scenes in Britain in the 1980s, including the midlands indie scene that produced bands such as the Wonderstuff, Crazyhead and Pop Will Eat Itself. In the late 1980s groups described as Baggy or Madchester bands emerged from the scene based around the mixture of indie and dance music being played at the Hacienda. Baggy reflected the loose trousers that became fashionable in the area, and Madchester was a term used by the band Happy Mondays for their *Madchester EP*. Singer Sean Ryder sang in a characteristically Manchester accent, and much like other Madchester bands such as The Stone Roses and Inspiral Carpets, they integrated guitar-based pop and rock with dance beats, employing electronic dance music DJs such as Paul Oakenfold and Andrew Wetherall as producers and remixers for their music. The Hacienda was one of the first UK clubs to play house, garage and techno music, perhaps due to the electronic proto-techno of New Order, who part-owned the Hacienda, and who had also mixed guitar and dance music cultures successfully. This mixture of dance beats, and British rock band culture helped Manchester to become the central focus of the British music scene. The bands involved were from working class backgrounds, and their local accents came through in the vocal parts of the music.

All of these guitar-based bands and scenes existed within a British music tradition, but interacted and shared influences with American musical scenes. By the beginning of the 1990s alternative or indie rock in the USA had much in common with its British counterparts. Bands like REM and the Pixies were also using a band format made up of drums, bass guitar and vocals with occasional keyboards, singing in their own local accents, having a group identity, playing their own instruments and positioning themselves as in some way alternative to or independent from mainstream culture.

I have tried to show in this section how there is long and continuous tradition of UK popular music that is focused on bands rather than solo artists, that reflects locality or refers to British culture, that is sung in British accents but has links with American musical culture and that has a conventional pop instrumentation. It was in the 1990s, however, that this tradition was given a name and a focus, being called Britpop.

Britpop

In Seattle a particular music scene developed around a local record label called Sub Pop. The founders of the label had deliberately constructed it in order to create a local scene or cult, creating the so-called Seattle sound (Azerrad 2001, p. 436). They had investigated other independent record labels and concluded they were all based around a sound or scene that was identifiably local, such as Motown in Detroit or Stax in Memphis. They also decided to promote this local scene in Britain, aware that there was also a history of local scenes from America becoming successful in the UK and subsequently becoming successful in the USA.

Soundgarden and Mudhoney did much to define the sound of Seattle, but the band that became the focus of what was also known as the grunge scene was Nirvana because of their widespread international success. Nirvana's break-through album was named *Nevermind*, after the first two words of the Sex Pistols' album *Never Mind the Bollocks*. The band dominated Seattle's music scene, and became the dominant power in the rock music scene in the UK and the USA. Other American bands benefitted from this, while the British music scene suffered, electronic dance music being the dominant UK popular music genre at the time. However, in 1994, Kurt Cobain died and three British bands, Blur, Oasis and Pulp, released albums that were to become hugely successful, triggering the development of a music scene that became known as Britpop.

> Britpop emerged fairly explicitly as an anti-American sensibility, dedicated to the celebration of a specifically British music tradition. This distinctive tradition, its proponents claimed, stretched back through Ian Dury and the Beatles to the days of music hall and was characterized by a now self-conscious mobilization of particularly 'British' themes and styles. (Morley and Robbins 2001, p. 178)

Blur released *Parklife*, an album that reflected British culture. The band was based in London, and vocalist Damon Albarn's singing on the album had a clearly cockney accent. This was not so pronounced on their most successful previous hit single, 'There's No Other Way'. Damon Albarn had been on tour in America, and said in an interview, 'I just started to miss really simple things … I missed everything about England so I started writing songs which created an English atmosphere' (Harris 1993). He also said that he wanted to get rid of grunge, oppose American culture and make identifiably British culture. Blur had been very much influenced by 1960s mod culture, what one could describe as the Britpop of the day. They had modelled themselves in particular on mod band The Who.

Like The Who, Blur brought an awareness of fashion to Rock music, Britpop was to be fashionable rock music, unlike the anti-fashion of much rock guitar music such as heavy metal. The Beatles, mods, punks and the Madchester scene had all also had specific fashions associated with them, something that helped them all to appeal to a mainstream audience, rather than only a rock'n'roll oppositional culture. The Beatles had been dressed in suits and given fashionable haircuts to change them from their rocker image, the Sex Pistols had emerged from Vivienne Westwood's clothes shop, and the Happy Mondays sang a song 'Loose Fit' about their preference for flared trousers.

Like all of those bands, Blur were a band not a singer with a backing group, they had a traditional rock line-up of instruments (drums, bass, guitar, vocal and occasional keyboards), and were clearly British. In the song 'Parklife' Blur particularly referenced British culture. The lyrics of the verses were spoken by actor Phil Daniels, who had played the lead character in The Who's film *Quadraphenia*, which was all about mod culture. His cockney accent exaggerated the Britishness of the song, connecting the swinging London of 1960s mod culture with Blur and Britpop. Blur represented London and the south of England.

Manchester and the north west of England had prepared the way for Britpop with the Madchester scene. Dave Haslam has investigated the musical culture of Manchester in more detail than is available here in his book *Manchester, England: The Story of the Pop Cult City*. He discusses in detail the evolution of the pop cult surrounding the city. Noel Gallagher had been a guitar technician touring with baggy band Inspiral Carpets. As well as his songwriting abilities, he brought his music business experience when he joined his brother's band, which was renamed Oasis. The band reacted against grunge, Nirvana and the Seattle scene, just as Blur had. Discussing the song 'Live Forever', Noel told MTV's Gonzo programme,

At the time it was written in the middle of the grunge and all that, I remember Nirvana had a tune called 'I hate myself and I want to die', and I was like, well I'm not having that, and as much as I like him, and all that, I'm not having that. I can't have people like that coming over here, on smack, saying that they hate themselves and they wanna die. That's rubbish. Kids don't need to be hearing that nonsense.

Lead singer of the band Liam Gallagher, sang in a characteristically nasal Manchester accent. Harris (2004, p. 120) tells us that Noel Gallagher had idolized Manchester pop icon Morrissey, but his songwriting drew heavily from his influences, such as the Beatles, The Kinks and T. Rex, often integrating elements of songs by these and other bands in his own compositions.

'Shakermaker' lyrically features 'Mr Soft' (the title of a Cockney Rebel song), as well as 'Mr. Clean' (the title of a song by the Jam), and also features the title of English chidren's programme Mr. Benn. The same song was sued for copyright infringement, having taken its melody from 'I'd Like to Teach the World to Sing' by the New Seekers. The first two lines of the melody of the Oasis song have the same melody as the first line of the New Seekers' song. The second line of lyrics of 'Shakermaker' is 'I'd like to build myself a house', in comparison to the less self-focused first line of the New Seekers' song, 'I'd like to build the world a home'.

The main guitar riffs for the Oasis songs 'Cigarettes and Alcohol' and 'Some Might Say' are taken from 'Get It On' by T. Rex. 'Whatever' was influenced by the song 'How Sweet to be an Idiot' by Neil Innes, who successfully sued for breach of copyright. The introductory chord sequence is very similar, and the melody of the first line is the same in both songs. 'Hello' by Oasis has material from 'Hello, Hello I'm Back Again' by Gary Glitter. Apart from a similar title, Oasis end their song with the beginning chorus of the Glitter song, complete with identical lyrics melody and music. 'Don't Look Back in Anger' begins with the same piano chords as 'Imagine' by John Lennon. 'Step Out' was not included as planned on an Oasis album due to the musical similarities to Thin Lizzy's 'Rosalie' in the verses, and because the melody in the chorus is also very similar to the Stevie Wonder song 'Uptight', featuring the lyric 'It will be all right' in comparison to Wonder's 'Ev'rything is alright'.

'Lyla' by Oasis is influenced by 'Street Fighting Man' by The Rolling Stones. The guitar introduction is similar and both melodies feature a characteristic four tone leap slurring up and down. 'Acquiesce' has lyrical, melodic and harmonic similarities to the song 'I Only Want To Be With You'. Although most of these references were to British music, Oasis were clearly influenced by American music as well. From the band's debut album *Definitely Maybe*, the song 'Rock'n'roll Star' begins with a line that has almost the same melody and lyrics as the first line of Creedance Clearwater Revival's 'Proud Mary'. The beginning chords and guitar parts to 'Morning Glory' are also the same as 'The One I Love' by REM and are even in the same key.

The similarities are not merely cosmetic; Noel Gallagher has discussed many of these similarities in interviews, and uses quotation as a compositional technique, just as bands like The Beatles had. The Beatles copied musical elements from various American musicians, as discussed earlier. In a documentary on the songs on his jukebox, John Lennon discusses how he used to write new melodies and lyrics based on the chord sequences and musical material of other songs, as his own understanding of music was limited.

In the early days, I would often write a melody, a lyric in my head to some other song because I can't write music. So I would carry it around as somebody else's song and then change it when putting it down on paper, or down on tape – consciously change it because I knew somebody's going to sue me or everybody's going to say 'What a rip off'. (Walker 2004)

Just as The Beatles built songs on other influences, or around existing songs, Oasis did the same, although they largely took these influences from earlier British bands, rather from African American sources.

As well as British accents and references to British culture in lyrics, in their image Oasis made explicit their British influences. The band were often seen wearing round coloured glasses much like those worn by John Lennon, the band wore mod parker coats, and sported haircuts that made them look like The Beatles or The Kinks. Like The Who, Oasis also featured the British Union Jack flag in their promotional material, and notably Noel Gallagher played a guitar with paintwork inspired by the flag, first using this guitar at a home-town concert at Maine Road, the ground of the football team Gallagher supports, Manchester City.

While Blur were from London and represented the south of England, Oasis represented the north of the country, and more specifically the north-west and Manchester. A rivalry between the two bands developed, leading their record companies to release singles on the same day, as a competition to be decided by sales. The publicity surrounding this helped to further boost the popularity of the two bands, and to further develop the Britpop scene. The competition between the bands harked back to the competition in the 1960s between the London based Rolling Stones and the northern Beatles. This played on the North–South divide in the UK, between the wealthier and supposedly more cosmopolitan South, and the less wealthy and more provincial North.

There were a number of other Britpop bands, some of which, such as Ride and Suede, did much to begin the Britpop scene, but the other band who would come to define the movement were Sheffield band Pulp. Pulp had existed for some time, but it was when lead singer Jarvis Cocker moved to London that he began to focus his songwriting on his observations about his Yorkshire upbringing, and the contrasts between his life experiences and those of the students he met in the capital. Much like the other groups already discussed, he sang in his local, Sheffield accent, and wrote lyrics about characteristically British life in a working class urban northern city. His lyrics describing woodchip wallpaper on the walls of terraced houses in 'Disco 2000', the life of 'Common People' and taking drugs bought in Camden Town in the fields of Hampshire in 'Sorted for Es and Whizz' resonated with British fans.

In 1994 the UK music industry Brit Awards were dominated by Blur who won awards in a number of categories, and Oasis achieved the same the following year. In 1996 Pulp lead singer, Jarvis Cocker, showed his own antipathy to a certain kind of American culture, when he ran onstage during Michael Jackson's performance at the same award ceremony, and waved his backside at Jackson. Pulp also went on to win a Mercury Music Prize for their album *Different Class* in that year.

This success of Britpop was supported by political changes that had led to the recognition of the power and commercial potential of a well-developed British popular music culture that was perceived worldwide as a part of the country's national identity. In the 1990s John Major took over as prime minister of Britain from Margaret Thatcher. One of the ways he attempted to reinvigorate the country was by boosting funding for culture. The Department of National Heritage was launched in 1992 and a National Lottery was also launched by this government.

The Lottery was used to fund heritage and culture, and the policy for this funding meant that funding was available for amateur and community projects as well as professional arts, and for all genres of music, popular music as well as art music. This reflected the growing breakdown of the boundaries between popular culture and high art in the UK. Up until this point, arts funding for music was almost all given to classical music. These changes coincided with developments in the British Phonographic Industry (BPI), the music industry trade association, and together they led to a greater appreciation of the contribution to the UK economy of the music industry, aided by the collection of more data about music industry employment, income and sales. Computer and digital audio technology was also allowing more data to be readily collected and analysed (Cloonan 2007, pp. 36–41).

During this period, Damon Albarn of Blur was invited to the House of Commons to meet with Labour party (the political opposition to the UK government of the time) leaders John Prescott, Alastair Campbell and Tony Blair in order to discuss how Albarn might help Labour's upcoming election campaign by reaching out to the youth vote. Prospective Prime Minister Tony Blair played electric guitar and was interested himself in popular music. He understood the power of music within popular culture (Harris 2003).

In 1997 Tony Blair led the (new) Labour party to win a general election, and his government created a Department of Culture, Media and Sport. The Labour party was traditionally supported by working class voters, whereas the previous Conservative government was more commonly associated with the wealthy and the upper classes. It is not surprising perhaps then that the Labour party further developed relationships with and supported the popular music industry, as a reflection of support for popular art forms rather than elite high art. An appreciation grew within government of the importance of British popular music as an export industry, and of the creative industries as employers and generators of wealth.

Labour wanted to show how young and funky they were in comparison to the previous Conservative government. Their campaign song had been dance anthem 'Things can Only Get Better' by D:Ream, and in July 1997 Noel Gallagher, Allan McGee from Creation Records, George Michael, comedian Harry Enfield, designer Vivienne Westwood, Anita Roddick and actor Tony Robinson (among others) were invited to a drinks party at 10 Downing Street to show the new attitude of the new, young prime minister. Although this has been seen by some as political spin designed to present the government as different but resulting in few real changes, Downing Street went on to be host to more media and sports figures, and the new government did mark a notable shift in engaging with popular culture. Damon Albarn chose to turn down his invitation to the party.

Meanwhile, the music industry was providing sets of figures that established how many people it employed, and using statistics such as the value of popular music to the UK economy to lobby government. The Music Managers Forum was formed in 1992, and in addition to the music industry controlled Brit awards, the BPI launched the Mercury Music Prize, which was branded as being based on musical quality rather than industry sales, with a panel of music critics to choose the winner. The popular music industry was beginning to formalize its processes to become more like any other industry. Britpop had emerged partly as a result of this support for popular culture.

The most visible latest incarnation of Britpop is the New Yorkshire scene spearheaded by the Arctic Monkeys. The effect of the governmental change in policy was felt in the band's home town of Sheffield, where state funding was used to establish and support a recording studio and music business training programmes, which the Arctic Monkeys had taken advantage of. A long list of bands in the Yorkshire region have become identified as singing in local accents, using conventional instrumentation, referencing local places, scenes and describing British life in songs that place themselves in Yorkshire, or elsewhere in Britain. This includes Reverend and the Makers, Milburn, The Cribs and The Kaiser Chiefs.

Influenced by the older Jon McClure, lead singer of fellow Sheffield band Reverend and the Makers, the Arctic Monkeys sang in their broad Sheffield accents and wrote songs about what surrounded them in Sheffield. The urban realism that can be heard in their first album describes the lives of these young men in Sheffield. In particular, one of their earliest tracks 'Fake Tales of San Francisco' comments on the tendency of British bands to sing in fake US accents. The lyrics describe the singer of a local band talking of San Francisco, but living in Hunter's Bar (part of Sheffield), and points out that the singer is not from New York City but from Rotherham (a town near Sheffield). Another song by the band tells of the prostitutes working near the band's rehearsal studios. Images on their record covers and videos are also recognizably British. In 'Fake Tales of San Francisco', the band take the unusual step for a Britpop band of taking an overtly oppositional stance towards the cultural imperialism of American popular music's huge influence on British culture, by criticizing other bands who do not sing in their 'natural' accent (Rothkopf 1997). The Arctic Monkeys are just the latest of a series of bands that have recognized the importance and power of reflecting their local culture in their music. The authenticity that this provides has supported a series of Britpop bands in creating a local cult focused around their music.

The local cult of popular music is one that can maintain and sustain the support of the local area, even after the band has stopped performing or the members have died. In Liverpool the city is enriched by Beatles based cultural tourism, with the city having established a Beatles Quarter, where there is a version of the Cavern Club where the band originally performed, a themed hotel, museum exhibits, tours to Penny Lane, Strawberry Fields and the band members' houses, and various other Beatle themed venues and activities. Fans come on pilgrimages to the city, and The Beatles have become an important part of the city's identity, its airport for example having been renamed after John Lennon.

What is significant about Britpop is that it shows the importance of local identity within popular music, and again and again shows how musical movements, cults of popular music, often grow from local scenes, and expand nationally and internationally. An in-depth investigation has also shown that Britpop did not arise in the 1990s, although that was when the term was coined. It was also not simply a revival of swinging London's 1960s scene.

It does seem to be characterized by (or features) popular music bands or groups rather than solo artists; singing in a local accent, often reflecting a working class urban culture; references in lyrics, artwork and promotional materials such as videos to local and British places, culture and people; songs that describe the lives of British (often working class) people rather than glamorizing a rock star lifestyle; a fashion consciousness, and a dress sense that is associated with the musical style; references to Britpop-type bands of the 1960s, or other previous local cults of British guitar music; an antipathy towards and yet influence from music from the USA; and a conventional popular music instrumentation, with drums, bass, guitar and vocals, with keyboards added occasionally. This pattern has been sustained through a succession of scenes, or local cults, growing up in different parts of Britain, including glitter rock, punk, Madchester, Britpop and new Yorkshire.

Ultimately Britpop was used as a marketing term, used to sell music magazines and periodicals, as well as to sell musical products. It is in the interests of record companies and the press to have categories such as Britpop in order to offer a defined scene, that includes dress, behaviour, culture and of course music. Britpop was not a new musical movement, but another in a long series of musical scenes to feature regional accents. However its emergence allowed the music business to market Britpop music as something new, something original, rather than a 1960s revivalist movement, or simply a reworking of the 'Madchester' scene. It also encouraged musicians to make music that reflected its locality, and focused this element of popular music culture.

Ultimately Britpop was separate from other rock music based British guitar band music scenes, and perhaps the reason why can be seen within the word Britpop itself. Rather than being called 'britrock', to underline the guitar-based focus of the music, it was regarded as pop music, rather than popular music. Pop music is focused on the music charts, is commercial music that is among the most popular of the moment, its music appealing to the mainstream, not just a group of fans within a subgenre, and it is usually focused on sales of singles rather than albums.

Sales of singles in the UK have for many years been a more significant part of the music industry than in other countries. According to the International Federation of the Phonographic Industry the UK accounted for 26 to 32 percent of all worldwide singles sales in the 1990s, making it the largest market for singles in the world, whereas it accounted for only 7 to 9 percent of album sales, making it only the third largest market for albums. Britpop was able to appeal to a wider audience than earlier rock music genres because it adopted the mod fashion sense of the 1960s, reconnecting with mainstream fashion and rejecting the alternative, oppositional anti-fashion of rock leather jackets, long hair, jeans and t-shirts. Unlike punk, baggy or grunge, the fashions of Britpop were mainstream enough for large numbers of girls to be attracted to the scene, and for it to appeal to cock rock as well as teen pop audiences.

For this reason the Spice Girls, a hugely successful teen pop girl band, became associated with Britpop after Geri Halliwell wore a dress featuring a Union Jack pattern during the band's performance at the 1997 Brit awards. Interestingly, this marked the end of the Britpop era. The massive success in the UK and the USA of the Spice Girls reorientated British pop music again as teen pop for young girls. Meanwhile, dissatisfied with being pigeonholed as Britpop, Blur recorded their next album in Iceland, influenced by lo-fi bands from the USA, abandoning their lyrical approach of writing about typically British characters and characteristics.

One long-time member of Pulp left, and singer Jarvis Cocker found the musical success that he had sought for almost 15 years in Pulp, as well as the fame that came with it, difficult to cope with, and Pulp's next album *This is Hardcore* was far less successful than its predecessors. The third album by Oasis was successful in the UK but less so in the USA, and not well received critically. By the fourth album two of the original members had left, and a succession of fights between the Gallagher brothers came to characterize the band. Repositioned as a rock band, their Beatles influences took an interesting turn when Ringo Starr's son Zak joined as drummer for a number of years, cementing the links of the band with the Beatles.

There has not been space in this chapter to cover all the different British local popular music scenes that have appeared, such as those in Scotland or Wales that have reinforced the national identity of those countries, or to cover local scenes in the USA. In particular it is important to note that many areas have local scenes that never spawned famous bands, and where the scene has not grown to become of national interest, where it has remained a local popular music cult that exists as a form of urban folk music, a local traditional music within the sacred popular.

Again, at the end of this chapter it is useful to see if typical descriptions of other religious cults fit the local cults of popular music. Many cults are specific to a particular region, especially in traditional societies, and membership is often what defines belonging to a community. Like local pop cults, membership in such cases is something that has different levels of involvement. Most local popular music cults revolve around a small group of charismatic leaders, the members of bands. Other key figures focus their activities around these leaders of music-based ritualistic activities like concerts, including managers, promoters and technicians. These leaders may not all claim explicitly to be gods, but they do offer access to the transcendental through the group based music experiences they offer, through the sense of connection to other people, the other worlds, states of consciousness and emotional states that can be visited with a select group of people within a localized community that members feel connected to. The pop stars at the centre of local cults are divinised, or offer access to these experiences that focus on the spirituality of the relationships between people. Like most cults, local pop cults focus around a group of sacred individuals who are either still alive or have not been dead more than 50 years.

Membership of a local pop cult usually involves a very high level of commitment in order to become fully integrated into the group. Continuing involvement means increasing levels of participation, which can often make it seem that relationships with parents and family members are damaged. Cult members are in general often young, and many pop cults are effectively youth cults, and as young people feel increasingly connected to the other members of the local scene, a feeling that family members do not understand the culture and behaviour of the cult can grow, with the local pop cult then seeming isolationist and secretive. It is local pop cults that are particularly associated with young members, it is rare that older aged sectors of the community have the time and interest to discover and participate in local popular music cults, often being more interested in music that is already more widely known.

Like most cults, local pop cults focus on recruiting new members or converts. Every band seeks to gain fans that are committed to them, yet despite this it takes effort to get to know enough to be credible as a fan, memorizing songs, knowing details of the lives of the band members and knowing how to behave and dress. Just as in many cults, local pop cults are associated with a particular dress code, or fashion, especially including hairstyles and clothing.

As well as trying to recruit members, like other cults local pop cults are focused on making money. Increasing the number of fans a band has is achieved by increasing record sales, which also generates more money. The band members around whom local cults revolve are usually ambitious and want their cult to grow to achieve national and international recognition. Fame, as well as the gaining of a greater number of recruits, is presented by most bands as more important than financial gain, but the two are of course inextricably linked. Cults are often accused of indoctrinating their members, and as in other pop cults this is somewhat the case in local pop cults, as is an association with mind-altering practices including drug taking.

This chapter has aimed to show the importance of locality in popular music cults. It has presented 'scene' as a term used to describe a local popular music cult, and as a term that carries with it the authenticity of the local. It has tried to demonstrate that many popular music scenes develop as a local scene, based in and representing a specific local area and its characteristic culture. If such a local scene becomes successful then this area will gain recognition as the origin of this particular genre or subgenre of music, and the two will be closely associated. It has investigated in particular the phenomenon of Britpop, aiming to define the term, and to explain why it is of interest. Similar points could have been made by discussing reggae in Jamaica, hip hop in the Bronx or Disco in New York City.

Local popular music cults provide a way of fostering pride in young people's local community, and helping them to connect with where they live. Many of the local cults that are most successful come from or reflect the culture of deprived or run-down urban areas where participation in a local music scene provides an increase in self-esteem, a pride in local identity. In an area that may be considered of low status financially, educationally or in terms of opportunities, a local popular music cult provides a site for the expression of identity, in which the culture of those taking part is respected and even championed. It offers the opportunity for the negative representations of a community to be re-enchanted, and more positively presented.

Chapter 6

Even Better Than the Real Thing: Virtual Cults of Popular Music

Elvis Presley was one of the first pop stars to semi-fictionalize himself through the use of film. His career moulded by svengali figure Colonel Tom Parker, Presley's success led to him featuring in a number of films that were essentially vehicles for his star persona. Who Elvis was, in the eyes of the public, became part-real, part-invented. His film roles rarely required him to act in a way that was different to his usual character. He usually sang in his films, creating further confusions between his own character, his music star personality and the various film roles he was playing. As discussed in the personality cult chapter, popular music weaves a complex mixture of the authentic and the fictional, with stars performing authenticity, performing their emotions and feelings, with such performances to some extent drawn from a mixture of their hopes, dreams and ambitions for themselves.

Elvis provides a bridge between earlier and later popular musicians. He was in many ways similar to crooners such as Bing Crosby, Dean Martin and Frank Sinatra, as he became as well known for being a film star as a singer, starting out as a popular musician. He also had much in common with later stars, as he was the first rock'n'roll star, and played overtly African American influenced music. In addition, when he first appeared, Elvis created a division between his young fans who adored him, and his critics who accused him of performing in too sexual and outrageous a fashion. Presley launched a rock'n'roll revolution that had resonances for many years to come, and, perhaps because he was the first icon of his kind, he had a peculiar level of success. His status was regarded as iconic or legendary, and there are a number of ways in which one might consider him a religious or cult figure.

Although Elvis is officially dead, there are many who have claimed he is still alive. For example The Elvis is Alive Museum website contains a plethora of documents, including a page where fans can write letters to Elvis that are displayed online. In a typical example, one person writes, 'I know you had a reason to fake your death, but I am looking forward to the day you come back to us and perform.' This has obvious resonances with Jesus Christ, implying as it does that Elvis is not really dead but will return one day to his loyal follow-ers. Another website, Letters to Elvis, is devoted to exhibiting letters from fans. There are a plethora of other sites, such as Truth About Elvis, also claiming that Elvis is still alive, with photos, stories, 'evidence' and a range of different conspiracy theories, all pointing to the fact that Elvis Presley is alive and well. Various books also attest to this theory, for example *Elvis Is Alive* By Robert Mickey Maughon (1997). Much as Catholics report sightings of Mary or other religious figures, fans report sightings of Elvis, some seeing him physically, others experiencing him in a more nebulous 'spiritual' manner.

Graceland, the former home of Presley, acts as a site of pilgrimage for fans who are encouraged by the official Elvis.com website to 'discover your inner Elvis'. Once more the religious symbolism is plain to see, Elvis being presented as like a spirit within the devotee. The date of his death is celebrated by fans with an Elvis week, advertised by the Graceland website. However it is not just his death, the Elvis equivalent of Easter, that is remembered, but the Presley Christmas, his birth, is also celebrated. In Elvis week an Elvis impersonator competition is held, as well as various other events. The Ultimate Elvis Tribute Artist competition held in Elvis week pits the winners of various qualifiers from previous rounds held across the USA against each other. There are a huge numbers of Elvis imper-sonators around the world, who dress as him and imitate him. According to Garber, 'the phenomenon of "Elvis impersonators," which began long before the singer's death, is one of the most startling effects of the Elvis cult' (1997, p. 369).

Also held at Graceland in Elvis Week is a candlelight vigil, to remember Elvis and his legacy. This is described in the *Fortean Times*,

Elvis Presley Boulevard, Memphis, 16 August, 2002: The normally traffic-choked state highway has been transformed from something quite different from its workday self. Candles flicker in the darkness, the rain pours down, and some 40,000 people keep their night long vigil. It's a bizarre scene, like some kind of Bergmanesque, mediaeval pilgrimage transported into the 21st century America, with tears and laughter, celebration and mourning min-gling in a tableau of devout humanity. (Sutton 2003)

It is events such as these that mean Elvis Presley is truly still alive. These events keep his memory alive, and the media construction that was Presley is perhaps more active now than it was when the man who was Elvis was living. Elvis is still performing in a cleverly constructed show that is now touring arenas around the world. Images of him singing are projected on large screens, his voice from the film accompanied by some of the musicians who played on his original recordings. He may be dead, but he is still able to perform beyond the grave, virtually performing as a screen icon with live performers adding concert authenticity. These performances consist essentially of crowds of Elvis fans collecting to watch recordings of Elvis, and the popularity of such concerts is testament both to his continuing existence and popularity.

A number of other important religious functions are associated with Elvis that imply that he can be seen as a leader of a cult. When he was performing in Las Vegas, Presley would hang scarves from his neck which he would pass on to adoring fans. He discussed religion and sang and wrote religious songs. An Elvis chapel has been constructed on land adjoining Graceland, and couples can get married there in themed weddings. In Las Vegas, where Presley performed for many years, there are a number of wedding chapels where one can be married by 'Elvis'. One such venue is Graceland Chapel where one can be married by an Elvis impersonator, who sings Elvis songs and conducts the ceremony. Many examples of Elvis themed weddings in Las Vegas can be seen online, for example on You Tube, in which the wedding party is often also dressed in Elvis-related clothing. Music stars like Jon Bon Jovi, Billy Ray Cyrus and Aaron Neville have married at an Elvis chapel, adding their own authenticity to the process.

The Elvis Cult has been discussed in a number of books, including *Elvis People: Cult of the King*, (Harrison 1992), *Elvis Religion: The Cult of the King* (Reece 2006), and *Elvis: The Messiah* (Mallay and Vaughn 1993). Reece sees Elvis as a popular rather than religious icon, but this is a somewhat difficult distinction to maintain. A number of films have enhanced the perception of Elvis as a religious figure, for example *Finding Graceland* (1998) telling the story of a magical individual claiming to be Elvis returning to Graceland.

Further to this there are individuals who specifically describe Elvis as a religious figure. This is sometimes done in a tongue in cheek, postmodern, fashion, or with varying degrees of seriousness. Some describe him as an 'other Jesus' or 'saint Elvis' (Gottdiener 1999a, 1999b). Others have actually formed Presley churches, for example the First Presleyterian Church of Elvis the Divine was set up as a satirical comment on religion, but has been taken seriously by a number of self-proclaimed Presleyterians, also known as Elvites. The distinction between Elvites or Presleyterians, who describe their following of Elvis as a religion, and those who describe themselves as fans may be an important distinction to some individuals, but their behaviours are largely the same, and this distinction is not really a clear one. As Plasketes tells us,

> Spirituality and the deification of Elvis continue to be among the most thriving dimensions of the Presley myth. The pious parallels are pervasive, with fragments of both traditional and non-traditional religions widely represented. The Elvis Lives phenomenon is but one manifestation of religious activity surrounding Elvis, The messianic movement includes a following of fanatics, true believers worshipping a deity, and spiritual and supernatural implications of conversion, resurrection, prophecy, and a second coming. The fundamental Presleyterian doctrine is that 'Elvis' is an anagram for 'lives'. Every year an estimated 12 million faithful make the pilgrimage, a Memphis mansion Mecca through the gates of Graceland. Elvis Presley International Tribute Week marks an annual August holy week

of candlelight vigils, cross-shaped floral arrangements, and weeping worshippers. (1997, p. 24)

Like Bing Crosby and Frank Sinatra before him, and Prince and Madonna after him, the association of the name of Elvis, with his image projected on screen, and his character fictionalized through the mix of acting, musical performance and 'real-life', has created a powerful dynamic. As the first major international rock'n'roll icon, it is perhaps unsurprising that his cult is one of the best developed within popular music culture. He now performs virtually, using multimedia technology to return from the dead, virtual reality allowing the creation and sustaining of a fictional virtual version of himself.

The mixture of the real and fictional, popular music and youth culture is enhanced enormously by the power of screen culture. Just as the earliest moving pictures caused people to jump out of the way of trains that seemed to be coming straight towards them, moving pictures continue to have the power to convince people that what they see is in some way real. The fact that the fast moving sequence of images on screen move as if they were real, and that the images on screen seem to be speaking or otherwise making appropriate sounds, is enough to convince our minds that what we see is a representation of the real world. Popular musicians like Elvis Presley have used the virtual realities that are created on screens to build their popular cults. Other musicians and bands that followed Presley have adopted similar approaches.

Like Presley, the Beatles also made films, first *A Hard Day's Night* (1964) and then *Help!* (1964). In both, the Beatles play themselves, and the films acted as promotional films for the band's albums. The Beatles are another example of an onscreen band that expresses a complicated mix of reality and fiction. The Beatles may have been perceived as being more authentic when they were playing rock'n'roll in the Cavern club in Liverpool or in Hamburg, but at that point they were not very successful. It was when the Beatles became the prototypical boy band that they became hugely successful, wearing suits that were made by London tailor Douglas Millings to look like the collarless fashions of French designer Pierre Cardin, and wearing Beatle boots, which were Chelsea boots with a Cuban heel, and mop top haircuts. These fashions were as much responsible for the success of the Beatles as their music.

The Beatles were also made into a cartoon series that ran in the USA from 1965–1967 (Axelrod 1999). The series caricatured the band members, and presented them much as they had been presented in their earlier films and television interviews. Each episode was based on a Beatles song's lyrics or title, and the song or songs were played during the show. This provided free television advertising for the Beatles' music and helped establish their personalities in the public imagination. The Beatles in the cartoon show were largely fictional however. Their images were cartoon exaggerations of them. The band's voices were performed by actors, an American playing Lennon and Harrison rather unconvincingly, while a British actor does a somewhat better job of voicing

McCartney and Harrison. This was a virtual Beatles, a fake Beatles, an imaginary Beatles; the real band's only contribution was when one of their songs was played during the show.

The band went on to make a cartoon film, *Yellow Submarine* (1968), which featured the band in the virtual world of animation, again with their voices spoken by actors. It was not important that the voices were not those of the real Beatles, a cartoon image of their faces, along with the use of their names and music was enough to tell the audience that it was the Beatles that was being referred to. This helped to sustain and develop the semi-fictional iconic characters of the Beatles, their mediaphemes (Johnson 2004). As well as developing these in the real world through interviews and live performances, the Beatles career was sustained by virtual performances in these cartoon appearances. In the USA in particular, television was a vital tool for the band to reach the far-flung corners of the country, and to be able to reach out into the homes of such a large population. The Beatles were hugely successful, so much so that In September 1965, the same month that the Beatles cartoon series was first shown, in the USA a production company decided to create a television show based on a four-piece band designed to be their own version of the Beatles.

The television Show *The Monkees* was launched on NBC in 1966 and the co-ordination of the launch of a hit single 'Last Train to Clarkesville' and the debut of the series, made the show, and the group, an instant success. The style of the show was inspired in the main by the Beatles' films, while the format was much like the Beatles' cartoon series, featuring one of the band's songs in each programme and promoting and being promoted by their records. In this case however the band was truly fictional, put together for the television show, with songs written by professional songwriters. The main lead singer was British actor and singer Davy Jones. Mickey Dolenz was a child-star actor who was taught to play the drums for the show, but who also provided lead vocals on some songs. Mike Nesmith and Peter Tork were previously unsuccessful musicians, who also featured, playing and producing. All four sang on the Monkees' recordings.

The band's albums were very successful. They went on to perform live, but there was a long-term struggle between the band, who wanted more control of writing, performing and choosing material, and the production company, who regarded the Monkees as principally a television show, and felt they were best placed to make such choices. The Monkees wanted to be a 'real' band, while the producers of the show wanted to use the best professional songwriters, producers and musicians available. The band eventually took control of their own destiny, sacking the producers who had created them in the first place. The producers were perhaps finally proven right, as this led to the band becoming less popular and then splitting up (Lefcowitz 1985; Sandoval 2005).

The Monkees were a media construction rather than a real band, that existed somewhere between reality and fiction. Just like the Beatles' band name, theirs was also a clever misspelling, which could be trademarked. This constructed 'boy band', put together in order to achieve the maximum commercial success, rather than having a mediapheme, actually *was* a mediapheme. The Monkees' Producer, Don Kirshner, went on to make a new cartoon television series *The Archie Show*, built around a cartoon pop band called The Archies that was based on characters from the Archie comic book. Just as the Monkees was based on The Beatles' *Help!*, The Archie Show was influenced by the Beatles cartoon series, and allowed the producers complete control, with no chance that the cartoon musicians could wrest control from them as the band members of the Monkees had done. The Archies had a major hit with the song 'Sugar Sugar', which the Monkees had turned down the opportunity to record, reaching number one in the US and UK charts in 1969. As in The Monkees TV series and The Beatles cartoon series, The Archies performed a song in every show, and released various singles and albums.

There were a number of cartoon TV shows that took the same approach, including musical performances in each show and characters that were members of a band, with session musicians performing the music, and musical releases and sometimes live performances associated with them. These shows included bands such as Josie and the Pussycats (one of the band's singing voices was the first success of future *Charlie's Angels* television show actress Cheryl Ladd); The Groovy Goolies (with characters taken from horror films); The Hardy Boys (based on the children's books); Butch Cassidy and the Sundance Kids (featuring Mickey Dolenz of the Monkees providing the drummer's voice); Cattanooga Cats (the band were cartoon cats and the drummer was voiced by Casey Kasem who also voiced the character Shaggy in the Scooby Doo series); The Chan Clan (based on Charlie Chan and featuring Don Messick who also voiced Scooby Doo); and The Neptunes (featuring a great white shark on drums). The Jackson 5 was also featured in their own cartoon series, as were The Osmonds. Cooper and Smay (2001) discuss these bands in some detail. Such bands were usually aimed at a market of young children, aiming to hook them on television shows and then sell records by taking advantage of the bands' onscreen popularity.

Each of these television shows was an invented fictional band, except the ones based on a real band such as the Beatles or Jackson Five, in which case the stories or behaviours were fictional. In the cases of the totally fictional bands, the music was constructed to fit the idea of the television show, with songs themed appropriately. The programmes used the idea of a popular music band as a framework for a fictional or mythical group of people. In the case of the real bands such as The Beatles or The Jackson Five, the process was adding to the mythology, the mediapheme, the media construction of the real people involved, complicated by the voicing of the band members by actors.

All of these bands were on television, each performed songs with cartoon characters animated onscreen, not actually playing the music, often with a different person performing the spoken and singing voice of each band member. One thinks of the Beatles as being four human beings, but in fact they are far more than that, a construction that mixes the real and the mythic, or virtual, with onscreen, onstage, and on record artificially constructed realities that contribute to the whole. In addition, what we think of as the Beatles was contributed to in part by others, such as ex-member Pete Best, manager Brian Epstein, designers such as Douglas Millings, extra musicians who played on recordings such as Eric Clapton, and producers and engineers such as George Martin, Phil Spector and Geoff Emerick. This is the case for every successful band, popular music is very much a team effort in nearly all cases, even for so-called solo artists.

Other bands were constructed in slightly less obvious fashion. The Bay City Rollers went through several incarnations before their manager found a group of musicians he was happy could achieve success. They went on to become one of the most successful UK pop groups of 1975–1976, hosting their own television show called Shang-a-lang. Many other musical acts mixed television and music careers, usually presented to the public as bands, often put together by record or management companies.

In 1999 pop impresario Simon Fuller created the band S Club 7 for a BBC television show called Miami 7. Fuller had run a very successful management company, leading the Spice Girls to international success. The Spice Girls were presented in the press with exaggerated versions of their own characters, and eventually made a film that again explored the line between reality and fiction, much like the Beatles' early films. Fuller gave each of the band members of S Club 7 a colour, and integrated the schedules of their musical releases and television shows. They made four series of the show, achieving worldwide success, winning Brit awards, and eventually performing live as well as on television. A second group, S Club Juniors, was formed after a television show that tracked auditions to be band members. As Fuller put it 'Pop music is about celebrity and not just about music ... Pop stars should be icons' (Robinson and Winkle 2004, p. 292).

Fuller also created the Pop Idol and American Idol television series, using a public search for pop stars as free television advertising during primetime slots, as well as a way to find the most popular future stars. These shows allowed Fuller and others to carry out research into audience preference onscreen, the winning acts having already proven their popularity with the public. The acts appearing on the shows were all signed up to contracts, the programmes cleverly disguising market research as entertainment. These series led on to X-Factor and similar shows, which have had a major impact on the music charts, providing a structured way to provide free advertising to large numbers of young viewers, mixing television entertainment and the music industry in a very successful fashion.

S Club 7 was not very different from a cartoon band. They mimed most of their performances on television, and their music career was constructed for television and managed carefully by music industry professionals. Faceless invisible session musicians provided the musical accompaniment, and session backing singers sang along to the band members' lead vocals, which were adjusted by auto-tuning, compression, enhancement, equalization, digital editing and other studio technology. The band members were very much aware of performing their onstage characters, and were chosen for their abilities to act as much as their singing ability.

Many similar boy bands or girl groups have been virtual bands at some level, existing to some extent fictionally as a media construction. The band members have been somewhat mythical, or legendary, to use a term often applied within popular music culture. They are icons, in the case of the cartoon bands they are drawings, much like traditional religious ikons. As the internet has become increasingly significant within popular culture, and as techniques of digital modelling, animation and video have developed, it has become possible for bands to appear who exist only in a virtual world.

In 1999 the lead singer of the band Blur, Damon Albarn, launched cartoon band Gorillaz with his friend cartoonist Jamie Hewlett. Albarn had found himself at the centre of the Britpop media storm, partly because he was in a relationship with lead singer of Elastica, Justine Frischmann. The British tabloid press featured the two heavily, and neither found the press intrusion easy to deal with. As lead singers in guitar-based bands they were used to press attention that focused on interviews by music press who discussed their musical work rather than their personal lives. The tabloid press in comparison were mostly interested in their personal lives, and the couple were plagued by photographers following them around and reporters hounding them. The media coverage of the relationship between the two contributed greatly to the success of Britpop, but also drove Albarn to seek to remove himself from the public spotlight.

Taking a break from working with Blur, Albarn set out to create a musical context where he could separate his music making from the culture of celebrity. In Gorillaz, Hewlett's cartoon characters took his place as lead singer, the front person who took the lead role in speaking to the press. In an interview Albarn stated,

> This is where I've wanted to get to in my life, just to have some control over everything ... Even though I was a frontman for many years I don't think I'm actually that comfortable with it ... That's the whole point of it ... It's like, let's deconstruct this celebrity monster that's been created in our society. (Purcell 2006)

Albarn had increasingly been writing about fictional characters in the songs he wrote for Blur, creating characters whose lives he discussed, so it was a small step to move on to create a completely fictional band. Albarn was certainly aware of how the press already fictionalized his musical success.

> If you're going to be a pop star, they should let you know in advance so you can prepare for it. But it happened overnight. The morning after we won

four Brits, we were pop stars and the paparazzi were chasing us round. The weirdest thing was the cartoon strip, The Blur Story, in the Daily Star. What an extraordinary time that was. (Lester 2003)

Having been featuring in a cartoon strip about Blur, seeing a caricature of him and his band living a fictional life, it was a logical step to form a cartoon band which would allow him to avoid the pressure of being a media celebrity.

In an interview Hewlett said,

There are very few truly original bands or singers or artists emerging any-more. Almost everything can be traced to something that happened 10 years ago … I don't believe these bands that I see on the TV … I feel it's all really false and contrived. And that just seemed to be the logical step with Gorillaz, well, let's make it up, but let's make it up and make it really good. And let's cut out that celebrity element that everyone seems to be so concerned with. (Thorne 2007)

Hewlett and Albarn created four cartoon characters who would be the public visual image of the band, and set about creating music for the band and an imaginary world for them to inhabit. A website was constructed that featured the Gorillaz home, where one could explore different rooms. The band would appear to visit the house by Albarn, Hewlett or others being online in the web-site chat room periodically where they could chat in real time to fans.

The group was so successful that in 2002 Gorillaz were nominated for a number of UK music industry Brit awards, performing virtually with the images of the cartoon band members projected on huge screens, while the musicians performed anonymously behind the screens. A DVD release featured cartoons, virtual tours around the website and a mock television documentary called *Charts of Darkness*, which had already been shown on UK television.

Gorillaz also launched a campaign attacking the idea of celebrity icons called Reject False Icons. People were encouraged to place stickers with the phrase 'Reject False Icons' on them, in public places. Stickers could be downloaded from a website or collected from record stores, and those placed in interesting positions were featured online. Many were placed on pictures of media stars in public places, such as on advertising posters. Albarn was continuing his battle against celebrity culture, although ironically he was using his power as a celebrity icon to do so. In the film *Bananaz*, a 2008 documentary directed by Ceri Levy about the band, Albarm describes American Idol. 'All of that is a sickness and they need to find a cure for it.' He places Gorillaz in opposition to commercial popular music, to constructed boy bands and girl bands.

Gorillaz was inspired in part by the Monkees and the cartoon bands described earlier. There are references to the Beatles in that the cover of Gorrilaz 2005 release *Demon Days* is very similar to that of the Beatles' *Let it Be* album. The name Gorrilaz is a bigger, badder development of and reference to the Monkees. Just as the Monkees is a misspelling of a small ape, Gorillaz is a misspelling of a larger ape, a blacker, darker, more powerful ape.

When James Hewlett is asked in the *Charts of Darkness* documentary what the inspiration was for the cartoon band's personalities, he names Rolling Stones guitarist Keith Richards; a baddy from Scooby Doo; stormtroopers; Peter Faulk (the actor who played Columbo); Brian Harvey (a singer in boy band East Seventeen whose career was marred by public admission of drug taking); minor UK television personality Matthew Kelly; and Star Wars villain Darth Vader. Many of these characters have both light and dark sides to their characters, and are perhaps anti-heroes.

While he describes these examples, other pictures show on the screen, including Daffy Duck; Peter Sellers (playing Inspector Clouseau in one of the Pink Panther films, the Pink Panther having also been made into a well-known cartoon); Shaggy from the Scooby Doo cartoon series; David Bowie; the child catcher from the film *Chitty Chitty Bang Bang*; Tom Sellick who played TV character Magnum; Laurel and Hardy; Chubby Checker and Fat Boys; a number of zombies; the cartoon character Popeye; children's television band The Banana Splits; cartoon TV series *Battle of the Planets*; Mr. T from the A-Team; Arnold from *Different Strokes*; the Thing from comic superheroes the Fantastic Four; cartoon character Dick Dastardly; John Carradine from TV series *Kung Fu*; The Monkees; characters from 1980s television show *Monkey*; and George Harrison from The Beatles.

It is interesting that The Rolling Stones, The Beatles and The Monkees all feature, which references the varying degrees of fictionalization in these groups. The Banana Splits represents the tradition of children's programmes based on fictional music bands already discussed. David Bowie, who also consciously created fictional onscreen characters, is shown. *Monkey*, a television show based on the Japanese series *Saiyūki*, is based on Buddhist legends. After the Gorillaz project ended, Albarn went on to produce an Opera based on the same stories. Overall, the list shows the fusion of reality and fiction that Gorillaz aimed to synergize.

Damon Albarn is responsible for much of the Gorillaz music, credited with vocals, keyboards, writing, guitars, bass and melodica. However Gorillaz is a collective effort, which features many different musicians. These include bass player Junior Dan; D12, a rap group who originally featured Eminem (who does not appear in Gorillaz); Terry Hall, the former lead singer of British ska revivalists The Specials; rap group Phi-Life Cypher; De La Soul (rappers on 'Feel Good Inc.'); singer Ibrahim Ferrer of the Buena Vista Social Club; rapper and remixer Dangermouse; singer Neneh Cherry; Dan Nakamura, a Japanese-American producer who specializes in rap and hip hop; rapper Del Tha Funkee Homosapien; Sean Ryder, lead singer of the Madchester group Happy Mondays (singing on 'Dare'); Pharcyde rapper Bootie Brown; Tina Weymouth and Chris Frantz of Talking Heads and the Tom Tom Club; Redman; Spacemonkeyz; scratch DJ and turntablist Kid Koala (on the debut album); Roots Manuva;

The Bees; singer Martina Topley-Bird; the London Community Gospel Choir (vocals on 'Demon Days'); Dennis Hopper; Booty Brown (vocals on 'Dirty Harry'); Ike Turner; the San Fernando Youth Chorus (vocals on 'Dirty Harry'); and Simon Tong. The website gorrilaz-unofficial.com provides a detailed list of featured musicians.

Dissatisfied with the semi-fictional world of popular music celebrity, unhappy with his position as a popular music icon, Albarn has shown how popular music can create virtual worlds. He found that within the cartoon band Gorillaz he was able to escape the expectations of his own mythology and make the creation of the mediapheme that surrounds his music an integral part of the creative work of popular music. Gorillaz was a successful popular music virtual cult, which encouraged participation from the audience, and interaction through online and multimedia resources. Unhappy with his own elevation to iconic status, Albarn created and presented Gorillaz as not spiritual, and indeed in opposition to god-like iconic status. However Gorillaz is a form of postmodern legend, drawing upon various other traditions that are drenched in meanings of various kinds. In addition one of the cartoon band members has spiritual powers, able to channel the spirit of a rapper, the rapper appearing as a ghostly ectoplasmic apparition above their head.

Conclusions

Film was the beginning of screen culture. Virtual worlds before film were within the imaginations of the individual, or perhaps within the text of books, but these were individual experiences not shared ones. In the past, churches and other places of worship have offered iconic representations of mythical and idealized figures, idols to be worshipped, and examples to be followed. They used music, imagery, text, ritual, drama and stories to create communal experiences of a semi-mythical spiritual world, the virtual world of its day. Church ikons were still and static, either statues frozen in the moment or paintings, flat against the wall. Many religions featured holy men, priests or shamen who were possessed in one way or another by the divine, whether dressed up in an elaborate costume and/or mask or channelling the deity filled with its spirit, this offered a closing of the gap between worshipper and worshipped.

In the twentieth Century it was hard for religious figures such as Jesus Christ to compete for the title of chief role model in Western Europe against the new icons and idols of screen-based culture. Unlike static images such as Christ nailed to a cross, these stars shone from and moved in the moving light of the screen. Instead of stories and parables written in archaic English telling moral tales from 2000 years ago, the new gods of the sacred popular told their stories themselves, acting out modern day parables in a miracle of moving light. As film turned to television they moved from the temple-like environment of the cinema to the home shrine of the television. This moving-light-box was placed at the centre of every home and families collected around it to be instructed in many ways, including cultural choice, good consumption, ethics, sexual attitudes, political information and ways of rebelling.

In contemporary society, television is the opium of the people. Nearly half of all free time in the USA, about 16 hours per week, are spent watching television. Viewers are found to be happy with watching television even though it has been linked by research to long-term personal unhappiness. Unhappy people watch more television than those who are happy, television acting as a refuge for people who are unhappy. Like a drug addiction or other addictive activity, television provides momentary pleasure but long-term misery or regret (Robinson and Martin 2009).

In comparing opium and television, one must remember the context of Marx's famous phrase, describing religion as the opium of the people. Opium was banned in China due to the detrimental effect it was having on the populace. This led to war with Britain, who had been selling opium to China in order to balance a trade deficit. Losing two opium wars with Britain, China was forced to allow the opium trade. This history is part of British imperialist practices, using the powerful addictive quality of opium to control markets and boost the UK's commercial profitability. Television has a similar role today, of providing an addictive remedy to individualized splintered communities and feelings of long-term dissatisfaction and unhappiness. At the same time it provides cultural imperialism, as hegemonic values, or USA television programmes, colonize the world using screens, bringing with them values, behaviours, practices, traditions, beliefs and consumer behaviours.

The quote from Marx says,

Religion is the sigh of the oppressed creature, the heart of a heartless world, and the soul of soulless conditions. It is the opium of the people. The abolition of religion as the illusory happiness of the people is the demand for their real happiness. To call on them to give up their illusions about their condition is to call on them to give up a condition that requires illusions. (Marx 1975, p. 244)

He was criticizing the need for illusions, for that which was beyond the everyday, the need for gods to worship, to obey, to follow. Yet the hierarchy he imposed instead, also used powerful iconography, required dogmatic obedience to a set of principles, was led by an all powerful unquestionable leader, and no more led to happiness than the religion that communism replaced. Religion, like Marxist doctrine, provided a way to construct communities, cultural practices to bond those communities together, and information systems to inform those involved how they should behave.

Watching television is passive, where entertainment is provided, and trains a passive reception and attitude, much like the effect of opium. Religion has traditionally played a pivotal role in bringing heart and soul to the people, in the words of Marx. This is seldom entirely passive, but participatory, communal and involving, thus I would say that rather than religion, television is more accurately described as the opium of the people, and in the West, popular music seems to be becoming the religion of the people. It is the (sacred) popular movement that brings heart and soul to a heartless soulless world, reenchanting as it goes.

Elvis Presley was not just a skin bag full of bones and flesh, the whole that is Elvis includes his actions and the effects that his actions has had and continues to have. In a very real way we are all still alive as long as we are remembered, our existence, our selves are sustained by the memories of others who are still living. Who we are, is partly constructed from what we stand for, what we represent, the ways that the universe is different because of what we do. Jesus, God, Mohammed, Buddha and the like all exist today, even if only in the way they are brought into existence by the beliefs of others. Whether one considers these are authentic or false beliefs, or beliefs in a falsehood, religious and cult figures are brought into existence and sustained by those who sustain their memory.

In some African cultures it is a very real belief that we are still alive as long as we are remembered, making lineages and genealogies significant cultural dynamics (Chernoff 1979). Our bodies exist whether we are alive or not. Our souls can be described as those things that show that we are interacting with others. If we conceive of our souls as our fields, with our bodies inside our souls, rather than our souls inside our bodies, we can perhaps better understand the effects that we continue to have after our bodies have ceased to function. Our field reaches out beyond our bodies during our lives, through the ways we affect other people and the society and culture in which we live. In that way we can understand how our souls outlast our bodies, as the body being a subset of the soul, rather than vice-versa. This definition of soul is extrapolated from attitudes to the soul in sub-Saharan African (Chernoff 1979), and the concepts of morphic fields of Rupert Sheldrake (Sheldrake 1988). Who a person is, is a complicated issue, and in the case of pop stars and icons, all the more so. The real, the imaginary, the mythical and the virtual interact in a complex fusion, especially within the cults of popular music.

Like other cults, virtual cults such as that of Gorillaz include semi-mythical characters presented as having god-like powers. The use of websites, chatrooms and other anonymous forms of communication, allows stars to be represented online by others. It also allows imaginary characters to be available to any number of fans without being restricted by the time this takes. Such cults are focused around recruitment of more members. As in other popular music cults, a great requirement of time, commitment and money is required to participate. The whole virtual world may be presented as some kind of artistic activity, but it is focused around money, selling products, and being commercially successful. Other virtual religions exist that are not financially driven, but virtual pop cults always have products, whether they are pieces of music, video or merchandising, that are for sale.

As in other pop cults, the virtual nature of the cults allow fans to spend huge amounts of time online, communicating with other cult members, other fanatics, using online messaging, posting on online boards, email and other methods. Being locked away in their bedrooms, developing an obsession with an absent virtual presence, can allow the cult member to be separated from reality, to replace their friendships and family and other relationships, and thus develop an us-versus-them mentality. This is particularly true of the vulnerable or those lacking social skills.

The virtual world can be a site of sensory deprivation, it being possible to control fully the output from a virtual pop cult, which can be viewed repetitively as many times as possible. There are elements of typical cult-like repetitious and brainwashing practices possible in the total immersion in the artificial virtual worlds that are constructed. The virtual characters are also not bound by usual human abilities, are able to partake in extreme activities, and behave in ways that the fan is not able to. In addition all of the usual cult-like artefacts of other cults of popular music may be present in a virtual pop cult, and in many cases the virtual pop cult is only a part of a wider pop cult that also exists in reality.

Virtual worlds, and screen cultures, allow pop cults to sustain the mythical existence of pop stars. The cartoon characters of Gorillaz are real; they exist in a virtual world that is part of contemporary culture. They are just as real and authentic as the members of Blur or any other popular group, or at least as real as the public's understanding of pop stars, the semi-fictional characters that we assume to be real pop musicians. As virtual reality and three-dimensional modeling techniques, and three-dimensional film and television increase in realism and detail, we can expect more virtual popular music stars, and further virtual pop worlds where the cult of the pop star can involve a completely artificial world, a media construction of epic proportions, only restricted by the imaginations of those creating and inhabiting them.

Chapter 7

Hope I Die Before I Get Old: Death Cults of Popular Music

The Construction of the Christian Devil

The devil of western culture is largely a construction of Christian cultural traditions, rather than one who comes from the Christian bible. The conglomerated character of a mixture of the Devil, Lucifer, Satan, the great dragon, the serpent, Baal and Beelzebub is presented as living in a hell of burning fire, with horns, goat-like legs, a toasting or pitchfork, coloured red, surrounded by similar winged demons, and is a complex construction mostly created by medieval Christianity. The Christian devil is a fallen angel, who appears attractive and beautiful to humans, tempting them. The biblical figure who appears to Jesus in the desert to tempt him is not the horny devil of contemporary mythology. The tempter of Genesis is of course the snake that tempts the proto-human characters of Adam and Eve with knowledge, control and the forbidden.

The apocalyptic visions of the book of Revelation include complex images and metaphors, which were aimed at the audience of the day and difficult for us to comprehend, the great beast for example is likely to mean Rome, which had an army of invaders who were occupying Israel. Apocalyptic images of the end times, of the end of the world, involving earthquakes, floods, death, demons and other beasts, were co-opted for a number of reasons by the Christian church as it spread across the Roman Empire.

Christianity had to compete against a wide variety of long-established belief systems in different countries. Even after countries were officially converted to Christianity, traditional beliefs still survived, and were practiced and maintained within cultural traditions. One of the ways that it managed to compete with such beliefs was to associate the deities of other religions with the Christian devil. Pan, Bacchus and Dionysus, for example, were gods of revelry, fertility and loss of control, as were many other similar gods in different cultures. They were associated with the underworld, but not necessarily with negativity or evil.

As Christianity became more centrally controlled and regulated in Europe, it developed a central power base that made and enforced decisions about how to behave. The bible became a set document, with a new testament made up of a set group of books chosen for a variety of reasons, with other books not making the cut. The focus of Christian theology began to revolve around fall and redemption, guilt and repentance. These polar opposites, the black and white distinctions between good and evil, are well represented by St. Augustine's views for example, who was himself influenced by neo-Platonic dualism. This became even more the case when these ideas were revived far later in Calvinist and Puritan theologies. During the early development of Christianity, the holistic, ecological and mystical perspectives of Celtic Christianity left too much spiritual and religious authority in the hands of individuals or local groups, and instead strands of Christianity that centralized power became more dominant. The Christian faith became increasingly enmeshed within political power systems. Christianity increasingly focused around the religious authority of a small number of priests, who were professional religious leaders. This made it important in terms of political and social control for Christianity to dominate as the official religion, and for other religious beliefs to be wiped out.

Associating traditional religious figures such as Pan, Bacchus and Dionysus with the devil or Satan allowed Christianity to literally demonize other religions, to associate them with evil, negativity and the taboo. This was carried out by making features characteristic of these deities, such as goats' legs, beard, horns, tail or a red colour, features of the Christian devil rather than that of a competing tradition. This was Christianity adopting these deities within its own traditions and for its own purposes, changing and transforming their meanings in the process. Along with the images of these gods, associated religious traditions, practices and beliefs were also presented as negative rather than positive.

Pan, Bacchus and Dionysus and the traditions that surrounded them were quite disobedient and irreverent, often involving loss of control. Becoming drunk, lively dancing to music, effervescent self-loss, mystical experiences, change, otherness, losing control of oneself, and a generally bodily spiritual experience were not behaviours that helped to build and develop the authority of the central church, and became increasingly associated with these newly demonized deities. The mystic in a trance prophesying, the direct experience of the deity, and general rather than special revelation, all decentralized religious power and authority, and thus were gradually discredited as ways to approach the divine.

Fear was used by religious authorities to stop people from carrying on with traditional religious practices. Eternal damnation in the hell that was presented as the home of this newly constructed devil, was the ultimate threat to the general populace to make them conform to the directions of the Christian church, backed up with torture and burning at the stake. Various literary and artistic descriptions and depictions of hell helped to enshrine the idea of the devil in the popular imagination, with demons torturing the damned that had failed to follow the advice of religious leaders. With the now set text of the Christian bible interpreted by priests and often only available in the Latin language that only they spoke, access to the divine became increasingly controlled by religious professionals. This was within hierarchical structures like the Catholic Church that were often as much political (secular) organizations as they were focused on spirituality.

Those who still practised pre-Christian traditions were sometimes branded sorcerers, and were condemned along with those whose sin was only that of heresy, of believing a different interpretation of Christian wisdom. Witches and heretics alike were burned alive or tortured so that they would confess. Opposition to centralized religious authority was crushed either by the fear of the fires of hell or the fear of the fires of the inquisition. A Satan was created who had a specific personality, who could possess people, who was the personification of evil. This character developed a life of its own, created and brought to life by the Christian Church, and was presented in books, the theatre, and films, developing its own traditions and mythology. By the middle of the twentieth Century, the devil was a creature of the popular imagination. The 'turn or burn' evangelism that presented Christianity as the only alternative to an eternity in hell used this Satan to try to scare people into seeking the safety and security of Christianity.

Unfortunately for Christianity, it began to lose its control of religious beliefs and practices in the West. Church attendance began to drop as the secular power of scientific belief began to challenge long held Christian traditions. Mass literacy, coupled with the translation and printing of the Bible, meant that anyone could make their own considered interpretation of Christian theology. Moral attitudes also changed as technology made birth control readily available to the masses. Science disproved many superstitions, and the fear of a mythical devil or the wrath of a disembodied God held increasingly less sway over an educated population.

In the twentieth Century it became clear that some of the proclamations of the Christian church were likely to be untrue, casting doubt on Christian doctrine in general. In an increasingly globalized world, other religious beliefs from around the globe were becoming more widely understood, and the primacy of any one religion became less possible to sustain, as was the demonization of any other. In this context the rise in interest in neo-paganism and other new age religions, though demonized by Christianity, increasingly problematized a simple meta-narrative that presented morality and spirituality as black or white, rather than dealing with the complex shades of grey which characterize the ethical problems of human lives.

The Demonization of the Blues

African American religious practices feature some of these same issues of the equating of traditional religious beliefs with the devil. The issue of racism makes these relationships more complex, as black was often equated with black magic, black arts, Satanism and evil, while white was equated with good and God. In America, white culture wanted black slaves to adopt western religious practices. Within African American culture references to Africa became seen as unsophisticated, until later periods when African culture was adopted in a more positive light by various movements including Rastafarianism, the Black Panthers and Afrika Bambaataa's Zulu Nation.

Many slaves taken to the USA were from West Africa. West African religion was not influenced by the mind–body duality of Roman and Greek culture, and was different in nature to the Christianity it interacted with in America and elsewhere. As Teresa Reed tells us,

> The diverse cultures of West Africa exhibit a common, unifying worldview distinct from that of the West. The lack of a sacred secular dichotomy in West African culture is directly related to the way West Africans experience those elements that in the West are considered spiritual, supernatural, religious or pertaining to the divine. (2003, p. 1)

West African traditional religion involved communication with ancestral spirits and the dead, involved a number of deities and direct communication with them and included possession rituals in which spirits entered people. It emphasized experiences of divinities and involved loud effusive rituals and ceremonies. It was highly different to the Christian religions it interacted with in North America, including the Calvinists and Puritans whose religious views had led them to leave mainland Europe.

It is easy to see how and why many elements of West African religion were associated with evil, the devil and Satan. West African religion bore many similarities to the pre-Christian folk religions that had been successfully repressed in Europe in the early days of the spread of the Christian faith. The worship of a number of deities, polytheism, and of gods other than the Christian God, was enough for the beliefs of African American culture to be regarded as evil by white (and later black) Christian culture. The possession rituals of West African religions were associated within Christianity with evil spirits, in particular with biblical references to Jesus having 'cured' or exorcized those possessed and the Vodou practices of spirit possession were equated with the demonic. The magical spells and sorcery that were common in West African traditional religions were another area long related within Christianity to evil.

West African religion does not distinguish so simply between good and bad. For example the Yoruba divinity Èsù is known as a trickster, but the tricks and deception involved is not always perceived as evil, just as is the case in some biblical traditions, where Satan acts with the agreement of God to tempt the individual, as in the case of Job. However, this was another deity represented by Christianity as related to the devil or Satan. Contacting the dead and ancestors was a common practice in West African religion, as it is in many religious traditions, but this had become associated with the occult in the West.

The interaction present in West Africa of all elements of life with religion also conflicted with Christian orthodoxy. Sexuality and body consciousness was somewhat repressed within Christian traditions, whereas it was less of a taboo or awkward subject in West African religion or culture. Achieving states of ecstasy through lively communal music and dancing, and becoming entranced was a normal practice in West Africa, and one that was neither secular nor sacred, not having such simplistic distinctions. Not only were such physical expressions of pleasure often condemned by the Christian church, this was particularly the case if they were within a religious context.

White Christian culture needed the slaves it had taken to America to fit in with and conform to the socio-political structures imported from Europe. Managing to get African Americans to adopt Christianity was be an important step in convincing them to submit to white authority, and accept and integrate into the social position chosen for them. The African derived elements of the cultures of African Americans had the potential to encourage organized opposition rather than submission, to the hegemonic powers of mainstream America. In order for the large numbers of African Americans to act as a cheap workforce it was important that Christian traditions replaced West African ones, cultural imperialism and religious imperialism becoming as important for the long-term success of conquest as weapons and superior technology. These issues are discussed more fully in books by Reed (2003), Magesa (1997) and King (1986).

Christian theology taught that evangelism was important, and that converting others to Christian beliefs was a moral duty. Ethically, Western Christians believed that converting others from their 'pagan' beliefs would save them from eternal damnation, and conveniently this also allowed them to assert the moral superiority of their own beliefs over those of others. As a result of this dynamic, African American religious culture became focused around Christianity and adopted a dualistic sacred/secular divide. Gospel music became a key element of sacred African American culture, while Blues music became associated with the secular. In West African culture music was fundamentally associated with spirituality and religion, the two were not considered separate, and it was not possible to entirely disassociate religion from musical culture, the two remaining linked. The secular world of blues and other African American dance music was associated frequently in relation to the sacred, with the profane of the Christian devil, rather than the strictly secular. As Fred Hay puts it in his discussion of the music of blues musician Sonny Boy Williamson, 'this dialectic of the sacred and the profane is, indeed, a central feature of the ongoing development and change in all African Diaspora societies, their worldviews and their music' (1987, p. 326).

As described in the sex cult chapter of this book, blues was presented as a secular method of escaping the difficulties of life for African Americans. Whereas gospel music offered a hope that that in a mythical or spiritual future, in heaven, the difficulties of life would be left behind, blues focused on pleasure in the present as a temporary escape from the oppression, discrimination and hardships of everyday life. Blues, and related musical forms such as jazz, swing, rhythm and blues, and soul focused on the moment, on the focus of consciousness being in the body, the present being left behind, lost in music, lost in the moment of simply being, dancing with others to music.

Secular African American music became associated with the other activities present at venues that played such music, including drinking (especially during the prohibition era), drug taking, gambling and prostitution, all of which also being practices that focus on the moment and the body. It became a place where some of the remnants of West African cultures could reside and be sustained and developed. Sustained periods of vigorous dancing became an important part of African American dance music cultures, as are discussed in the possession cult chapter of this book. The close association of dancing and music in African American musical cultures is in stark contrast to many of the white music scenes that have developed from them. These white cultures have often removed the element of dance that exists in the forms from which they developed, such as within the rock music that developed from rhythm and blues.

The association during the USA prohibition era of blues, ragtime and jazz music with speakeasies put it directly in opposition with the American Christian holiness movement, and other conservative Christian religious traditions of the day. Blues in particular was regarded as the devil's music. The bent notes and modal tonalities, rambling structures, repetitive lyrics, improvised sections and syncopated rhythms of blues were regarded as having roots in African music, which is to some extent the case, and thus as being evil.

Blues musicians were often itinerant, travelling from place to place to earn money. They typified a lifestyle that opposed the values of the African American church. Many blues musicians had careers as both Gospel musicians and blues musicians, such as Blind Willie McTell and Blind Willie Johnson. So polarized were attitudes, that some did so by adopting a false pseudonym, in order to avoid criticism from their sacred audience, thus Blind Lemon Jefferson worked under the gospel name of Deacon L. J. Bates, Charlie Patton became Elder J. J. Handley, and Blind Boy Fuller became Brother George and his Sanctified Singers (Young, 1997). Many gospel music fans would not buy records by artists who also made blues recordings.

However, gospel and blues music both had roots in earlier forms such as spirituals, and there were many similarities and crossovers between the genres. White American Christian traditions often regarded the effusive physicality of African American churches as ungodly and having elements of heathen or West African culture integrated into it, and criticized it as much as members of the African American church often criticized blues. The Pentecostalism common in African American churches with its speaking in tongues, and being filled with the spirit, is very similar in nature to West African possession trance rituals, and has roots in those traditions. Gospel music also uses sliding notes, seventh chords, improvised sections, and other musical traditions that contain influences from West African traditions, so it is ironic that blues musicians were criticized by the African American church.

There were many examples of crossover forms, such as the work of Thomas Dorsey, a gospel pioneer who integrated elements of blues style into his gospel music and vice versa, performing blues as Georgia Tom. As rhythm'n'blues developed into rock'n'roll, African American performers began to integrate the showmanship of the gospel preacher into secular performance styles, Little Richard being a good example. Elvis Presley, with a background in gospel music, integrated a gospel style into his work. Elvis began as a raw country blues shouter, scandalizing the general public with his sexual blues moves and racy lyrics, but as early as 'Are You Lonesome Tonight' he used the spoken voice tones and close harmony of gospel music in a secular context. He later sang overtly gospel songs alongside secular rock'n'roll tunes.

Rhythm and blues singer and pianist Ray Charles recorded perhaps the first soul song with 'What'd I Say', which featured call and response backing vocals, and a verse structure taken from gospel music, but with the sexual moans and sighs of blues lyrics. This style, mixing gospel and R'n'B came to be known as soul music, named using a sacred term, even though it was a secular music. Many soul musicians were gospel musicians before beginning to make secular music. Sam Cooke had been lead singer with the Soul Stirrers gospel group, Aretha Franklin had performed with her father who was a well-known gospel singer, and James Brown and the Famous Flames had previously been the Gospel Starlighters. Drawn by greater levels of fame and fortune, many gospel artists replaced 'Jesus' with 'baby' in their lyrics, and switched from being gospel stars to soul singers.

Some singers took gospel songs and wrote 'new' material based on gospel songs. 'Stand by Me', by Ben E. King is a well-known example of a gospel song that was made into a popular song. Others who would go on to be rock'n'roll or soul music stars, also had been brought up singing in church, and many would mix their sacred and secular careers. Little Richard left his secular career in order to follow his religious beliefs, later returning to musical performance. At a July 2007 performance I attended in New York, he handed out religious books to audience members, but performed a set made up of his secular hits. Singer Al Green carried on parallel careers as a pastor and musician.

Soul singer Solomon Burke was born to highly religious parents, his grandmother having had a dream that she would have a grandson who would be a religious leader. She founded a church that Burke now leads. His brand of soul music is exemplified by the song 'Everybody Needs Somebody To Love'. It features a spoken introduction, complete with gospel style affirmations, gospel chord sequence and backing vocals. Its message is very general however, not specifically Christian, and sits on the boundary between the secular and sacred. This kind of 'inspirational' song, message music but not referring specifically to Christianity, was also written by various other singers, such as Curtis Mayfield (whose grandmother was also a preacher), the Staples Singers, Marvin Gaye, the Temptations and Stevie Wonder. Stevie Wonder's career as a gospel musician was cut short when he was caught singing secular songs in public, but he continued to make inspirational music, this style mixing with 1960s counter-culture and black consciousness causes to produce music that was highly meaningful, community based and filled with spiritual metaphors and meanings.

Although in reality blues and gospel have interacted in many ways and have much in common, whereas gospel has been associated with Christianity, God, and good, as already described, blues has often been associated with the devil and evil. For example, it is a common misconception that 'Crossroads Blues' by Robert Johnson is principally about him selling his soul to the devil. Johnson was rumoured to have met a sinister figure at a crossroads, who gave him an uncanny musical ability on the guitar in return for his soul.

In reality this is a myth that arose for a number of reasons. As a youth, Johnson was an untalented guitarist, although he had family connections to blues greats like Blind Lemon Jefferson. Later in life Johnson left home for a year, and when he returned he had improved immensely at playing the guitar. His 'magical' improvement in guitar playing led to rumours that he had sold his soul to the devil, whereas in fact he had spent time away from home learning to play. It seems that the principal motivation for his demonic reputation was the jealousy of others who could not understand why it was that Johnson could play the guitar better than they could themselves. Although evidence is a little unclear, he may have learnt to play partly from a blues musician called Ike Zinnerman. Zinnerman was a guitarist who claimed he learned to play in a graveyard, and who cultivated an association with the occult, probably to gain notoriety. Johnson understood the kudos of associations with the occult within blues circles, and did little to dispel the rumours.

Many virtuosic musicians have been rumoured to have sold their souls to the devil, including classical violinist Pagannini, and the story of Johnson at the crossroads may have been influenced by this story. Crossroads are often places where spirits would wait in West African and African American traditions, as they represented intersections between the real and spirit world. In addition juke joints were often placed at road intersections, and such places have numerous metaphorical meanings. Johnson's song in fact makes no specific reference to the devil at all, although his songs 'Hellhound on my Trail', and 'Me and he Devil Blues' do reference his reputation. In reality, Johnson had a cataract that gave him an 'evil eye' look, which added to the rumours. Jealousy over his 'miraculously' acquired skills and intolerance of his womanizing, hard-drinking lifestyle also added to his reputation.

Another somewhat later blues and rock'n'roll musician, Screamin' Jay Hawkins, actively embraced satanic imagery in order to increase his popularity and notoriety. Hawkins would appear in a coffin onstage, and wear capes, dressing like a vampire or other character from a horror film. Many other musicians copied this idea, and Hawkins felt he never received recognition for pioneering this approach.

I got fed up. I went to Honolulu for ten years because I figured the world wasn't ready for me. In the meantime, all these people are recording my goddamn stuff. Nina Simone, Alan Price, the Animals, Creedence Clearwater Revival, the Who, Them, Manfred Mann, the Seekers, Arthur Brown. Melvin Van Peebles copied my whole act and put it on Broadway ... At one time or another, they've all taken a little something from me, and I get the impression that everybody's going places with what I was doing fifteen goddamn years ago. Everybody but me ... (Screamin' Jay Hawkins in Tosches 1999, p. 162)

Other musicians would take and expand Hawkins' idea of encouraging the idea that his music was the devil's music.

Within blues and rhythm and blues lie the musical roots of rock and heavy metal music. The reputation of the blues as the devil's music was an influence on both rock and metal and is an important feature of both. Religious imagery from African American and West African culture, including spirit possession, communication with the dead, a number of deities identified with the Christian devil, sorcery and magic were all imported into European rock and metal cultures, connecting and resonating with pre-Christian European folk traditions. It also brought into the music's cult and culture a morality that was in opposition to Christian beliefs, in particular as regards sexuality and drug taking. The elements of the demonic, Satanic and apocalyptic that were used to describe and condemn West African folk religious traditions in general, and blues music in particular, were also imported into Europe within blues culture.

Christianity had created an image of Satan and the devil in order to stop people from practising similar folk traditions in Europe to those that came from West Africa into African American traditions, and to focus on Christianity. In doing so it had created an understanding of such ideas in the popular consciousness. The lack of a clear delineation between the sacred, secular and profane in African American culture meant that the popular culture secular music of the blues was imbued with a range of religious aspects, allowing it to become a part of the sacred popular, and develop cult-like properties.

The 27 Club

As blues music became popular in the UK, the lifestyle associated with the blues became associated with British musicians. As rhythm and blues, soul and rock'n'roll developed into beat and then rock music, musicians adopted a lifestyle that involved promiscuous sexuality and drug taking. This made rock stars into iconic legendary figures, that lived lives that others wished to emulate. As has been described in the drug cults chapter, drugs have been associated with popular music scenes for many years. In the 1960s, swinging London saw musicians taking drugs such as cannabis, LED, cocaine and amphetamines.

These 'rock gods', were in reality inexperienced young men and women, often with little education, and large amounts of time to kill travelling between gigs. They took drugs to give them energy to perform, and in order to fulfil the expectations of the fans, who came to expect pop stars to behave in increasingly extreme fashions, as part of their performance. Stars had enormous and suddenly achieved wealth, staff to do their bidding, and a plentiful supply of drugs and alcohol. They also regularly had experiences onstage of great excitement, intensity and god-like hero worship. In comparison, everyday life must have been somewhat mundane.

Some pop stars believed in their own legend, and lived a lifestyle involving an endless stream of drinking and drug taking. As Shapiro puts it,

> The likes of Noel or Liam Gallagher, Johnny Rotten, Keith Richard or Janis Joplin are blank slates on which young people inscribe a multitude of tantalising vicarious experiences. It's almost part of the pop star job description to be bad on our behalf, so that we can carry on as normal when the show is over. That's partly why so many of those with the worst reputations don't survive; they transfer those audience expectations into their own private lives and play out their own mythology. (1999, p. 163)

This was an unsustainable lifestyle and inevitably some died tragically young. One of the most interesting groups of those who died largely due to over-indulgence are those in what has come to be referred to as the 27 club. In July 1969, Brian Jones, the leading light of the Rolling Stones, drowned in a swimming pool. The following year Jimi Hendrix died, choking on his own vomit after taking too many drugs. Janis Joplin also died that year of a drugs overdose. Exactly two years later, to the day, Jim Morrison died, probably also from drug-related causes. All four of these leading musicians of the era were 27 years old.

Perhaps a sadder postlude to this group of musicians was the death of Kurt Cobain of Nirvana and the disappearance of Richie Edwards of the Manic Street Preachers. Both suffered from psychological problems. Cobain suffered from depression, was aware of the 27 club, and had said as a child that he wished to join it (Cross 2002). Edwards had psychological problems and was known for self-harming, most notably carving the phrase '4 Real' into his arm in front of a journalist to prove his and the band's authenticity. Cobain committed suicide, and Edwards is missing presumed dead, both were aware of the existence of the 27 club. Cobain was 27 when he died and Edwards last performed in public on the evening before his twenty-seventh birthday, disappearing a few weeks later.

Many other musicians have died young as a result of the lifestyle they led, the lifestyle expected of and associated with being a rock or pop star. Drug taking is perhaps the largest killer, sometimes death being caused by a cocktail of drugs and alcohol. Brian Epstein, Rory Storm, Gram Parsons, Nick Drake, Tim Buckley, Paul Kossof of Free, Gary Thain of Uriah Heep, Tommy

Bolin of Deep Purple, Elvis Presley, Keith Moon of the Who, Sid Vicious of the Sex Pistols, Steve Took of T. Rex and blues guitarist Mike Bloomfield are all examples of popular musicians who died from either deliberate or accidental drug overdoses. Charlie Parker, Billie Holiday, Lowell George of Little Feat, Art Pepper, Phil Lynott of Thin Lizzy, Graham Bond, Mama Cass Elliott, Denis Wilson of the Beach Boys, Michael Hutchence and John Bonham of Led Zeppelin all died in ways that were contributed to by their drug or alcohol habits (Shapiro 1998, pp. 229–33).

Others died in the fast cars they wrote about, or through crashes of planes, cars or buses transporting them between concerts. Hanoi Rocks' drummer Razzle died in a car crash, Motley Crue singer Vince Neil was the driver, who was jailed for drunk driving and manslaughter. Marc Bolan died in a car crash; Eddie Cochran died in a taxi while on tour in the UK, Gene Vincent surviving the crash; Ronnie Van Zant, Steve and Cassie Gaines of Lynryd Skynryd died in a plane crash between gigs; another plane crash also killed the Big Bopper, Richie Valens and Buddy Holly. Other stars have been shot, for example John Lennon being shot outside his apartment by a psychologically disturbed fan. Freddie Mercury, well known for his promiscuous lifestyle, died of AIDS. It is perhaps a surprise considering the promiscuity of many popular musicians that this has not been the cause of many more deaths.

Blues and soul musicians seem to have had a particularly bad run of luck, and this has been put down by some to the result of associating with the devil, although they are more reasonably the result of unusual and extreme lifestyles, including drug taking and promiscuity. Robert Johnson is thought to have died of hypothermia, frozen while sleeping on the street. Johnny Ace died playing Russian roulette, Dinah Washington overdosed, Sam Cooke was shot, Otis Redding died in a plane crash, the death of Clyde McPhatter of the Drifters was hastened by his alcoholism and drug problems, Donny Hathaway fell to his death from a fifteenth floor window, and Marvin Gaye was shot by his father. Latterly rappers Tupac Shakur and Biggie Smalls were shot dead, probably due to rivalries between them and those associated with them, and Michael Jackson was killed on the verge of his comeback series of concerts, by drugs administrated by a doctor.

The careers of some other stars have been halted by drug taking, Syd Barratt of Pink Floyd, Peter Green of Fleetwood Mac and Brian Wilson of the Beach Boys being good examples of talented musicians whose careers were ended following psychological problems triggered by drug taking. The drug taking of the Happy Mondays brought their career to an end and bankrupted their record company Factory records. Eric Clapton spent a number of years unable to play due to his alcohol and drug problems, and he took many years to recover his guitar-playing skills after cleaning up. Boy George's drug taking has led to him being imprisoned and pilloried by the press for his habits. Blues legend Leadbelly was sent to prison for murder and subsequently for attempted murder before being discovered there by Alan Lomax.

Popular music stars have long been associated with illegal and highly risky behaviours that have led to deaths. This is more extreme than in other types of celebrities, there is not a similar list of film stars who died young, or of sports of political figures. The film stars who have died young have similar stories of death from drugs and fast cars, James Dean dying in a car crash, River Phoenix dying of a drugs overdose, Heath Leger died surrounded by drugs, and John Belushi, also a musician, also died from a drugs cocktail.

The lives of pop stars are supposed to be extreme, performing for the audience even when not onstage. These behaviours have often led to the death of the stars involved. When a popular icon or star dies their public persona is frozen in time. If the star is particularly successful, that means that they will never have to be seen growing old or becoming less successful. They will never have continued to try to make music after fashions have moved on, they will never have albums or singles that do not sell, they will never become old and less attractive. When a popular icon dies at the peak of their success, the real person may die, but the public persona continues. The star that dies young will never grow old, their public self will remain young and successful forever. A number of songs reference this in their lyrics, the Who singing 'I hope I die before I get old' in 'My Generation', and Blondie titling a song 'Die Young, Stay Pretty'.

Most pop stars get older and fade away, being replaced by newer, cooler, younger, more attractive and up to date stars. The dead pop icon becomes much like a saint, especially if they have died due to what appears to be adhering to a rock'n'roll lifestyle. Those who have died young by taking too many drugs, or crashing a car, will always leave their audience wanting more, always wondering what music they might have made if they had carried on. In most cases they would have made less successful new music, and relied on the popularity of their old hits until even these are no longer in fashion, but they never have to suffer this indignity.

Dying is the ultimate way for a popular music star to be enshrined as a popular music icon, saint or deity. The dead pop star lives forever as a young, brilliant performer at the height of their powers, through recordings and video recordings, validated by the authenticity of believing so much in their music that they effectively died for it. Thus the list of bands who have had someone die is like a who's who of popular music, including Elvis Presley, The Beatles, The Rolling Stones, Led Zeppelin, The Who, The Clash, The Sex Pistols and the Beach Boys.

As Bono from U2 put it in a 2009 interview on BBC television's The Culture Show,

Bono: One of the things we like about rock and roll is this religiosity. And genuinely people do want you to die on a cross aged 33 with a glass of Jack Daniels in your hand.

Lauren Laverne: Self-destruction is part of rock and roll, that's part of the rock and roll mythology.

Bono: Yeah, It's a death cult, and so to give in to it is to be made beautiful by it. People are disappointed we didn't die in an air crash, or, you know, at least choke on your vomit one of you. But we haven't, we don't believe in that game. Our job is to part derail a mythology that isn't helpful to music or musicians.

U2 are one band that understood the pressures of rock superstar lifestyles and the dangers of living out the expectations of fans. U2 have created outrageous rock star characters that they have performed as part of the mythology of the band in which they perform. Bono and the Edge have names that are made up, the beginning of creating larger than life characters that can exceed the limitations of ordinary humanity and reach for the extremes required for major popular music success. Bono went on to create other personas, such as the Fly and MacPhisto, as part of the band's mediapheme (Johnson 2004), their carefully constructed media identity.

The Fly is a caricatured rock star, wearing leather clothing and huge sunglasses. MacPhisto is a more interesting concoction. Bono had become known for being a Christian and making preacher like statements about political and social causes. MacPhisto undermined that perception, having devil-like horns. He is a trickster, and at concerts would ring up famous politicians, while the tens of thousands in the audience listened in. This allowed U2 to associate themselves as a band with the dark side of their character, and to tie into all the history of such dark identities present in blues, pop and rock music.

Other stars have constructed their identity in this way, some realizing the attraction to the public of being associated with imagery that opposes Christian values, and engaging with ideas that were supposed to scare people away from blues music, the dark images that had become associated with blues rather than gospel African American musical culture. Just as Screaming Jay Hawkins had associated himself with horror and the occult, so others have realized the power of this kind of imagery and association. In a number of ways and for a number of reasons, rock and metal music have become associated with traditional Christian attitudes to Satanism, the devil and the pagan.

Heavy Metal and the Dark Side

A young British band called themselves Black Sabbath in the 1970s after a horror film of that title that was showing over the road from their rehearsal studios. They wrote lyrics that reflected the shadow, dark side of the human psyche including fear and paranoia, reflecting the dark and heavy, distorted, powerful guitar sound of their music. The heavy blues sound of bands like them came to be described as heavy metal. Music of this kind focused on representations of power, as 'musical articulation of power is the most important single factor in the experience of heavy metal' (Walser 1993, p. 2).

Such expressions of power, and exploration of the shadow, offer pleasures to the audience including (the largely male) bonding of fans within a scene or subculture, as discussed by Weinstein (1991). Three 1970s bands in particular formed the focus around which heavy metal developed, Deep Purple, Led Zeppelin and Black Sabbath. All took the distorted electric blues guitar music of African American musicians like Howling Wolf, Muddy Waters, Otis Rush and others, and made it more extreme. Jimi Hendrix had pioneered a heavier, more distorted take on the blues in songs like 'Purple Haze', emerging out of a blues explosion in Britain, as white British musicians discovered the music of African American blues musicians.

Out of that scene came Alexis Corner, The Rolling Stones, Eric Clapton and the Yardbirds. Within blues was a blueprint for heavy metal music. Singers shouted and roared their vocals, allowing their voices to crack and distort to imply extreme emotional power. Guitarists like T-Bone Walker would play their instruments loud, fast and distorted, using their teeth and lips to play or playing the instrument while doing the splits (Till 2007). The guitar had become a central instrument to the blues, especially once it had been electrified. It signified the phallic power of the male dominance of the performance of both blues and metal.

When Jeff Beck left perhaps the most famous early British blues band, the Yardbirds, his old school friend Jimmy Page took over as guitarist. When the rest of the band left, Page recruited new members to fulfil a tour that was booked for the band. He changed the New Yardbird's name to Led Zeppelin, who went on to become one of the best-selling acts of the UK and USA. The band's first album was largely made up of blues covers. However, the band integrated a mysticism that drew upon lyrical themes from Tolkein's 'Lord of the Rings', a world that included war and darkness as well as more positive images. Echoing the African folk religion references of blues, the band's lyrics discussed spirituality from an other-than-Christian perspective, plugging in to the new age references evident in the hippie scene.

This also drew upon Jimmy Page's interest in the occult. Page bought Alistair Crowley's old house, Boleskine House, which was bought by Crowley because it was perfect for particular magical rituals. The band, led by Page, named their fourth album after four images chosen by the band members. Bass player John Paul Jones and drummer John Bonham chose symbols from *The Book of Signs* by Rudolf Koch (1930, pp. 32–3) and singer Robert Plant chose the symbol of the feather of Ma'at, the Egyptian goddess of justice and fairness. Guitarist page chose an enigmatic symbol that read zoso or zofo, the meaning of which is unclear, raising suspicions of links to the occult. As mentioned in the chapter on personality cults, it has been described as a sigil or occult sign used in spells, representing Saturn, which is Page's star sign (*In The Light*, online).

In the band's live concert film *The Song Remains The Same*, each musician is featured in a fantasy scene that seemingly presents an exaggerated view of their personality. Singer Robert Plant is shown as a god-like beauty, with his wife and children, in a typical English pastoral scene. Jimmy Page is seen with demonic red shining eyes, perhaps representing the hermit from the tarot pack, which can also be seen in the artwork of the inside of Led Zeppelin's fourth album. The band had a sequence of misfortune, including the death of Plant's son, which some blamed on the band's occult links. All of this served to enhance the mystique of the group. Led Zeppelin in general, and Page in particular, firmly grasped the dark heritage of the blues.

Deep Purple similarly address issues of power, but also issues of ethics and control. Songs like 'Highway Star', 'Space Trucking' and 'Speed King' address freedom, power and drug taking. The song 'Black Night' implies occult references, and 'Child in Time' discusses lyrically the line drawn between good and bad. The band is less overtly involved in mysticism than Led Zeppelin, but their music is similarly driven by power and distortion. Singer Ian Gillan screamed and wailed, distorting his voice, and keyboard player Jon Lord fed the sound of his Hammond organ through a Marshall guitar amplifier in order to distort its sound.

Guitarist Richie Blackmore brought classical techniques and virtuosity to metal guitar playing. Like Jimmy Page, he had worked as a recording studio session musician, but his classical approach was more precise and complex than the blues and folk influenced Page. Guitar virtuosity continued to play an important part in metal music, especially after Eddie Van Halen introduced a further level of complex techniques to the genre in the 1980s. Metal music is often virtuosic, virtuosity signifying in the musician power and control. 'The virtuoso not only possesses unusual technical facility but through music is able to command extraordinary, almost superhuman rhetorical power' (Walser 1993, p. 76).

The supernatural skills of the virtuoso guitarist are often associated with the Devil, who is himself often referred to as a player of a stringed instrument (violin). This link refers back to Robert Johnson's virtuosity being associated with the devil, and also to that of Paganini. It has helped the blues to transmit pre-Christian ideas of religion and spirituality to rock and metal musicians and fans.

The textual content of metal contains the most obvious references to a dark flavour of mysticism.

> The names chosen by heavy metal bands evoke power and intensity in many different ways. Bands align themselves with electrical and mechanical power (Tesla, AC/DC, Motorhead), dangerous or unpleasant animals (Ratt, Scorpions), dangerous or unpleasant people (Twisted Sister, Motley Crue, Quiet Riot), or dangerous or unpleasant objects (Iron Maiden). They can invoke the auratic power of blasphemy or mysticism (Judas Priest, Black Sabbath, Blue Oyster Cult), or the terror of death itself (Anthrax, Megadeth, Poison, Slayer). (Walser 1993, p. 2)

Doogie Horner has created a fascinating taxonomy of heavy metal band names (online). He breaks Metal down into five categories, deadly things, death, badass misspellings, animals and religion, which are then further categorized.

Metal: Metallica, Metal Forge, Metal Church.
Deadly Things: Anthrax, Napalm Death, Venom, Poison, Skid Row, Overdose, Drowning Pool, Death from Above, Biohazard.
Death: Megadeth, Stormtroopers of Death, My Dying Bride, Corpse, Carcass.
    Metaphorical: Sepulchral Doom, Grim Reaper.
    Dark: the Darkness, Dark Angel, Dark Throne, Dark Tranquility.
    Pleas for Help: Sick of it All, Suicidal Tendencies, Disturbed, Paranoid, Pit of Anger.
    Adolescent Poetry; Cradle of Filth, System of a Down, Bless the Fall, All That Remains, Thine Eyes Bleed.
    The Occult: Angel Witch, Burning Witch, The Conjuring, White Zombie and The Cult, Black Woods, Bloody Wall of Gore, Gore Hearse, Gorefest and Burning Tomb.
    Faulkner References: As I Lay Dying, The Sound and the Fury, Corncob Rape.
Badass Misspellings: Korn, Led Zeppelin, Deth, Eyehategod.
    Puns involving 'hell': Helloween, Hellbilly, Hellelujah.
    Foreign Sounding: Queensryche.
    Actually Foreign: Dimmu Borgir, Borknagar, Pantera, Sepultura, Voivod, Borknagar.
    Umlauts; Motörhead, Blue Öyster Cult, Spinal Tap, Dëthkløk, Fetüs.
    Double Umlaut: Mötley Crüe.
    Pointless Misspellings: Mercyful Fate, Def Leppard, Lawnmower Deth, Alcatrazz.
Animals:
    Imaginary: Goat Snake, The Cancer Bats, Behemoth, Iron Butterfly, Whitesnake, White Lion.
    Extinct: Mastodon, Queens of the Stone Age.
    Real: Ratt, Budgie, Manowar, Scorpions, Black Widow, Wolfmother.
Religion: Faith No More, Ministry, Black Sabbath, Judas Priest, Cathedral, Shotgun Messiah, Black Mass.
    Angels: Morbid Angels, Death Angel, Dark Angel, Angel Queef.
    Satanic: Crippled Lucifer, Satan's Loneliness, Satan's Blind Date, Satan's Awkward Gropings, Satan's Child.
    Pagan: Baal's Balls, Wiccan Guidance Counsellor, Heathen Tomb.
    Biblical: Lamb of God, Testament, Babylon, Leaky Stigmata, Exodus.
    From the Book of Revelation: Ragnarok, Armaggedon, Sign of the Beast.
    Mediaeval: Dragonforce, The Sword, Flesh Castle, Agathodaimon, Wizard.
    Viking: Hellhammer, Loki, Odin's Beard, Viking Crown.

This complex list shows up the number of European pre-Christian or neo-Pagan references. Also present are many Christian and other religious references. There are many references to death, the dark, to damaging objects, dangerous animals, mythical beasts or characters, and to horror and fear. There are also numerous references to the other, and to the ancient or gothic, sometimes through the use of umlauts, or through misspellings, pointing to a time before spelling and language was not set, aiming to call to mind a world of medieval castles, witches, knights and battles.

There is not time here to fully analyse such a list, and there is far more to say especially if one also took into account song titles, song lyrics, stage costumes, scenery and props, the artwork of record and CD covers, imagery on other merchandising, and imagery in promotional videos. It is clear that metal has fully engaged with, welcomed and adopted many elements of the West African spirituality transmitted from Blues music culture through the filter of African American culture. These cultural elements had been transformed by white Western culture into demonized Christian references that had resonances within Europe to pre-Christian religious beliefs and practices, or oppositional and rebellious attitudes to religion.

An interesting example is metal band Iron Maiden's Eddie. Eddie is a zombie figure, human in shape but looking like a rotting corpse. He is a monster-like character, appears as a giant puppet or animatronic figure on stage at concerts, and appears in various guises on artwork and merchandize associated with the band. Eddie is a creation of Iron Maiden, they have created a fictional character who is presented as the visual personification of the music, linking the band to horror films and a range of pseudo-religious imagery.

Whereas heavy metal is rarely presented as overtly religious, with imagery being used to attract fans, set a tone or create an atmosphere. Satanic imagery is used to imply rebellion and opposition to mainstream culture. Such imagery was adopted to separate the music further from mainstream culture, to present it as different, oppositional and other. Some bands have adopted more than images though, and have actually associated themselves with the religions and beliefs that for a band like Black Sabbath were only ever a fictional but interesting and attractive cover story.

Extreme Metal

The heavy rock, blues rock and heavy metal music of the 1970s mixed with punk influences in the 1980s to create thrash metal, death metal and black metal.

> Under the influence of punk, early 1980s bands such as Venom began to develop more radicalised forms of Metal. These forms, including Thrash, Death, Black and Doom Metal, eschewed melody and clear singing in favour of speed, downtuned guitars and growled or screamed vocals. Whilst each

style has distinctive features and distinct networks of fans and musicians, they share enough to be frequently referred to by fans and musicians as 'Extreme Metal'. (Harris 2000, p. 14)

These more extreme forms of metal were also more extreme in terms of their lyrics, their image and their associations. From only their names one can tell that thrash bands like Metallica, Megadeth, Slayer and Anthrax took a more extreme attitude to their music. The instruments and voices in the music were more distorted, all the instruments played faster, and lyrics were full of horrific subjects and monstrous language. This became more extreme in terms of image in death metal bands. Of the four thrash bands mentioned, Slayer's content was the most violent, including faster more extreme music, and lyrical content more focused on violence, death and Satanism. Death metal largely developed from Slayer's music, along with other bands like Venom who had adopted an overtly Satanist image. The music's lyrics involved growls, gutteral roars, distorted vocal sounds and screams that all made it particularly difficult to decipher. This was music that was not intended to appeal to the mainstream. Musical structures were often odd, the music often used strange, constantly changing time signatures, was very dense, and of little interest and difficult to understand to the uninitiated. The cult following death metal bands was extremely committed to a set of musical, cultural and conceptual elements that were often the opposite of mainstream values.

From death metal emerged black metal. Many of the bands originally involved were from Norway, such as Mayhem, Burzum and Darkthrone, although the genre later spread across the world. Musically there are many similarities with death metal, although vocals often feature high-pitched shrieks or screams rather than low growls. The main feature of the music is the specifically anti-Christian nature of the lyrics, and of the beliefs of the bands involved. Most of the bands' works promote paganism, Satanism, occult beliefs, atheism or other non- or pre-Christian beliefs. In Norway a number of religious movements had begun to revive beliefs based on Norse or Viking mythology, and this had an effect on Norwegian black metal.

Satanism to these groups did not necessarily mean the worship of the Christian devil. Rather it was presented as going back to pre-Christian traditions, reclaiming them from their presentation by Christians as negative or evil. It was a rejection of the mainstream of religious opinion, and religious control. It was the adoption of mystery and rebellion, but also of the cultural roots and origins of Norway, rather than those of Christianity. For many black metal musicians, the use of the term 'Satanism' is abusive and inaccurate. Self-proclaimed Satanist and heavy metal musician King Diamond has said,

Satan, for me, is not like the guy with two horns and a long tail. I don't believe in hell being a place where you burn for eternity. That's not what Satan is all about. Satan stands for the powers of the unknown. (Toledo 1987, p. 84)

Despite the different more positive possible approaches to Satanism and other pre-Christian beliefs, as in death metal, black metal music often involves lyrics referring to death, violence and somewhat negative material.

Black metal bands' images often feature inverted crosses or pentagrams, and a number of bands wear so-called 'corpse paint' make-up, black and white make-up sometimes with added blood red colour. Band members often adopted new stage names, such as Oystein Aarseth of Mayhem who was known as Euronymous. Aarseth opened a record store in Oslo, which became something of a centre for the developing Norwegian black metal scene. In 1991 Per Yngve 'Pelle' Ohlin, known as 'Dead', committed suicide. He was found by Aarseth, who photographed the corpse before phoning the police, and reputedly made necklaces from pieces of Dead's skull. The publicity surrounding this event made this scene grow and allowed it to become better known.

Aarseth himself was shot by Varg Vikernes. Vikernes, also known as Count Grishnackh, had created his own one-person successful black metal band, Burzum. He later joined Aarseth's band, Mayhem. Vikernes was one of a number of black metal musicians who burnt down historic Christian churches in Norway. They seem to have been acting not specifically as Satanists, but representing a range of 'heathen' views, including neo-pagan and Odinism, in supposed retaliation for the repression handed out by Christians through-out history of those who were not Christians. Over 50 churches were burned down, allegedly by musicians and fans from the black metal scene.

In 1993 Vikernes stabbed Aarseth to death. He was sentenced to 20 years in prison, but was released on parole in 2009. He was also found guilty at the time of four church arsons. On his arrest, explosives and ammunition were found in large quantities at Vikerne's home. He has also been linked to a number of fascist groups. Details of these events, and of the Norwegian black metal scene, can be found in *Lords of Chaos: The Bloody Rise of the Satanic Metal Underground*, by Michael Moynihan and Didrik Søderlind (1998).

Death Cults in Metal Music

Again we turn to typical characteristics of cults to see if we can see different types of heavy metal and its associated culture as a cult. In a simple surface fashion, it seems that there is some evidence. Band names like Blue Öyster Cult with their song 'Don't fear the Reaper' and The Cult with 'She Sells Sanctuary' would suggest that those involved in the scene consider themselves involved in cultic behaviours.

As in all the pop cults this book investigates, the death cults of popular music are led by individual, characteristic human leaders, who are presented as god-like, and able to provide access to the divine or transcendental. Jay Jay French of metal band Twisted Sister tells us,

You walk on stage some nights and you feel more muscular, you just all of a sudden feel like the power is pouring out of you, the tune is just ripping itself through your body, out of the speakers, out of the PA blowing people away, and you haven't even broken a sweat yet. The night's just beginning and they're already going crazy, and you're just cruisin' in first gear. Then you move it up a notch … And you lay it out, then put it into third, and then it's one of those nights, and the audience goes even crazier, and you're just blowing away, and you're just lookin' at yourself and you go 'Gee, I am God!' and then you kick it into fourth, and the whole night's amazing. (French 1989, p. 12)

French is indicating his power to connect people to the divine, to channel power and manipulate experiences. Steve Vai describes his own mystical musical experiences, with a somewhat extreme approach, literally locking himself in a room to make an album, the process involving fasting, visions and bleeding on his guitar (Walser 1993, p. 100).

Many of these individual pop icons, or iconic groups, are still alive, however some have died within the last 100 years, and the cult of their personality has carried on, and in many cases been enhanced, by and since their death. Fans copy the iconic leaders of these cults by dressing like them, wearing similar clothes, reading about them, and buying their records and other products. They go to communal events like metal or rock discos and concerts, to take part in ritualized communal celebrations, dressing in special costume. Cult members wear particular clothing that identifies them as being either members of the death metal cult, or the thrash metal cult or another. They have characteristic haircuts and sometimes make-up, and in some scenes will have characteristic tattoos or piercings, something that is common for example in extreme metal circles. It is also normal for fans to wear band T-shirts or patches identifying the names of the groups or individuals leading the cult or cults they are involved in. Like many others, these cults are often linked to new forms of paganism, including Odinism, Heathenism, witchcraft, Satanism, druidry, Wicca, which is a characteristic of many other cults.

Membership of pop death cults involves a very high level of commitment of time to the group, which often damages relationships with family members. Walser recounts this example.

I am a 16 year old guitarist who's been playing since I was six years old. I switched from laying country to rock music when I was 10 and decided that one day I would be among the masters. I started pushing myself with eight hours a day, then slowly but steadily it increased. I now usually practice 16 hours daily, all day and sometimes all night. Recently I was expelled from school due to my continuous absences when I was practising. I have become a skilled player, but I am losing sleep and my social life is hurting. My philosophy is practice makes perfect, but my friends, my school and my parents say I have blown my life out of proportion with it. I could cut my practising down, but with the excellence among today's players, I fear I will not stay in the game. (Walser 1993, p. 100)

Like other pop cults, this cult requires insider knowledge to take part and understand it, and it takes a while before a fan is considered an authentic member of a scene.

Further evidence of cult like behaviour is the opposition of Christian groups to Heavy Metal. For example, in Carl Raschke's 1990 book *Painted Black: from Drug Killings to Heavy Metal – The Alarming True Story of How Satanism Is Terrorizing Our Communities*. The PMRC's opposition to heavy metal parallels the opposition of cults by anti-cult groups. Tipper Gore's 1987 book *Raising PG Kids in an X-Rated Society* devotes a whole chapter to heavy metal for focusing on the dark side of life.

Some have even tried to prosecute metal artists, essentially for their music containing references that clash with Christian ideas of morality. These cases bear similarities to the approach of the inquisition, mediaeval witch trials or the hysteria of the Salem witch trials, a moral panic driven by fear. A legal case brought against Judas Priest in the USA accused them of disguising pseudo-Satanic messages within their music by recording them backwards, after two of their fans committed suicide. A long running similar urban myth claims that Led Zeppelin's 'Stairway to Heaven' contains a similar backwards masked message. Ozzy Osbourne was also prosecuted following the suicide of one of his fans, over the lyrics to his song 'Suicide Solution'.

Marilyn Manson was also accused of being responsible for the death of a fan. Manson has constructed a media image designed to be shocking, choosing a female first name to shock, just like Alice Cooper, adopting anti-Christian imagery, wearing make-up, creating an androgynous image and choosing controversial lyrical material. Manson is an honorary reverend in the late Anton LaVey's Church of Satan (Wright 2000, p. 374).

However he is anti-organized religion rather than being a devil worshipper. He says,

I see what I do as a positive thing. I try to bring people closer to themselves. That may be further away from God but that's closer to themselves. I think that's a good thing. I think that makes people stronger ... I'm trying to tell people to believe in themselves because that's all that they have to believe in. I think that's a positive thing. (Wright 2000, p. 375)

Manson has been the target in recent years of a series of attacks by Christian groups.

Reverend Donald Wildman's evangelical American Family Association and the Religious Right, best known for their tenacious campaign against 'pornographic' art funded by the National Endowment for the Arts (NEA), singled out Manson's 1997 tour for demonstrations in several American cities (and ended up in a legal wrangle with Manson's lawyers after posting false 'affidavits' on the Internet claiming that the band had distributed drugs, sexually abused audience members and incited its fans to kill animals). (ibid.)

Manson has been described as a cult leader.

> Lynda Fletcher, executive director of the Lower Mainland Purpose Society, an organisation that counsels 'troubled teens' – has called him a 'cult leader' who leaves his 'victims ... so brainwashed ... that they literally cannot separate fantasy from reality'. (Brunet 1997, p. 42)

Metal music has often been accused of brainwashing young people into doing the things that are described in the music, whether this is having sex, using drugs or committing suicide. This repeated listening to music is presented as a form of brainwashing, a typical accusation of cults.

The interest in pop cults that address rather than repress the dark side of the human psyche, its shadow side, is perhaps a result of Christianity's repression of such discussion, making it appear taboo and exciting. Christianity's labelling of elements of traditional ancient folk beliefs as evil and negative has in some ways encouraged, enhanced, sustained and publicized them. The labelling of blues as the devil's music has made it more popular not less. When the blues became popular in Europe, the pagan-like associations given to the blues were happily adopted by musicians and fans, rather than putting them off the music as might have been hoped. The caricatured profane blues lifestyles of sex, drugs and alcohol, and the extreme behaviour associated with a heathen or pagan life were adopted as expected norms for successful musicians. The result of living out that lifestyle in reality, rather than performing it within the media, was the death of a number of significant popular music stars, and years battling addiction for others.

Religious folk traditions from West Africa passed into the blues via African American 'secular' music culture, enhanced, sustained and given oppositional cultural authenticity by gospel music and Christianity's labelling of it as 'the devil's music'. This connected with similar pre-Christian religious folk traditions in Europe, and as rock and metal developed from blues these two traditions fused to provide a strong connection with the dark side of the human psyche, Satanism, neo-paganism, and other non- and anti-Christian traditions which more readily addressed issues such as fear, horror, death and mystery without enforcing the control of power dynamics. It took more and more extreme behaviours to create something shocking within metal genres as they developed, making them increasingly cult-like, resulting in the Norwegian Black Metal scene, which ended up being at the centre of murders and arson.

The death cults surrounding metal and rock are one of the more obvious and convincing examples of a pop cult. Death, however, is a significant part of life, and although sometimes portrayed as negative, to address fear, horror, death and war is important within any religious system. These should perhaps instead be called power cults, as it is power, and the knowledge of how to control that power, that is really at the heart of the cults of rock and metal. Discussing metal, Walser states that 'it mediates social tensions, working to provide its fans with a sense of spiritual depth and social integration' (1993, p. xvi).

He adds that,

> If religion functions both to explain the world – providing models for how to live, tenets of faith and empowerment, and comfort for when they don't work – and to offer a sense of contact with something greater than oneself, the heavy metal surely qualifies as a religious phenomenon. (ibid., p. 154)

An understanding of death helps us to connect with the past, and deal with the death of loved ones when this comes close to us. The remainder of a person after their death, is their memory or history, and remembering allows us to keep the dead alive, and connect with our ancestors, something considered very important in most religions, including Catholicism, in which saints play an important role. We cannot contact the bodies of the dead, but we can still interact with what Sheldrake (1988) might call their remaining morphic field, the results of their actions on Earth in the memories and behaviours of others. Maintaining the memory of dead, popular icons help fans to explore and practice the way they relate to and respect the dead.

In liquid modernity time is problematized, video and audio recordings of people, as well as photographs, allow us to experience the dead as they were before they died, allowing us to time travel. Just as advanced technological music such as electronica gives us a glimpse of the future, the music of Jimi Hendrix allows us to travel back to the 1960s, and the dead pop star is remembered the same now as when they died. Thus dead pop icons provide stopping off points to where we can travel back in time, their music triggering associated memories. Because Mick Jagger is still performing, he does not transport us back in time the way that Jim Morrison can. Pop death cults are perhaps a method of time travel, just as the global cults of world music allow us to travel across space. The death cult of heavy metal has gone from strength to strength, and thrives on the negativity sent its way. This is particularly the case in terms of the criticisms of the Christians who seem to most fear it, and in criticising it power it with counter-cultural authenticity. As long as it continues to find and understand ways to instigate and control the reactions of fear and shock in Conservative elements of society through expressions of power and representations of that considered by the mainstream to be profane, it will surely continue to grow and thrive.

Chapter 8

God Is a DJ: Possession Trance Cults of Electronic Dance Music*

Introduction

This chapter explores the possession cult of electronic dance music culture (EDMC) and its relationships to trance, religion, meaning and spirituality. It briefly outlines some of the existing work in this area, before presenting evidence of elements of cultic behaviour and religiosity found in EDMC. A brief explanation of the historical roots of EDMC is followed by an investigation of transcendent experiences, of how these are perceived, of the use of drugs to trigger them and of how they relate to trance and possession. Evidence from the field of ethnomusicology is discussed in relation to EDMC, as is the way that music and dance interact. The effect of individualization within postmodernity is discussed, as is EDMC, as a ritual technology for social construction, creating community and openness with others. In conclusion, the possession cult of EDMC is defined and discussed.

I have used the term EDMC as it describes a coherent group of activities and cultural practices, including those in some nightclubs, at free parties and festivals, and focuses on music genres such as trance, techno, house and drum and bass, while excluding mainstream chart music, rap and hip hop, which have different cultures. EDMC can in this case be also used to mean electronic dance music cult, and I will aim to show those elements that make this particular culture much like a cult. I have avoided using the term club culture, as it infers a restricted range that is based within nightclubs, and therefore tends to include too much mainstream or 'townie' culture, as well as excluding festivals. I have also avoided using the word rave as there is some question about its authenticity in the UK, and as it also refers to a particular subgenre

*Material from this chapter appears in a different form in Till, R. (2009), 'Possession trance ritual in electronic dance music culture: A popular ritual technology for reenchantment, addressing the crisis of the homeless self, and reinserting the individual into the community', in Chris Deacy (ed.), *Exploring Religion and the Sacred in a Media Age*. Ashgate, pp. 169–87.

of EDMC popular in the UK from 1987 to 1990. Rave is perhaps the opposite of club culture in that it tends to be used to refer to those events outside of nightclubs, which are held outdoors or illegally. In short, club and rave cults and cultures add together to form EDMC. This chapter is focused principally on England, although it resonates with and relates to EDMC worldwide.

Within EDMC there is no one author. The club is the text, and both the experience of it and its substance are different for each clubber. It is very much a part of postmodernity, and demands a multi-levelled interdisciplinary approach to describe its many facets. An author-based approach is reflected here in ethnographic field study and interviews, discussing those who have created EDMC. This chapter results in part from my own ethnographic study, which involved long-term participant observation, drawing from Chernoff's (1979) methodology. This has resulted in a presentation one might describe to some extent as emic, as I have been a musician, clubber, DJ and event promoter working within EDMC since 1990, and as I was attending EDMC events before I began to study them.

My research has included discussions with clubbers and event organizers, and included attendance at numerous EDMC events and venues. Many of these events were in the north of England, including those in Sheffield (Headcharge, Planet Zogg, Destination Venus, Sundaze, the Arches), York (Sweatbox, He La Hu), Leeds (The Warehouse, The Gallery), as well as in Cambridge (Clueless), London (The Fridge, SEOne, Tyson Street Studios), Manchester and at various music festivals and free parties. The cult of EDMC is a close-knit community, which is difficult to understand or penetrate unless one is within it, and I am indebted to those I met at these events for the information presented here.

Insider knowledge of EDMC is important as its illegal elements bring with them secretiveness; EDMC initiates having a greater level of access than outsiders to all of its activities. However I have aimed to maintain an intellectual distance in this research where possible, in order to ensure some level of objectivity, aided by the fact that I am no longer substantially involved in EDMC. A textual approach to this study is used to some extent, in order to interpret cultural meanings and analyse content. This chapter also addresses sociological analyses of EDMC, as well as exploring it through praxis, by involvement in composing, performing and creating club events. It has endeavoured to integrate concepts from fields such as the sociological study of religion, intrinsic religion, theology, philosophy, sociology and cultural studies where relevant.

This interdisciplinary methodology has been the case in other chapters, but is mentioned here in particular, as EDMC is at its centre neither concert music or music to listen to at home, and requires a particularly broad method of study to understand it. It is within the trance music subgenre of EDMC that overt religious references are most common, and so it is the trance music scene within EDMC that will be focused on principally here, although elements of religion and spirituality pervade EDMC in general to some extent. Many publications have investigated the relationships between religion, spirituality, meaning and EDMC.

Gordon Lynch's interviews with clubbers made it clear that clubbing was meaningful for them, 'There is reasonable evidence that club culture did perform religious functions in some sense for the majority of participants (Lynch 2005, p. 177). Graham St. John's ethnographic research presents clubbers as parts of neo-tribes, with trance based ritual part of their culture, discussing EDMC as involving fearless leaps into uncertainty (2004). Gauthier (2004) has commented that rave is 'a manifestation of the religious "fete", or celebration', and has investigated EDMC in Canada as implicit religion referring to commitments, integrating foci and intensive concerns with extensive effects (2005).

Olaveson (2004, p. 86) suggests that 'rave' cultures 'do in fact exhibit many features of new religious movements and, while that phrase may lack precision here, the dance culture phenomenon of the past fifteen years demonstrates sociocultural revitalization on a massive scale'. He found 'raving' to be a 'highly meaningful and spiritual practice for many ravers' and that 'dance events are meaningful and transformative'. Lynch and Badger (2006) describe EDMC as a secondary institution. It has also been described in terms of cultural religion (Sylvan 2005), home (Rietveld 1998) or temporary autonomous zone (Bey 1985). It is clear that for those involved in EDMC it fulfils many of the traditional functions traditionally served by religions, and that it bears many of the hallmarks and typical features of cults, religion and spirituality.

Implicit and Explicit Religion in EDMC

During visits to EDMC events, I found many references to religious or spiritual elements. For example the Celestine Prophesy by James Redfield (1993) was a popular text among clubbers, and one that came up again and again in conversation. The book was a world wide best seller in the 1990s, and discusses spiritual insights and synchronicity. Through this book co-incidental events were reified, imbuing clubbing with meaning and mystery. Some practised Reiki, healing, massage or reflexology in club chill out rooms, often surrounded with spiritual imagery and paraphernalia referencing Buddhist, Taoist, Hindu or vaguely 'Eastern' spirituality, mixed up in a new age melting pot.

Clubs' chill out rooms were places where clubbers could sit and talk, rest from dancing, or escape from the intensity of the main dance floor. For example a monthly chill out club called Sundaze, based in Sheffield, was set up as a deliberate attempt to create a secular equivalent of a meditation or church event on Sunday nights, as a centre of culture and community for clubbers outside of the frenzy of mainstream clubbing. Inspired by Frigid, a similar event in Sydney, Australia, Sundaze featured down-tempo music, video projections, art happenings, sofas, candles and customers recovering from a weekend's clubbing before returning to work on Monday. The group developed links with a number of similar UK events and organizations, such as the Mellout, IDSpiral, Liquid Connective, Small World Stage and the annual Big Chill festival. These events had artefacts of, or similarities to, religious organizations, but were presented as secular events.

Some other EDMC events have an overtly spiritual agenda. London club Return to the Source (RTTS) was developed by Chris Decker in London, in 1993. He drew upon his experiences while travelling, in particular the full moon parties he attended in Goa. He stated in the accompanying booklet to one of the RTTS albums,

> At Return To The Source it is our vision to bring back the dance ritual. A ritual is a sacred act with focused intention. Our intention is to create a modern day temple, a positive space created with love, where we can join as one tribe to journey deep into trance just as our ancestors did long ago. We view the dancefloor as a sacred space, a place to connect with our power. (Decker 1995)

A trance music scene (or subculture) developed in London, based around the Brixton venue where RTTS and another similar night, Escape From Samsara, were held, and these helped to inspire trance events to begin throughout Britain. The EDMC trance scene is now a global phenomenon, developing from this London scene, as well as from other areas where this music was popular, including Goa and Israel. Before RTTS events commenced, a shamanistic ritual would precede the opening of the club, and participants taking along 'tribal' instruments like drums and dijeridoos to play would pay a reduced price for entry to the event. Mixing its trance music with imagery and other elements focused on spirituality and hedonism, Buddhism and psychedelia, world music, techno and drug culture, it provided a model for later events.

The Boom festival in Portugal developed more recently. It features a number of different areas, including a 'liminal village' which features meditation, yoga and Tai Chi sessions, and explores spirituality through workshops, seminars, discussions of new age issues, exhibitions and art. Boom's website discusses its liminality as being,

> characterised by ambiguity, openness and indeterminacy. One's sense of identity dissolves to some extent bringing about disorientation. Liminality is a period of transition, during which your normal limits to thought, self-understanding, and behavior are relaxed, opening the way to something new. According to the anthropologist Victor Turner the liminal stage of a ritual is a period during which one is "Betwixt and between", "Neither here nor there". (Boom Festival website)

Boom describes itself as

> bringing together the latest in psychedelic audio and visuals, art installations
> and workshops, this weeklong event is a harmonic convergence of people,
> energy, information and philosophies from around planet Earth and beyond
> ... Reflecting a harmonic balance of the organic and the cyber-technologic,
> Boom 06 maps the metaphysical framework in accordance with Peace, Love,
> Unity and Respect. The tone is set for a transformative experience in celebra-
> tion of the perpetual cycle of creation and re-creation – from the beginning of
> the whole to the Eschaton. (Boom Festival website)

Boom is held in a remote location in the mountains of Portugal every two
years, and the journey to the venue is something of a pilgrimage. Many miles
from any major city, entry to the festival is by a single road, and the 20,000
participants have had to queue for as much as twelve hours in their cars to get
from the main road to the festival site. Despite this people come from all over
the world to attend. Figure 8.1 shows a tree of life or axis mundi sculpture at
the centre of the main dance floor, which is also the central focus of the festival.
Figure 8.2 illustrates the audience before a concert at Boom participating in a
Buddhist prayer.

A bibliography on the Boom website includes texts relating to religion and
spirituality such as *Tao: The Watercourse Way* (Watts 1973), *Cosmic Trigger*
(Wilson 1995), *Supernatural* (Hancock 2006), *Transfigurations* (Gray 2001),
Techgnosis (Davis 1999), *Secret Life of Plants* (Tompkins and Bird 1989) and
The Mysticism of Sound and Music (Khan 1996). Some at Boom were interested in such philosophy and spirituality, others there have a more hedonistic
philosophy of taking drugs, dancing and having fun, which is also clearly a
part of the Boom philosophy, or at least its practice. Boom clearly has elements
of and references to spirituality and religion. St. John describes Boom in more
detail in his paper 'Neotrance and the Psychedelic Festival' (St. John 2009).

The Synergy Project was another EDMC event that specifically engaged
with issues of spirituality. It was based in London, and organized monthly
events, which attracted several thousand people. Before its doors opened to
the public, participants gathered together in a circle and held a short ritual
that began the event. The organizers aimed to create a space where clubbing
could be explored in a conscious and spiritual fashion, instead of with a purely
hedonistic approach.

> Synergy Project was a magical indoor festival, combining musicians,
> DJs, VJs, performers, and artists from all corners of creativity, joined by
> various proactive NGOs and charities with the expressed aim to make a
> difference.

In a society which generally perceives clubbing as a form of escapism
associated with values of transgression, The Synergy Project re-invented the

Figure 8.1 The 'Tree of Life' at the centre of the Boom 2008 dance floor (author's photo)

clubbing experience by transforming it into an 'educational' tool, associating healthy values of sustainability and social justice to strong role models such as respected artists and performers of the entertainment industry. Creating awareness with more efficient means to reach directly a young audience

Figure 8.2 A Buddhist prayer at Boom 2008 before a music performance (author's photo)

that might be otherwise reluctant to receive, respect, and incorporate such messages when proposed by conventional sources.

Offering a wide arrange alternative techniques such as Shiatsu, Reiki, Massage and Reflexology to name just a few, the healing area provided a space where people could enjoy relaxation and health/stress awareness therapy. Training workshops and information about alternative health practice and contacts with healers throughout the country are provided. Synergy also utilized a large crew of welfare staff whose primary focus is to ensure that attendees have the best possible/safest of times. (Synergy Project website)

The Synergy Project has developed into three separate organizations, a club event Luminopolis, a charity/community project The Synergy Centre and a music café called the InSpiral Lounge.

EDMC events involve numerous rituals. Clubbers collect before an event in homes and bars to talk, dress, listen to music and purchase or distribute drugs, preparing for the night ahead. Finding out about, finding and travelling to events is sometimes difficult, with advertising often being via specialist media such as flyers and posters in specialist record shops, through websites or (for illegal events) carefully guarded phone numbers passed on by word of mouth or via the internet.

Queues to get into EDMC events have their own associated cultures. Dress restrictions for those arriving at a nightclub are sometimes applied, creating a coherence of identity of the club members. Entering a club or event is a rite of entry and passage, door security staff choosing who can come in by their own varied criteria, or searching people as they enter. Clubs often turn away those wearing clothing that did not fit in, in order to ensure the required atmosphere, as well as allowing well-known faces to skip the often long queues. Queuing rituals provide a transition from the outside world to the fantasy world inside, a sense of delineation between the profane or mundane outside and the sacred or special inside. Ehrenreich tells us that music/dance based

> rituals serve to break down the sufferer's sense of isolation and reconnect him or her with the human community … because they encourage the experience of *self-loss*, that is, a release, however temporary, from the prison of the self, or at least from the anxious business of evaluating how one stands in the group or in the eyes of an ever-critical God. (2006, p. 152)

Other elements of EDMC contain references to religion that are less specific. Its lyrics rarely have the same youth culture themes as pop or rock music. Instead lyrics have different themes, often uplifting, encouraging or overtly sexual. In many cases the music has no lyrics, and this is a mark of difference to other popular music forms in the more underground scenes and subgenres of music, a mark of not being commercial or mainstream. EDMC trance music originally almost never had lyrics, although chart trance music has developed that does have lyrics, and is aimed at a more commercial market. Some lyrics point out the religious nature of EDMC. The song 'God is a DJ' by Faithless states that 'This is my church, this is where I heal my hurts'. 'God is a DJ' by Pink states that 'Life is a dancefloor, Love is the rhythm, You are the music'. There are various other examples.

EDMC music itself is not designed for individual consumption, for playing on the radio or purely for listening, but is specially designed for the communal ritual of clubbing, for groups of people to dance together. The design of clubs is often similar to that of churches. The DJ booth is often placed high up in the air, much like an organ loft or pulpit, above the audience, and there is often a gallery. Indeed there is a long history of the use of old churches as clubs. The Que club in Birmingham, for example, was originally the city's Central Methodist building. One description of the Que Club is 'The House of the Techno Gods, where the infectious grooves will make your booties move' (Williams online). Promoters Obsession who ran nights like Freedom at the Que club state on their website,

> there is something seductively religious about a club that is located in what used to be a place of worship. The DJs now occupy the altar, playing to a

congregation of around 1,600, many of whom know what it truly means to have seen the light. (Obsession website)

Obsession and Freedom are typical of the use of religious references in names used for EDMC clubs and organizations. Other examples of clubs that use terms related to religion include House of God, God's Kitchen, The Ark, The Monastery, Mass and Heaven (referencing sacred space and a sense of community); Heresy, Sin, Seven Sins and Temptation (transgression); Passion, Release, Joy, Sublime, Blessed, Lost in Love, Ascension, Awakening, Rapture, Lifted and Bliss (transcendence); Source, Pure, Best, Revelation, Renaissance, Positiva, Empathy, Freedom, Liberty and Future Perfect (utopianism); Devotion, Praise, The Trinity, The Cross, Spirit of Soul, Labyrinth (Christian references); Cosmos, Voodoo, Destination Venus, Dionysus, Escape from Samsara, Return to the Source, The Gathering presents Highway to Hell and Earthtribe (various neo-pagan or new age references). All of these names were taken from a single issue of EDMC magazine *Mixmag*. Clearly the organizers want to signify that something like a religious experience will happen.

Clubbers can often be seen raising their hands up towards the light(s) in a fashion very reminiscent of a Pentecostal church service. Raising one's hands was a sign for clubbers I spoke to of release, rapture, escape, ascension and ecstasy, as they reached upwards and outwards towards lights that came down from above the clubbers, framing their heads like a nimbus or halo, a signifier of divinity in religious art of the sacred or divine, all set within heaven-like smoke machine generated clouds. Moving light is also manipulated by technological lighting effects using moving mirrors, and in the complex use of video projections. Light is used much like religious art, to set the space apart from the mundane, to create an impression of the earth and heaven meeting, bringing the divine into the present. Images from nature, science fiction and fantasy on décor and video screens add to the otherworldly effect.

The imagery present in clubs often references religious themes, as can be seen by looking at Shamania, an EDMC music festival. The 2006 festival featured a number of hard trance music sound systems with workshops, stalls and other content derived from new religious movements such as Paganism, Wicca and groups influenced by Shamanism. Figure 8.3 is a wall decoration from the festival featuring self-similarity, entoptic imagery and magic geometry. I often saw similar images at other club events. Such geometric patterns can be seen in pagan images such as the supposedly Satanic pentagram, in Masonic and Gnostic imagery, in prehistoric rock art, in Buddhist Mandalas and in Christian knot-work.

Other Shamania decoration included a painting of a bird spirit leaving a shaman holding a drum, accompanied by the words 'There is a fire burning in Bird Spirit land, My Bones smoulder I must journey there'; circles and tunnels of dots and stars; Yin and Yang symbols; a complex mandala with an Om symbol at the centre; adverts for 'green witchcraft', 'sensory solutions' and

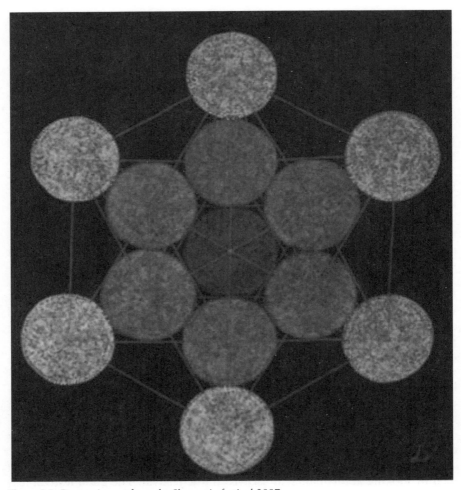

Figure 8.3 Decorative art from the Shamania festival 2007

'herbal remedies'; an advert for 'the shaman's apothecary plant allies teachers and healers – rare psychotropic and visionary plants and herbs'; publicity for 'Murgen's Keep, the pagan festival stall', with 'witches parking only, all others will be toad', '666' and 'Give me that old time religion' all visible.

'Club décor' would in many circumstances have religious imagery, such as angels, demons, Hindu gods or magical geometry. There were often the kind of entoptic images or Turing patterns often associated with 1960s psychedelia. Figure 8.4 shows an example featuring a naked image of a female 'demon' surrounded by fire. She is smiling and sexual, and is placed on a psychedelic background pattern designed to play with perspective. Festival-goers told me how their perception of this image changed after they had taken liquid LSD, ecstasy or other drugs, from

Figure 8.4 Décor image from Boom festival 2006

a flat painting to a realistic three-dimensional red and white room or tunnel, with the female image floating inside in the foreground. This typical EDMC imagery is transgressional and sexual, a demonic temptress from the Christian tradition, mixing elements of pan and other horned gods with 1960s influenced psychedelic imagery. EDMC décor also routinely uses paints and colours that react to ultraviolet (or black) light to create other three-dimensional effects.

Angels and Demons, often feminine and sexualized, are featured regularly in EDMC. Plastic angels' wings and devils' horns are often worn by clubbers, and demons, angels and wings are tattooed on clubbers' backs and shoulders. A key element of EDMC is its separation from mainstream culture. Clubs are a place of escape, of transgression, of release. They are also sites drenched in postmodernity, and as such witness the frequent clash of extremes, of sacred and secular, old and new, organic and technological. Christianity is usually the target of this transgression. Almost never does one see in EDMC a transgressional approach to Islamic, Hindu or Buddhist imagery or content, in fact instead these and other religions are usually presented in a positive light. Despite borrowing substantially from Christian culture, it is this mainstream religion of USA and British culture that is opposed and transgressed.

EDMC's oppositional and transgressive stance has been discussed in terms of its subcultural identity, Thornton describing how subcultural capital is gained. 'The social logic of subcultural capital reveals itself most clearly by what it dislikes and by what it emphatically isn't. The vast majority of clubbers and ravers distinguish themselves against the mainstream' (Thornton 1995, p. 105). As Hebdige (1979) has explained, subcultures are often created as cultural resistance to a hegemonic form. In this way it is an anti-religion (Demerath 2002), or a-religious approach, socio-political as much as religious in nature, but no less meaningful.

One of the reasons for the oppositional nature of EDMC is its reaction against the idea of a single reading of what is healthy or constructive, the will to choose one's own path, an approach typical of postmodernity, and in opposition to the singular presentation of truths within modernity. EMDC involves the knowing transgression of what the mainstream regards as healthy and constructive, accompanied, authenticated and advertised by the moral panic of the tabloid press over the use of drugs. It is this that gives EDMC much of its oppositional subcultural capital, an identity enhanced by the use of unofficial or unlicensed venues (the 'Free Party' scene); the use of uncleared samples and opposition to traditional ownership and copyright (Beadle 1993); the use of deregulated, unlicensed white label recordings; the focus on specialist, independent EDMC record shops and websites and the use of micromedia for advertising, such as flyers, posters and websites.

It is clear that EDMC has elements of religion, spirituality and meaning, although Christian influences are often imbued with a sense of transgression. This is partly a reaction to the history of repression of ecstatic music and dancing practices in Europe by Christianity, particularly by Puritan and Lutheran traditions. This history has become ingrained in dualistic western European attitudes to the body.

> Whereas Western dance forms control body movements and sexuality itself with formal rhythms and innocuous tunes, black music expresses the body, hence sexuality, with a direct physical beat and an intense, emotional sound – the sound and beat are felt rather than interpreted via a set of conventions. (Frith 1983, p. 19)

> Popular music has stayed especially close to 'the body' – compared to the art music of the European aristocracy and bourgeoisie – and that this intimacy has increased in the twentieth century. (Ibid., p. 258)

It is in the African American dance genre of disco that we first see many of the essential elements of EDMC fully developed. EDMC began within 1970s disco, an African American dance form, not as 1980s house music as is often thought. From Black and Latino gay disco culture, elements of Christianity (from black/gospel church culture), African trance culture (from African American secular music culture) and 1960s psychedelia were transmitted into later EDMC. Like its predecessors jazz, blues, rhythm and blues, rock and roll, and soul (Till 2007), house music, little known in the USA, crossed the Atlantic into British white culture, became hugely popular and eventually migrated back to the USA.

Although the Sanctuary's Francis Grosso ... invented DJ'ing in the modern sense (long sets "beat-matched" to sustain a nonstop groove), it was Mancuso who pioneered the we-are-family vibe central to house culture and the idea of the club as total experience, with every aspect—audiophile sound system, lights, decor, free food—micromanaged for your pleasure ... The scene's combination of overwhelming sound, trippy lighting, and hallucinogens was indebted to the late-'60s psychedelic culture. Mancuso still uses the Timothy Leary catchphrase "set and setting" to describe the art of creating the right vibe at parties. Part of the fascination for the Loft era is that it's about as far back as you can trace the roots of today's dance-and-drug culture. The New York dance underground described by Siano—clubs with house dealers, audiences hyped on a polydrug intake, trippy lights synchronized to a hypnotic beat, DJs working the crowd into mass hysteria—was essentially rave culture in chrysalis. The Paradise Garage, founded in 1976, was a members-only club with resident DJ Larry Levan playing to a mainly gay, black and Hispanic crowd. That same year Levan's friend Frankie Knuckles moved to Chicago to take up a residency at the Warehouse, transplanting the New York underground ethos and in the process fathering house music. (Reynolds online)

EDMC's prehistory in African American culture explains its recurring Christian musical references including the use of gospel style vocals, pianos and organs. That gay disco is the primary route of transmission of this culture explains that EDMC references to Christianity are most often made transgressionally and oppositionally, following the persecution and proscription of homosexuality by traditionalist Christians. Pan, Bacchus and Dionysus, gods of revelry and pleasure, are celebrated by EDMC as positive, reclaimed from their demonization by Christianity. The appropriation by the Christians of the horned gods to represent all that was evil and feared, makes them ideal figures to act as EDMC signifiers of transgression, freedom from conformity and hedonism (as in rock and metal music).

Transcendent Experiences

The most conclusive pieces of evidence of spirituality and religion within EDMC are the innumerable accounts of transcendent experiences described by clubbers themselves. These are some examples that are typical of the kinds of experiences described to me by clubbers.

'I felt really amazed ... made me fell like I'd left my body briefly ... I thought I was in the matrix'.

'Many deep meaningful conversations, hallucinations, perceptions, realisations of putting my life in order, connected completely to everything and everyone, stomping music where all on the dancefloor were dancing exactly to the beat in such rhythm ... parties let me be part of a wider sense of reality ... I've become more open minded ... (when dancing) often like meditating when you feel like you are the universe and nothing else exists – a feeling of complete oneness'.

'I forget my everyday worries and remember how to just have fun. Often a great night out dancing puts things I'm worried or stressed about into perspective for me'.

'I feel transported away to somewhere else, I lose myself in dancing. I feel like I'm connected to my body in a special way ... it gives me a chance to celebrate life'.

'I remember feeling an understanding of the world, of the universe, that faded after a while ... drugs, partly a group of cool people all there to have a good time and respecting one another'.

'I get to a point where I am not focused on anything except dancing. That is the only thing that matters. I am just thinking about moving my body, and me, my body, the music are all one. The music and my dancing are the same thing, it is like the dance is another form of the music. I am not really conscious of anything else and my body just feels indescribably alive and wonderful ... There were times when I was connected to other people when the whole dancefloor was like one person ... when I felt I understood life and existence in a perfect way, when life made complete sense'.

'Unconcerned by the realities of everyday life ... nothing else matters except enjoying that moment ...'

'It is the disappearance of the conscious self, my body moving instinctively in time with the beat of the music ... no sense of how long it goes on for ... just a sense that this is good, feels right and makes me happy'.

'The most spiritual experience I have ever had was post-clubbing ... we went back to someone's house and I had my first ketamine experience ... I lost any sense that I had a body or ever had had one, and thought that I was a clicking noise that had existed for all time! Gradually I morphed into the entire universe, which was encapsulated in a single atom and, as such ran the universe and I suppose was God by proxy ... gradually my vision returned as did a sense that I had arms and legs'.

These are mystical experiences of transcendence and rapture. Writer Simon Reynolds relates a similar experience,

Borne aloft in the cradling rush of sound, swirled up and away in a cloud of unknowing, for the first time I truly *grasped* what it was to be 'lost in music'. There's a whole hour for which I can't account. (1998, p. xxvii)

Perception of EMDC Behaviour by Clubbers as Non-Religious

Perhaps due in the main to inherited transgressional attitudes to Christianity, most clubbers made it very clear in interviews that they do not see themselves as religious, and do not see EDMC as religious or indeed as spiritual, in contradiction to the clear references to elements of religiosity described above, and the elements of religion and spirituality that seem to be present. This is perhaps because I interviewed UK clubbers, and they were differentiating themselves from Christianity, the predominant traditional British religion. These are comments made by clubbers when asked if they were religious or if clubbing was.

'Absolutely not'

'An altered state yes, but I associate spirituality with clarity and I'm not sure I've felt much of that when I've been clubbing'

'I think a lot of the feelings stem from the drugs, but that's not to say it's insignificant ... I would feel naive to say clubbing is spiritual (it has a dirty side too), but the experiences I've had through my time of intensive clubbing and outdoor parties have certainly altered who I was'.

'They are good experiences for me, for my spirit/soul/id, but I don't get a sense that they are experiences directed by some higher force'.

(I am) 'anti religious, I find the codification of spirituality into religion almost the antithesis of spirituality'.

(Of religions and spiritual practices) 'Loathe the lot especially the ones that seek to foist their ideas onto you without being asked, these practices are evil'.

'I've always put it down to the drugs and consequently have reality issues about the whole thing'.

'I have never felt the presence of God or any one supernatural deity'

In fact the description of EDMC as not being religious, depends on a very restricted definition of religion that is based on a modern definition of Christianity, such as clarity rather than confusion; not using drugs; control by an external higher power; and evangelism and prosthelytism. Even Christianity does not always conform to this definition in all its different forms, and other religions certainly do not. However, these clubbers seem to define religion in terms of their criticisms of Christianity.

Because EDMC is sometimes an escape from life and often involves the use of drugs, clubbers often do not recognize their activities as religious or spiritual. This does not mean necessarily that they are not. Bailey has explained how those within social institutions such as EDMC may not see their activities as religion, if this religion is implicit rather than explicit. 'It will not be seen, by the actor, as religious' (Bailey 2002, p. 9), other terms being used instead of religion such as philosophy, world-view, life-style, way-of-life, ideal or identity.

Bailey describes the need for a three-dimensional discussion of religiosity that includes the sacred, the profane and the everyday to make sense of experiences such as those in EDMC. The implicit religion he describes as arising from the everyday includes concepts also significant in EDMC, such as commitment, identity and integrity. Despite the eloquence of many of the interview respondents I have quoted, they lack 'a discourse that would enable them to describe their experiences' (Lynch 2005, p. 181), having no traditional religious context. The dimensions of the sacred experience and the human encounter are clearly present in EDMC, but the dimension of the holy, the encounter with God, seems to be missing and to be rejected. Clubbers had no interest in an external organization or deity whose opinions, obedience or control was enforced or required. Encounter is with other people and the self, although there is a sense of the infinite, the transcendental and the void, and it is partly the language, traditions and history of religion that are rejected rather than its philosophical essentials. Certainly, if 'The sacred … is that which is special and set apart' (Bailey 2001, p. 78) it would seem that EDMC is sacred.

Drug Taking in EDMC

The widespread taking of illegal drugs in clubs is described in some detail in numerous texts including for example Reynolds (1998), Shapiro (1999) and in Deehan and Saville (2003). The illegality of the recreational use of drugs that are commonly taken within EDMC in the UK, such as ecstasy, LSD, ketamine, cocaine, amphetamines, amyl nitrate, nitrous oxide and cannabis, has created a prohibition culture similar to that of the USA in the 1920s, with the same associated gun crime, criminalization of supply and underground chic of illegality. The rituals of finding drugs, smuggling them into clubs, taking them, discussing them and recovering from them are an important part of the ritual practice of EDMC.

Ecstasy (or MDMA) has been the most prominent and common EDMC drug taken, and the initial growth of EDMC in the UK in 1988 coincided with the introduction of widespread use of ecstasy. This drug floods the brain with serotonin, the chemical related in the brain to happiness and well-being, and dopamine, which stimulates motor activity, speeding up the metabolism, causing overheating, filling the person with energy and encouraging them (in an EDMC context) to dance for hours on end. Reynolds (1998, p. xxiv) describes ecstasy, its history and effects, very clearly. The initial effects of the drug can cause nervousness, discomfort, distraction, stomach-aches and vomiting, and this fits in well with Rouget's (1985) descriptions of the crisis that occurs before a possession trance ritual.

It is following such a crisis that possession takes place, typical symptoms being loss of time (as the participant is focused on the passing of musical time, normal time often passing unnoticed) and a different consciousness. Within EDMC, once a clubber has overcome his/her crisis, and started to feel happy and comfortable, has overcome this first period, he/she is described as having 'come up'. As serotonin and dopamine floods the brain, and the heartbeat is raised by fast dancing and the effects of the drug, a powerful euphoria is often experienced. This period is commonly known as 'rushing', when physical and emotional pleasure 'rushes' through the clubber.

There are a number of typical behaviours or rituals associated with having taken ecstasy and other drugs in EDMC contexts, including the developing of drug distribution networks, often small scale and involving friends providing drugs for one another; the smuggling of drugs into clubs past bouncers; comparing the potency of drugs taken and their effects; sharing drugs with other people; giving and receiving massages; spending time cooling down and talking intensely to other people (or often just one person) in a chill out room, bar, on the floor of a corridor or any other space; taking drugs in toilet cubicles (toilets being key social sites in clubs and providing privacy); looking after other people who are struggling to cope with the effects of drugs; loss of awareness of the passing of time; loss of memory; coming up; coming down and sharing water on the dance floor.

Ecstasy interferes with the body's ability to control its temperature, and accompanied by long periods of dancing this can lead to overheating and dehydration. Water is drunk to control this temperature fluctuation, but this can put excess demands onto kidneys that are already working hard to cope with the effects of drugs, and a number of high profile deaths from ecstasy have been as the result of drinking too much water. Set within this context, the sharing of drinks of water on the dance floor is an important ritual of social bonding in EDMC.

Clubbers often collect after an event at each other's houses, at after-parties or in the houses of people they had met that night, to discuss the night's events and recover. Coming down is the process of returning to an everyday sense of consciousness as the effects of drugs wear off. A 'come down' on the other hand, is a mild form of depression, usually experienced a few days after taking ecstasy or other drugs, apparently due to the detrimental side effects of drugs including the depletion of serotonin levels in the brain. Some studies have indicated that ecstasy may disturb the balance of serotonin in the brain and cause long-term depression among users, one of a number of the negative side-effects of drug taking. Drug taking is clearly a powerful ritualized process for clubbers, and it is important to note the sense of transgression and excitement granted within EDMC by illegality, by the legal and physical risks involved in taking potentially lethal unregulated narcotics.

Clubbers who have taken ecstasy have described to me feeling their whole bodies glowing with pleasure, a physical and mental experience of being flooded with joy, ecstasy and love for those around them. Many clubbers told me that this is an experience that cannot be fully understood if one has not tried it, that it is a key part of EDMC, and that the first time taking it was an initiatory experience that changed their perception of EDMC. They commented that ecstasy had changed perspectives on life, opened them up to other people, and allowed and freed them to have closer friendships and greater levels of emotional intimacy.

Ecstasy users described to me how they felt an enormous empathy and connection with each other, a connection that was not the same with someone who had not taken the drug, that they would feel a deep intimacy with a person within minutes of meeting them. This was something that bonds clubbers together, and has created an insider world within clubbing that was impenetrable to anyone who had never taken drugs. Ecstasy is of course an illegal drug. Clubbers understood but played down the negative aspects of the drug, such as depression, mood swings, disruption of serotonin production or even death caused usually by mistreatment of symptoms of the drug. Drug taking was clearly a powerful ritualized process for clubbers that played an important part in achieving trance-like and altered states, and it is important to note the sense of transgression and excitement granted by illegality.

Trance and Possession

EDMC has many similarities to possession trances that exist in some traditional cultures. As Sylvan puts it 'connections between music, rhythm, dance, and trance induction are consciously recognized by ravers, and the induction of the trance state is a specific goal of the music' (2005, p. 68). One clubber told me that 'All concept of time disappears' when clubbing having taken ecstasy. Loss of memory is an important indicator of a trance experience. Malbon (1998) describes EDMC altered states as oceanic experiences. Saunders et al. (2000) and Reynolds (1998) both discuss EDMC in terms of trance rituals and ecstatic states. Robin Sylvan (2005, p. 90) regards EDMC as having taken its trance traditions from African Yoruba and Fon traditions, via African American music.

Rouget (1985, pp. 11–14) describes trance as involving movement, noise, being in company, crisis (or altered state), sensory overstimulation, amnesia and no hallucinations, as well as trembling, protruding eyes and thermal disturbances. These are typical conditions for a clubber in an ecstasy induced EDMC altered state. Rouget defines two kinds of trance, possession, in which the entranced has little control over his experience, and shamanic where the entranced journeys on a voluntary voyage to visit the world of the spirits (1985, p. 23).

The latter shamanic type of trance seems to most resemble what happens in EDMC, but it usually involves the shaman making his or her own music. More similar still to EDMC is the trance culture of the African Pygmies and Bushmen (Rouget 1985, pp. 139–47), where the trance is a shamanic one, but unusually one in which the music is made for the shaman, something that is characteristic of possession trances, an unusual position between possession and shamanism, which is similar to that within EDMC.

Rouget describes how hallucinatory drugs are sometimes used to trigger trance (ibid., p. 25) as is continuous loud drumming (ibid., p. 53), and how a person's character changes during a trance. He describes the crisis that precedes a trance state, the difficult transition from a normal to a trance state (ibid., p. 44); how more recent initiates react more strongly and are more likely to achieve a trance state, the more experienced having more control over whether they go into a trance; and that music usually accompanies trance and is generally thought to induce it. He states that this music includes rhythmic breaks, complex rhythms, changes in stress and rhythmic irregularities, speeding up and getting louder and the musical collapse, or breakdown. Trance dancing is described as frenetic and repetitive, as 'acting the music rather than simply undergoing it ... substituting a totally or partially passive relationship to music with an overtly active one' (ibid., p. 91) while undergoing the effects of the music. 'The possessees are the ones who do the dancing ... the music is played for the purposes of dance' (ibid., p. 114). 'Dancing ... brings about modifications in the dancer's state, both at the physiological and psychological level' (ibid., p. 117).

These descriptions by Rouget of elements of traditional trance are similar to what is found within EDMC. Similarly, the trance dance movements mentioned by Rouget are ones I have seen often in EDMC, and will be familiar to any clubber, 'packed one against the other, the dancers bend their knees in time with one another, accompanying each beat with a kind of pounding of the ground and a back-and-forth swaying of the body' (ibid., p. 312), and 'an alternating movement consisting of swaying the entire body from right to left and left to right while the head oscillates from one side to the other' (ibid., p. 301).

Music interacts with dance in two ways, acting to trigger trance and then sustain it. This is either done directly, in which case the trance makes people dance, or indirectly, in which case the music triggers dancing, which itself triggers trance. Music and dance integrated. Dancing is a key element of EDMC. Barbara Ehrenreich (2006) makes it clear in her book *Dancing in the Streets* that there is a long tradition of vigorous dancing to music in England, a tradition that was systematically suppressed by the hegemonic institutions controlling society as it was seen as containing elements of disorder in an enlightenment world struggling to make the world a more controlled place.

'Music and dance act in conjunction to produce an emotional state favourable to possession' (Ehrenreich 2006, p. 182). Ehrenreich describes the history of the loss of these traditions in some detail. She also makes it clear that this kind of activity is a core part of traditional human activity

These ingredients of ecstatic rituals and festivities – music, dancing, eating, drinking or indulging in other mind-altering drugs, costuming and/or various forms of self-decoration, such as face and body painting – seem to be universal. (ibid., p. 18)

According to Rouget 'The universality of trance indicates that it corresponds to a psychophysiological disposition innate in human nature' (1985, p. 3). Rouget also makes it clear that throughout the world trance is usually associated with religion and ritual as well as music and dance.

> To dance is to inscribe music in space, and this inscription is realised by means of a constant modification of the relations between the various parts of the body. The dancer's awareness of his body is totally transformed by this process. Insofar as it is a spur to dancing, therefore, music does appear to be capable of profoundly modifying the relation of the self with itself, or, in other words, the structure of consciousness. Psychologically music also modifies the experience of being, in space and time simultaneously (ibid., p. 121).

Nettl describes this association of music and dance as universal.

> The importance of music in ritual, and, as it were, in addressing the supernatural. This seems to me to be truly a universal, shared by all known societies, however different the sound. Another universal is the use of music to provide some kind of fundamental change in an individual's consciousness, or in the ambiance of a gathering ... And it is virtually universally associated with dance; not all music is danced, but there is hardly any dance that is not in some sense accompanied by music. (2000, p. 469)

Lomax's (1968, p. 16) cantometrics project found two basic types of music, that which is individualized and that which is integrated, or groupy. The music of the rainforest pygmies and the bushmen has already been described as having much in common with EDMC, and it could also be described as the epitome of this kind of groupy, communal music, where dance and music are integrated and the whole is built in to cultural life, and in which the interlock of musical technique is both a metaphor for and practical technique for increasing the closeness of the culture's sense of community. Its style is distinctive, with many individuals making individual notes or sounds that are built together to create a continuous flow of music. Grauer describes it as 'intensely group oriented, but also individualised' (2006, pp. 15–17). 'This would appear, at least on the surface, to be a musical culture of great artistry and sophistication, an expression of well being and joy in a peace-loving, harmonious society which values creativity, fellowship, and individual expression' (ibid., p. 44).

This musical interlock is also present in EDMC, where the music consists largely of interlocking rhythms, often with no harmonic motion or vocal material. This group orientation, the use of music that features interlock, to form social bonds, within EDMC, is a response to mainstream culture. As Rietveld puts it, 'In a capitalist society which alienates the individual from the larger social fabric, a celebration of a temporary community can lead to an intense, yet temporary experience' (1998, p. 196).

Grauer describes the principle of socio-cultural inertia, which he defines as 'a tendency on the part of any human group to retain the most deeply ingrained and highly valued elements of its lifestyle until acted upon by some outside force' (2006, p. 10). He tells us 'There is nothing "natural" or intrinsic about cultural change, it does not just happen on its own, for no reason' (ibid., p. 12). This use of groupy musical technology to form social bonds, of using dancing to interlocking musical grooves to maintain community, has been such an important part of human culture that it is seen in Africa in a similar fashion as within EDMC, despite the individualization of contemporary western culture.

Crisis, Individualization and Ritual as Social Technology

Chernoff states that the most fundamental musical aesthetic in Africa is 'without participation there is no meaning' (1979, p. 23), that 'we can clearly perceive African musical forms only if we understand how they achieve their effectiveness within African social situations' (ibid., p. 30). He compares this with Western attitudes where

> we see art as in many ways something separate and distinct ... we isolate the work of art from the social situation in which it was produced in order to concentrate on our main aesthetic concern, those qualities which give it integrity as art. (ibid., pp. 31–2)

Frith states that 'the musical experience has been individualized. Music is no longer a necessarily social or collective affair' (1996, p. 237). In comparison, 'African music is not set apart from its social and cultural context' (Chernoff 1979, p. 33).

The differences of cultural histories in traditional African and modern Western cultures are borne out in their musical cultures.

> In the African world music has played such a central role in the life of its people for so long that there is often no separate word for it in indigenous languages. Like religion, music permeates the societies of sub-saharan Africa in a way difficult to understand in the west. An essential vehicle for communicating with God and the ancestors, a key determinant in rites of passage from birth to death, a tool for healing the ill, educating the young, settling disputes and entertaining the communities of both rural and urban Africa, music is perhaps *the* essential foodstuff for the African mind, body and spirit. To paraphrase Kango scholar Dr. K.Kia Bunseki Fu-Kiau: "To understand music is to understand life itself". (Gray 1991, p. 15)

It is this striking temporal, physical and social continuity that has perme-
ated every aspect of African life, in the rituals that embody their skills and
knowledge in agriculture, in the working of metals, in the weaving and
dying of cloths, the building of houses, the design of villages and towns,
the making of musical instruments and the complimentary arts of costume,
masking, musical performance and dance, themselves thought of as a single
unity, the great performance art for which we lack a name (unless it be
celebration). All of these have been devoted to one end, which Davidson
calls the art of social happiness. 'Few others', he says, 'dealt in the raw
material of human nature with more subtlety and ease, or so successfully
welded the interests of community and the individual. The Africans practiced the art of social happiness, and they practiced it brilliantly.' (Davidson
p. 82). One might say that the intelligence of Africans is devoted to learning how to live well in the world, rather than to mastering it, and they do
not imagine, as does the scientifically-minded European, that the latter is
necessary in order to achieve the former. (Small 1987, pp. 21–2)

Trance is usually associated with a crisis. The crisis that is associated with
EDMC seems to be related to the individualization of society, the loss of and
discomfort with traditional forms of community, religion and ritual, and the
loss of communal celebration and regular connection to the essence of existence. This has created what Ehrenreich (2006, pp. 143–4) describes as, 'the
terrible sense of psychic isolation – "the unprecedented inner loneliness" – that
a competitive sink or swim economy imposed' (quoting Weber 1992, p. 104).
This is not a new problem. Lawrence wrote in 1929,

We are unnaturally resisting our connection with the cosmos, with the
world, with mankind, with the nation, with the family ... We *cannot bear
connection*. That is our malady. We *must* break away, and be isolate.
We call that being free, being individual. Beyond a certain point, which we have
reached, it is suicide. Perhaps we have chosen suicide. (1931, pp. 101–103)

Heelas and Woodhead discuss the rise of the secondary institution within
counterculture, as a response to the individualization of society and the 'homeless self' (2001, pp. 43–4), quoting Marx, 'all that is holy is profaned' (1977,
p. 224), and Weber, 'a world once charged with religious significance had been
"disenchanted" by "the tremendous cosmos of the modern economic order" '
(1992, p. 181). A secondary institution is a useful term for EDMC, as, unlike
Christianity, they provide no '*order of things* to be obeyed ... and therefore
provide much greater freedom for people to exercise autonomy' (Heelas and
Woodhead 2001, p. 53). EDMC is a process of re-enchantment, of addressing
the problem of the homeless self.

Reinsertion into Society, Ritual as Social Construction

This sense of togetherness was important to the clubbers I met. As one told me, 'If you're dancing to the same beat as everyone else and equally loving it then, yeh, there's a feeling of connection'. The use of drugs in this context for pleasure rather than as medicine is a recreational use of medical technology and an act of bricolage, the oppositional reuse of an object for other than its original purpose (Hebdige 1979, p. 104). As Rietveld puts it, 'by destroying a sense of self, the merging with technology becomes a cyborgian rite of passage which needs to be repeated for as long as the identity crisis prevails' (2004, p. 59), and the destroying of the self allows a bonding with the group.

The crisis of self in an industrialized world brings machine and humans together musically, ritually, but also pharmacologically. By taking ecstasy a clubber uses chemical technology to short-circuit the lack of traditional ritual, cultural and social technologies that they have available to them, in order to feel completely inserted into the dynamic of the group. Clubbers take a short cut, a direct route into trance that bypasses the need for some of the artefacts of religiosity usually found in traditional or 'ethnic' trance traditions. As Reynolds puts it, ecstasy is self-medication for the societal illnesses caused by rampant consumerist individualization in the 1980s,

> The Ecstasy experience ranges from open-hearted *tête-à-tête* through collective euphoria to full blown religious rapture ... In the rave environment, Ecstasy acts as both party-igniting fun-fuel *non pareil* and the catalyst for ego-melting mass communion ... MDMA takes you out of yourself and into blissful merger with something larger than the paltry, isolate 'I', whether that trans-individual is the couple-in-love, or the dancing crowd, or the cosmos. MDMA is the 'we' drug. It's no co-incidence that Ecstasy escalated into a pop cultural phenomenon at the end of the go-for-it, go-it-alone eighties (the real Me Decade). For Ecstasy is the remedy for the alienation caused by an atomized society. (1998, p. xxii)

Rietveld has discussed EDMC in terms of providing a sense of home.

> One may even go so far as to call a dance space, which involves the consumption of house music, a kind of night-time 'church', where an experience can be achieved of a self-effacing identity which becomes part of a community. (1998, p. 195)

Rietveld also describes the disc jockey as a mother-figure (ibid., p. 195), and as being like a shaman (ibid., p. 196), reflecting on the womb-like heartbeat of the 'four-to-the-floor' bass drum, and the sense of rebirth, drug-induced trances and infant-like features of EDMC.

As traditional community foci in Britain have become deconstructed, club-bers have sought out new places where they feel part of a community, in which 'music becomes a focus for values as it mediates the life of a community' (Chernoff 1979, p. 37), and 'the collective voice is given precedence over the individual voice of the artist or composer' (Hebdige 1979, p. 11), art leading the re-enchantment of culture and society (Gablik 1991, pp. 167–83).

Ehrenreich describes the rise of carnival traditions and other ecstatic dance/music traditions of blacks in the Americas in general (and the Caribbean in particular) as 'ecstatic, danced religions in which music and the muscular synchrony of dance are employed to induce a state of trance interpreted as possession by, or transcendent unity with, a god' (2006, p. 169). She explains that festivities and ecstatic rituals act to dissolve rituals and other forms of social difference (ibid., p. 44), and that this was one reason why they were repressed. She uses Turner's (1969) term communitas, 'the spontaneous love and solidarity that can arise within a community of equals' (Ehrenreich 2006, p. 10), as well as Durkheim's term collective effervescence, 'that which leads individuals to seek ecstatic merger with the group' (ibid., p. 14). Lynch also describes Turner's 'communitas' in terms of EDMC as,

> a temporary unstructured form of community in which all participants are, for a brief time, regarded as equal. This idealised form of human community offers a brief respite from the hierarchical nature of day-to-day society, and provides an important reminder of people's essential quality and of the importance of treating people with proper regard. (Lynch 2005, pp. 30–1)

The Boom festival and psy-trance subgenre's mantra of PLUR (peace, love, unity and respect) is an example of EDMC actively trying to create communi-tas, and indeed, as discussed earlier the Boom organization quotes Turner on their website. Sylvan equates communitas very closely with EDMC,

> Traditional rites of passage emphasize the liminal quality of this transition from adolescence to adulthood by separating the initiates from the rest of society, stripping them of their normal social identity, placing them in their own temporary form of alternative community – which Turner called com-munitas – and initiating them through a powerful encounter with the sacred. Raves do all of these things in exactly the same sequence. (2005, p. 102)

As Small puts it,

> The nature of recorded music and, in particular, its function in human life, remains the same as that of 'live' musicking; to put it briefly, it remains a performance, in which the relationships which go to make up the partici-pants' sense of identity are explored, affirmed and celebrated. (1987, p. 395)

Becker tells us,

> Whereas it is the individual who experiences trancing, it is the group and the domain of coordination that triggers trancing. There must be changes in the neurophysiology of the trancer for trancing to occur, but those changes are not attributable simply to the brain/body of a self-contained individual. They occur through the group processes of recurrent interactions between co-defined individuals in a rhythmic domain of music that is intrinsically social, visibly embodied, and profoundly cognitive. (Becker 2004, p. 129)

Rouget also describes this process of community reintegration.

> Possession essentially is a process through which the individual is reinserted into the whole that surrounds him, and, as a corollary, that the role of music and dance is to reconcile the torn person with himself. Whether the "whole" referred to in this reinsertion process is the cosmos, as Plato thinks, or the society, as I do, is of secondary importance. (1985, p. 212)

Possession trance consists of a change of identity, from an individual to a part of the group. Music puts the individual experiencing the trance in tune, in phase, in time with the rest of the group.

> The music is the instrument of communication between the subject and group ... Creates a certain emotional climate ... leads the adept towards the spirit possessing him ... provides the adept with the means of manifesting this identification and thus of exteriorising his trance ... It is the only language that speaks simultaneously to the head and the legs ... it is through music that the group provides the entranced person with a mirror in which he can read the image of his borrowed identity and to reflect this identity back again to the group in the form of dance ... A means of reasserting the unity of the group and reinforcing awareness of that unity among all of its members. (ibid., pp. 325–6)

Membership of an EDMC possession trance cult begins with acquisition of subcultural capital, getting to know about its hidden, esoteric traditions. Initiation comes when a participant first takes ecstasy (or another drug) while at an EDMC music event.

The possession ritual itself relies on advanced knowledge of appropriate ways to behave, the correct cultural etiquette. It begins with preparation, as special ritual clothing or costume is donned. The identification of and journey to the event can be significant, followed by ritually entering the temporary autonomous zone. At some point the drug is consumed. A crisis period of 'coming up' is undertaken, followed by 'rushing', loss of self, loss of a sense of time and achievement of ecstatic states, altered perception and liminality. A feeling is engendered of melding with the rest of the group, of immersion in a group consciousness. Strong bonds are formed with other individuals taking the same ritual path.

Dancing and music allow the body to be synchronized to the time domain of the music, the external clock of the repeating bass drum, pounding at a loud level, overloading the senses and entraining the body to its rhythms. Violent movements of the head and body backwards and forwards and stomping of feet are normal, as in many other trance dancing traditions. I encountered a number of clubbers whose heartbeat had become completely synchronized with the music, each heartbeat coinciding exactly with each bass drum beat. As Shapiro puts it, 'a combination of the repetitive 4/4 house music beat and ecstasy consumption produced dancers who entirely synchronized their bodies to the music' (1999, p. 182).

Dancers maintain multiple cross rhythms in different parts of the body while dancing, triplets or syncopated semi-quaver rhythms perhaps danced by the hands, with quavers represented by bending the knees, crotchets by head movements and the torso moving swaying side to side each bar. Such co-ordination of body and music has powerful effects, further confusing and disrupting any clear perception of a simple, normal flow of time, and locking the body to the various beats.

EDMC music is specifically designed to have this effect. Even in a disco track such as Giorgio Moroder and Donna Summer's 'I Feel Love', the simple repetitive driving 4/4 beat is complicated by a syncopated triplet cross rhythm played by synthesizers, and the intricate syncopations of the voice. By the time the first house music track was released that used the Roland 303 bassline electronic instrument in the acid house boom of 1988, the music was described by the track's creators as aiming to affect clubbers like a drug, 'it takes you over. People go into a trance, they just lose it' (Reynolds 1998, p. 14). What they lose is their self, the dominance of the subconscious by the conscious mind, and as a result they lose track of time. LSD and other drugs were popular in the Music Box nightclub where the track was first played, and the trance states and time loss of an acid trip or other drug experience was an influence on EDM in its formative years.

The physicality of dancing takes the body and mind out of its usual time frame, aided by drugs and expectation. This continues for a sustained period, with beat-matched music that is designed to seem like one sustained musical stream, far from the typical western individual three-minute pop song tradition, which breaks time down into easily recognized four-minute periods. Not all clubbers take drugs, but most do. Not all achieve an ecstatic state each time, and after repeated use, the effects of ecstasy diminish. An initial 'ecstasy honeymoon' period (when the user first takes the drug) is perceived as most rewarding, and eventually most clubbers move on from such drug experiences, taking part less often and with less vigour.

A large number of members of the group all take this ritual journey together, hearts synchronised and minds stilled, the dancing providing a focus for the cult member's consciousness, which can move from the brain into the body, allowing the instinct and subconscious to become stronger, freeing the participant from inhibition and individualization. Holding their hands in the air, lights and smoke whirling overhead, perception dominated and sensory inputs overloaded, carried on in the euphoria of group dynamic and with brains flooded with drug-induced dopamine and serotonin overloads, EDMC cult members have participated in a kind of millennium fever for the end of the twentieth century, becoming a major cultural movement between 1988 and 2000. Exhausted by the night's exertions, the ritual ends by small groups of participants returning to homes, coming down, discussing the events of the night and listening to slower music, sustaining the effects of the trance gently as the effects of the drugs slowly wear off.

EDMC is a reaction against and a result of postmodernity. It is an effort by postmodern culture itself to create its own forms of religion, spirituality and meaning. As Bauman tells us,

> postmodernity ... brings 're-enchantment' of the world after the protracted and earnest, though in the end inconclusive, modern struggle to dis-enchant it ... Dignity has been returned to emotions; legitimacy to the 'inexplicable', nay *irrational*, sympathies and loyalties which cannot 'explain themselves' in terms of their usefulness and purpose ... Fear of the void has been blunted and assuaged ... we learn to learn to live with events and acts that are ... inexplicable. Some of us would even say that it is such events and acts that constitute the hard, irremovable core of the human predicament. (Baumann 1993, p. 33)

Studies have shown that music may actually be able to lock or entrain brain-wave activity to a specific frequency, and directly assist the achievement of trance states. The repetitive beats of EDMC, with its driving rhythms, high volumes and pervasive sixteenth note subdivision, added to strobe and other lights flashing in time, facilitation by drug taking and participants dancing vigorously to the music, may act to entrain the rhythms of body and mind in time to the music, helping the brain to slip into an altered state of consciousness or trance state. Di Paolo (1999), Turow (2005) and Clayton, Sager and Will (2005) have all discussed in detail the entrainment of the mind by music.

> More generally, several cognitive psychologists hold that perception, attention, and expectation are all rhythmic processes subject to entrainment. In other words, even when a person is only listening to speech or music, their perceptions and expectations will be coordinated by their entrainment to what they hear. Entrainment is fundamental then, not just to coordinate with others, but even to perceive, react to, and enjoy music. Music, as an

external oscillator entraining our internal oscillators, has the potential to affect not only our sense of time but also our sense of being in the world. (Turow and Berger 2010, pp. 26–7)

Thus music takes EDMC participants away from their everyday experience and entrains them to the pulse of the music and cult surrounding them. For two rhythms to be entrained they must be coupled together. It is the common culture and cult of electronic dance music, and the shared ecstatic experience of music and dancing, that couples people together, entrains them into community and connection.

EDMC trance experiences are leaps into the void, into irrational enchantment, into the sacred away from the everyday. It is religion 'without a strict and comprehensive ethical code ... making a wager on human moral intuition and ability to negotiate the art and the usages of living together' (Bauman 1993, p. 33).

Small describes African American derived popular music as 'a powerful means of affirming and celebrating identity, in a society whose tendency is increasingly to render the majority of its members powerless and faceless' (Small 1987, p. 395). He also states that

The central musical culture of the west in our time, which despite the commercialisation and the star-making inflicted upon it remains a music of participation rather than of spectacle, in which all are invited to join, and through which even the most downtrodden member of industrialised societies can come to define themselves rather than have definition thrust upon them. (ibid., p. 425)

Black people in the Americas, North and South, and in the Carribean, have found ways of engaging, through their musicking and their dancing, with fundamental human questions of identity and community which, as industrial states in our time become more oppressive, have become the vital questions which all of us must confront if we are to keep our power to say, "This is who we are", and to explore, affirm and celebrate our sense of who we are, in relationships with our fellow humans that are not just the crude instrumentation and exploitative relationships of industrialism. (ibid., p. 428)

Musicking is essentially a communal occupation ... the relationships that are established between the participants during a performance ... are much richer ... since the listeners (and the dancers, should there be any) are not mere witnesses at a spectacle but active participants ... relationships between the participants in a performance are not hierarchical; the performers do not dominate the audience, nor are they dominated by any outside person such as a composer or conductor ... As a tool for self-determination and for the building of community, Afro-American musicking is an activity of profound seriousness and significance, even at its most frivolous and lighthearted. (ibid., pp. 644–5)

The art of social happiness is the supreme human art, to which all other arts, and the sciences also, must contribute. The arts, and especially that great performance art of music-dance-drama-masking-costume for which we lack a name, are vital means by which human identities and relationships are explored, affirmed and celebrated. (ibid., p. 480)

The lack of distinction Small discusses between music and dance (and in fact religion) is significant, and is reflected in EDMC. In art music there is a clear definition between what is dance and what is music. This is not the case in EDMC, and

> In large parts of Africa, for example, the identification between communal dance and music, on the one hand, and what Europeans might call "religion" on the other, was profound. The term the Tswanas of Southern Africa use for dance (*go bina*) also means "to venerate," and in the Bantu language group of southern, central and eastern Africa, the word *ngoma* can mean "ritual," "cult", "song-dance" or simply "drum". (Ehrenreich 2006, p. 157)

Merker goes even further, in his discussions of the origins of music, describing how the ability of a group to synchronise musical gestures to a shared rhythm over a range of tempi could well have been the beginning of human musical activity, and a key part of human development of language, culture and communication. He also describes how dancing would have helped to keep this rhythmic synchrony, and been an integral part of music, with dancing motions being drawn from the hominid bipedal walking and running that emerged at a similar point of development.

> Such an ancestral adaption for entrainment to a repetitive beat would supply, in other words, an ancient biological foundation for the musical pulse no human culture has failed to feature among its musical means of expression. Indeed, if the present argument should turn out to have any merit, this adaption for entrainment supplies an irreducible biological root of human music ... The net result of these conjectural developments would be the emergence among our hominid ancestors of a novel and unique social adaption, namely, a behavioural forum featuring synchronous singing and dancing on the part of a higher animal. (Merker 2000, pp. 319–20)

If Merker is right, then the development of dancing and music came as the first humans developed, and could be an important part of this developmental process. He describes how female sexual selection and other biological imperatives could have developed music and dancing abilities and effectively coded these abilities into human DNA as it was developed. It is at least further evidence that dancing rhythmically to music is a core element of human culture.

Freeman makes it clear that these cultural activities are hard wired into humanity through biological and evolutionary development.

> Music and dance originated through the biological evolution of brain chemistry, which interacted with the cultural evolution of behaviour. This led to the development of chemical and behavioural technology for inducing altered states of consciousness. The role of trance states was particularly important for breaking down pre-existing habits and beliefs. That meltdown appears to be necessary for personality changes leading to the formation of social groups by cooperative action leading to trust. Bonding is not simply a release of a neurochemical in an altered state. It is the social action of dancing and singing together that induces new forms of behaviour, owing to the malleability that can come due to the altered state. It is reasonable to suppose that musical skills played a major role early in evolution of human intellect, because they made possible formation of human societies as a prerequisite for the transmission of acquired knowledge across generations. (Freeman 2000, p. 422)

Freeman places the development of music and dance before or alongside fire, tools and shelter, as this method of communication and building the coherence of the group would have been necessary for retaining knowledge and the effective use of these inventions.

Openness with Others

The importance of this building of community and reinsertion within the group is clear from responses I had from clubbers.

> Usually the best nights are when I meet a great new person or have a really good time with friends ... One of the first times I went clubbing and ended up at an after party the next morning, I met a woman who gave me some acid. We had a great time and I'm still friendly with that woman now, years later ... It was a way of meeting new people (who weren't a part of 9–5 living), having an extended social circle and just having an interesting conversation with a person I've never met ... When I'm out and about in Sheffield I see a lot of people I know. I know there's another world out there which is very different from that of work and I feel my mind has been opened up to differences – I'm more open minded.

> ... particularly at outdoor parties, the feeling of closeness of friends and being part of a 'secret' world. Also making contact with new people and striking up interesting conversations ... I remember mostly making a connection with people I had only just met.

It has made me more open to meeting different types of people ... the closeness and acceptance with/of other clubbers ... I really learned how important it is to let other people know how you feel.

I enjoy the music & the openness of the friendships/interaction at clubs ... there was a community spirit that transcended the clubbing itself ... As well as accounting for the majority of my present social circle, clubbing has also resulted in a (positive) realignment of my base emotional state, given me a greater sense of empathy and has increased my ability to talk to people I don't know.

Meeting certain people who will probably be friends for the rest of my life ... the place and my/their state of mind leading to a certain empathy that is difficult to replicate in any other social situation. That sense of empathy on a broader level ... ecstasy has rewired my brain and I now get emotional when I see something's on TV/at the cinema/theatre that would not have affected me before ... I don't dwell on it.

These comments were typical and reaffirmed many times. What cannot be easily perceived from the small sample of comments provided above is the long-term significance of this process in the small communities formed by clubbers. Many clubbers spoke to me of the way that the short-term effect of an ecstasy-fuelled clubbing experience allowed them to feel more emotionally open, more able to express their feelings and to open up to other people. They discussed how dancing in a non-predatory but open sexuality allowed them a more comfortable attitude to their own physicality.

They also mentioned that they enjoyed the group dynamics of clubs, a feeling of being part of a group, a community, without any stated demands, rules or dogma except from the self-imposed responsibility felt to respond in kind and with care. Although these were short-lived experiences, many clubbers described to me how they felt their life was affected by these experiences in the long-term. Outside of clubs, and years after many of them have stopped going clubbing, these clubbers still have strong individual friendships and small communities of close friends, having first formed friendship bonds while clubbing. They talk of having learned to be closer and more open to other people and more comfortable with themselves. They still find ways to dance to music and find a place of self-loss and transcendence, but it is less frequent, less intense and/or less likely to require the use of drugs to achieve it.

EDMC Spirituality

Lynch has identified three elements of EDMC spirituality, a deeper connection with the self, the finding of this connection through an essential non-verbal form (dancing, ritual) and the enjoyment of freer and more intimate relationships with others (2002, pp. 88–9). These elements combine and mix together in various ways. EDMC spirituality involves many elements including the creation of sacred spaces; the emulation of images of heaven using clouds of smoke and moving lights; out of body, otherworldly experiences; opposition and transgression; subcultural authority and authenticity; ecstatic journeys; ritual possession trance practices triggered by dancing, drugs and music; no reference to an external deity that has an absolute right to obedience; and the replacement of priests by DJs, drug dealers and promoters whose jobs are to facilitate and enhance the mystical experiences of the clubbers.

It is a democratised, postmodern, re-enchanting, reconstructive spirituality. It is autonomized, subjectivized, both individualized and rational/holistic, both individual and group/communal, emotionally intelligent and explorational, seeking sensation and ecstasy, mystical, and involves power and spiritual authority being owned, not passed or delegated. It relates to somethingism, connection to the earth, Gaia theory, the neo-pagan, direct connection with others and God, general (rather than special) revelation, the experiential, body positivism and liberal attitudes to sexuality. It is focused around community facilitation and celebration, communitas and collective effervescence. Ethical decisions within EDMC spirituality are the responsibility of the individual, in line with Zygmunt Bauman's *Postmodern Ethics* (1993), rather than an 'absolute line of reference' (Lynch 2005, pp. 94–5) or external power, and are sometimes guided by the concept of PLUR.

EDMC is a significant cultural phenomenon. Figures showed in 1996 that 42 percent of the general population of the UK visited clubs at least once per year, 43 percent of 15- to 24-year-olds visited a club once a month or more often (Mintel 1996) and 1.8 percent of 16- to 59-year-olds used ecstasy in 2006/2007, a figure that has stayed roughly the same (between 1.5 and 2.2 percent) since 1995 (Nicholas et al. 2007). These figures suggest that in any one year more people might go to a nightclub than go to Christian church in the UK. The percentage of the UK population that are taking ecstasy (1.8 percent) is larger than taking that part in pentecostal (1 percent) or charismatic evangelical (1.2 percent) Christian churches (Ashworth and Farthing 2007). Although not all these clubbers are attending underground or trance EDMC events, some are more commercial 'townie' clubs, there are also many denominations of Christian church with widely carrying beliefs, and the figures underline the significance of clubbing in the UK.

It may be that like other popular music forms, EDMC will be a short-lived cultural phenomenon. Perhaps it will be looked back on by history as a millennial phenomenon, responding to pop star Prince's call to 'party like it's 1999' (1983). EDMC has been criticised for maintaining its participants in a liminal state of continual infancy, and its endemic drug use may be causing brain damage to a generation of young clubbers. Lynch asks 'if club culture does serve religious functions for some people in Western society, this raises normative questions of whether it does so in ways that are healthy and constructive' (2005, p. 178).

I have tried not to cast value judgements on the merits of EDMC, one could just as easily ask the same questions of Christianity or any other religion, of whether they are healthy and constructive. Healthy or not, EDMC remains popular worldwide, and reflects some of the needs of society and culture and the failures of traditional religions and contemporary society to meet them. It helps us to understand the importance within our cultures of traditions, rituals, communities, transcendence and dancing together to music.

EDMC contains elements of spirituality, meaning and religion. As mainstream culture has become more individualized and less community orientated, and as it has lost its celebratory traditions, rituals and religions, some of the original roles of organised religions have been replaced by EDMC and other popular music cults, which act much like a religion. EDMC's possession cult draws upon those traditions around it in a pick and mix, postmodern fashion, using material from various wisdom traditions. It has adopted elements of Christianity from African American music culture, but because of their transmission through secular black music culture and gay disco, these elements are referenced in a transgressional fashion.

Also transmitted through African American music traditions are trance practices that have their roots in African possession rituals, with particular similarities to Pygmy/Bushmen traditions. These trance practices are reinforced by the use of illegal drugs to cybernetically enhance the effects of the trance, and add to a sense of subcultural authority and transgression, the illegality providing a barrier to re-absorption into the mainstream and a resultant process of disenchantment and deconstruction.

The crisis that this trance is in response to is that of the individualization of society, the homeless self, and the trance ritual acts to help the individual feel reconnected to or reinserted into a community. Clubbers do not see this activity as religious, but this may be because the religion is implicit rather than explicit, with clubs acting as what some have described as a secondary institution. However EDMC acts much like a religion, providing a site of escape and transcendence, a sacred space separate from everyday existence and a key focus of community and identity.

As the traditional dominant religious Christian tradition dies away in the UK and elsewhere, many young people in particular have had no religious context in which to practice ritual together, have group mystical experiences or develop communities of like-minded belief. The fundamentality and universal human desire for such activities is shown in that EDMC in general, and the trance scene in particular, have grown to provide these functions for a large body of young people. Chill out rooms provide the equivalent of prayer, meditation and spaces to meet and discuss, and the dance floor provides a liminal space or temporary autonomous zone akin to communal worship, offering self-loss within the group.

On the dance floor, music entrains and replaces thought and takes people out of their minds into their bodies, and out of normal time, drug taking exaggerating the experience. This is a youth cult, lacking sustainability, becoming less attractive as participants age or have children, who cannot generally participate. As musical trends change and shift it is uncertain whether the EDMC trance cult will continue or die out, but there remains much to consider, study and evaluate about this musical religious movement of postmodernity.

Dance Cult

This chapter has endeavoured to show how EDMC acts as a form of possession cult. It is not identical to African possession cults, but it has most of the primary characteristics of a trance form, including expectation, initiation, crisis, possession brought on by dancing to repetitive loud music leading to a perceived loss of time and ritualised use of drugs.

St. John has described the way that his descriptions of neotribes, neotrance and technomads within EDMC are linked to cult-like behaviours.

> Possessing some resemblance to what I have referred to as "tribal", the cultic involves those who, while not forming organised religions (i.e. churches or sects), nevertheless participate in groups and networks forming around shared beliefs. (St. John 2009, p. 43)

Like other cults within the sacred popular, membership of electronic dance cults does not require obedience to a set of behavioural standards. Like other cults it is linked to neo-pagan movements, many of which are evident, as has been described. Musicians, DJs, promoters, drug-dealers and others are priest-like figures who direct, facilitate and organise the behaviours of the cult, although individuals negotiate their experiences of the divine themselves, and the divine power that enters and controls the dancers is music. This music is created by musicians, and the music they create is perhaps their spirit, which enters the dancers channelled through and by the DJ, who mediates between the source of the music (musicians) and the dancers. This makes the musicians distant unseen figures, with control of and access to the entrancing music held by the priestly caste of the DJ.

There are various levels of cult membership, including the new neophyte club first timer who has never taken drugs (if they do not choose to take drugs they may not progress any further); the initiate who has taken drugs; the regular who is known to many others and is often granted special privileges; the VIP, often with access to backstage or special areas not available to all; the club (or event) staff including bouncers, bar and cloakroom staff (who do not participate in the trancing). Those putting on the event have their own hierarchy, including flyer distributor, décor designer, VJ, promoter, local DJ, national DJ, superstar DJ.

Like other cults, electronic dance music cults are often secretive, partly due to illegality involved in the scene. They can involve large amounts of commitment, whole weekends regularly set aside for participation, and create an us-and-them mentality, largely between those who have taken drugs, and those who have not, the latter not considered to be able to understand the drug experience, including work colleagues and family, clubbing activities often as a result being disguised or secretive.

Drug taking is endemic within EDMC, and this is a typical cult characteristic, the trance practices involved equating to supposed 'brain-washing' repetitive techniques. The sexual arousal triggered by some drug taking means that sexual activity or experiences are a feature of EDMC, linked to drug taking and ritualised trancing, and thus another characteristic considered typical of cults. Although some EDMC events are not financially driven, others are very much so, including superclubs like Cream, Gatecrasher and Ministry of Sound, which have risen from humble EDMC beginnings to become large international brands. Codes of dress and haircut identify clubbers as belonging to different musical subgenres, as is the case in the other cults described in this book.

Another consideration that reinforces the perception of EDMC as a cult is its opposition by the mainstream, largely on moralistic grounds. EDMC has been attacked due to the ecstasy use evident in the scene. The father of Lea Betts, a young girl who died having taken ecstasy, launched a campaign about the use of ecstasy, and other groups have been similarly critical. However, Betts died largely due to a lack of understanding of the effects of the drugs (having drunk too much water), through poor education and the criminalization and prohibition of the drug, which limits the information available and prevents users from knowing what is being taken and in what dosage.

Warnings of the dangers of ecstasy ignore the implicit evidence of the millions of people who have taken the drug without dying. The UK government has ignored the advice of experts who have advised that the legal status of ecstasy in particular be downgraded due to its lack of harm in comparison to heroin, crack cocaine or crystal meth. That is not to say that the drug is safe, or may not lead to long-term harm, but the principle danger to EDMC cult members is buying the drug from untested sources, and the lack of knowledge and research on the drug due to its illegal status. In addition to the Lea Betts campaign, and those like it, the UK press launched an anti-EDMC moral panic when the acid house scene first emerged in 1988. This is detailed in Thornton's (1995) book, for example.

The most remarkable testament to the power of EDMC as a cult is the opposition in the UK by the creation of the Criminal Justice and Public Order Act of 1994, created specifically to clamp down on illegal or unlicensed raves characterized by what the act describes as being wholly or predominantly characterized by the emission of a series of repetitive beats that might distress the local community. Other laws have been brought in that aim to make venues and promoters criminally liable when clubbers in their venues or events are found to be taking illicit drugs. In the USA the RAVE (Reducing Americans Vulnerability to Ecstasy) Act addressed 'rave' events as well as ecstasy use in 2002. The Illicit Drug Anti-Proliferation Act of 2003 incorporated much of this legislation, but added the responsibility of managers for drug taking in their venues, much like had been introduced in Britain (Sanders 2006, pp. 7–8).

What is unusual about the Criminal Justice and Public Order Act is that it attempts to define and criminalise EDMC in particular. It was deemed important that EDMC events were not allowed to happen outdoors in unlicensed public spaces, but that any other kind of music subgenre could hold a similar event without prosecution. This was therefore specifically legislating against a particular kind of music. The evidence of having legislation specifically introduced to oppose it is perhaps the final testament to the power and significance of EDMC as a cult of some importance.

Chapter 9

Do You Believe in Rock and Roll? Musical Cults of the Sacred Popular

Traditionally in Western Europe, religious songs were pieces of music with references to religion and spirituality in the lyrics that were performed in a communal setting that had religious context and ritual setting. Are not pop songs like this? 'Imagine' is song about belief and meaning in a postmodern age, an anthem of utopia, a call for global unity, peace and tolerance, with added meaning due to the death of its author, John Lennon. Lennon had become a leader within US counter culture, a significant figure in the anti-Vietnam war movement, in addition to his extraordinary level of fame as a member of the Beatles and subsequently as a solo artist. His music addressed the hippie spirituality of peace and love, writing 'All You Need Is Love' for example to be played during the first worldwide satellite television link up. Asked to write something that could provide a global message, the performance of the song featured a panoply of sacred popular icons including Eric Clapton, Mick Jagger, Marianne Faithful, Keith Richards, Keith Moon and Graham Nash, singing along in the chorus, and was a key event in the history of postmodernity and the globalization encouraged by television and international communications (Lewisohn 1988, p. s120). Lennon eventually died as a result of his fame. He was aware of the earlier death of John Lennon the man, as John Lennon the public figure and Beatle had taken over. He was quoted in *Newsweek* in 1980 as saying,

> I was used to a situation where the newspaper was there for me to read and after I'd read it, somebody else could have it ... I think that's what kills people like Elvis and others of that ilk ... The King is always killed by his courtiers, not his enemies. The King is overfed, overdrugged, overindulged, anything to keep the King tied to his throne. Most people in that position never wake up. They either die mentally or physically or both ... and that's how the Beatles ended. Not because Yoko split the Beatles, but because she showed me what it was like to be Elvis Beatle and be surrounded by sycophants and slaves who were only interested in keeping the situation as it was. And that's a kind of death. (Shapiro 1999, p. 219)

Lennon consciously stepped down from his position as a pop idol, abdicated from being a king. He withdrew from public sight for a number of years, only later re-emerging as a solo musician, focusing on his private and family life rather than his public life and pop star persona. He did not have a mansion with tight security, or a bodyguard at all times, as one might expect of a major star, political or religious figure. He seemed to consider that if he could not live his life as a free human being, then he had suffered the death of John Lennon at the hands of his popular mediapheme. He thus had little protection against being shot, and died anyway at the hands of John Lennon the famous Beatle, as it was his fame that meant that someone wanted to kill him.

The death cults of popular music are full of examples of pop icons that have been martyred on the altar of the life of a musician. Buddy Holly died in a plane crash along with a number of other stars, a victim of the incessant travelling of a performing musician. Don McLean wrote the pseudo-mystical 'American Pie' about the day the music died, asking 'Do you believe in rock and roll, Can music save your mortal soul'. The song is full of obscure references to religion and the occult, such as 'the fire is the devil's only friend', and the meanings of the lyrics have been much discussed. It is a song that is often sung by groups of people, I have certainly been in situations where groups of people joyfully sing together with gusto the lyrics 'this will be the day that I die', as hymn-like a popular music experience perhaps that one can have, singing together of the death of the popular saint Buddy of Holly, and of death and the power of music.

Popular music has become increasingly important at ritualized moments in people's lives, for example at weddings and in funerals. In 2009 a British Anglican vicar, Father Ed Tomlinson, was widely reported as having complained that religious hymns and prayers were being replaced at funerals with popular songs and eulogies. In response another vicar, Geoff Stickland banned pop songs at funerals. Stickland claimed it was 'not right' to play pop songs at funerals. He went on to say,

> We have changed to a culture that I find incredibly hard to accept ... I am 68, have been a priest for 44 years, and do not want to change ... When any momentous event happens in their lives, such as a funeral, they want us to perform in their culture. (Hough online 2009)

He seemed not to understand that the words of a long dead Victorian in a hymn, in archaic language and music with no cultural relevance to those present, is not an effective choice as a ritual way of understanding and dealing with the complex emotions surrounding death. The vicar perhaps had a lifetime of experience singing such hymns, in school as a boy and in church as an adult, but much of society has no such experience or reference. If someone wants music that will speak to them at a funeral, be meaningful in such a key rite of passage, a popular song is often a better choice than a hymn that the dead person may not have known, liked or believed in the content of. The Christian church is so culturally out of touch with the rest of popular culture and society in the West, that it still considers hymns that are relics of Victorian religious practice, in some way significant, and the leaders of such religious groups seem to prefer that their church die than keep in touch with contemporary culture.

According to the BBC, many people have discussed what song they would like played at their funeral and the top ten popular funeral songs in 2009 were:

 1 My Way – Frank Sinatra/Shirley Bassey
 2 Wind Beneath My Wings – Bette Midler/Celine Dion
 3 Time To Say Goodbye – Sarah Brightman/Andrea Bocelli
 4 Angels – Robbie Williams
 5 Over The Rainbow – Eva Cassidy
 6 You Raise Me Up – Westlife/Boyzone/Josh Grobin
 7 My Heart Will Go On – Celine Dion
 8 I Will Always Love You – Whitney Houston
 9 You'll Never Walk Alone – Gerry and the Pacemakers
10 Unforgettable – Nat King Cole (BBC online 2009).

Fifty-eight percent of funerals featured popular music, despite clergy sometimes rejecting choices which they deemed inappropriate.

People often play popular songs at weddings, and indeed increasing numbers choose to marry in a secular setting for a number of reasons. This may be simply because they do not believe in Christianity, being an agnostic or atheist, but is often because many churches are unwilling to fulfil a cultural role as a site of ritual for the whole community no matter what their beliefs. The lack of cultural reference points in Christian weddings, and the cultural conservatism of many churches, effectively drives people away from the few rites of passage where one would expect people to be drawn towards religious venues in order to mark the event involved with an appropriate ritual that ties one in with history and tradition.

For these and other reasons, in contemporary Western culture, pop cults, popular music based new religious movements (NRMs), have replaced many of the functions traditionally served in traditional cultures by religions, as those traditional religious cultures have become increasingly culturally irrelevant, refusing to discard outdated traditions that have little to do with the literature or teachings of the faith itself, but rather are often accumulations of cultural habits that have become associated and intertwined with the belief system itself. Since popular music and culture have entered the field of the religious, it is useful to use language and methods that have developed to understand and discuss religion to study them, rather than using methodologies developed to understand scientific subjects or rational traditions. Religions are not rational or logical, nor are cults of popular music, and in order to understand their function it is useful to use relevant language and concepts. This can reveal patterns, behaviours and structures that might not otherwise make sense or be understood.

Religions have numerous discrete functions within cultures. They have developed within human cultures as ways of structuring society and controlling behaviour. Youth culture developed in Western culture after the Second World War as greater disposable income, independence and free time were available to the younger sections of society. Largely excluded from the power systems that controlled government and religion, this sector of society had cultural tastes that were changing more rapidly than ever before, driven as they were by globalization and developments in communication. As a result of this, popular music cultures, and cults, developed to fulfil for youth culture, functions formerly associated with the major religions, offering ways to structure society and setting codes of behaviour that were in tune with their own choices and preferences. Thus, pop cults became key sites and foci for the development and structuring of the communities and cultures of young people, and for developing patterns of behaviour.

Religions have in the past provided context for the powerful emotions and passions that surround human behaviours of all kinds. Sexual behaviour and interpersonal relationships are an area where attitudes have in particular developed and changed in contemporary popular culture. Religions have helped to provide ways of understanding the dissolution of self that takes place in moments of sexual activity, and to relate these experiences to other ecstatic practices. They have in traditional cultures often had the responsibility of helping to provide sexual safeguards and boundaries to safeguard the young and vulnerable, and to explore limits on what is appropriate, trying to control activities that may cause harm. As contraception became more widely available, and attitudes to sexual activity outside of marriage (as well as to homosexuality and other forms of sexual activity that Christianity, for example, opposed) changed in the second half of the twentieth century, young people looked to places other than traditional religions in order to understand and develop attitudes to sex. The numerous links between sexuality and popular music made this a key site for such explorations of sexuality, especially in the West, where popular cultural attitudes and opinions had changed enormously in the latter half of the twentieth century.

Christian religious literature was written in a context where there was little availability of contraception, and where childbirth outside marriage was extremely socially problematic. In addition, many Jews in biblical times would have been promised to marriage at a young age. The bible speaks little of sex outside of marriage, mostly dealing with adultery by a married person. It has attitudes to homosexuality designed to address male temple prostitutes, ignoring lesbians, and in a culture where it was not acceptable for long-term same-sex relationships to exist. Attitudes to sex and sexuality have become problematic issues for a church that still considers equality of women (in priesthood at least) and homosexuality an issue, in a culture where the equal rights of women and gay couples are enshrined in law. The massive gulf between moral attitudes taught within Christianity and normative values within popular culture has provided a significant reason why the exploration of post-modern modes of sexual practice has often been explored within pop cults rather than traditional religions. A steady stream of sexual scandals, whether related to gay priests, priests having sex with their parishioners, or to child abuse, have also meant that discussions by Christians of sexual morals are widely discredited.

Sexual ecstasy is not the only type of ecstatic experience which religions have avoided dealing with, while pop cults have embraced them wholeheartedly. The mind–body duality of Western Christianity, the rejection of the body and focus on the mind that has dominated Christianity in particular since the reformation, enlightenment and renaissance, has left much of Western culture somewhat disconnected from physicality, and from physical expressions and explorations of spirituality in particular. Pop cults in the UK and the USA are heavily influenced by African American music, whereas in Western culture, mainstream religions are separated off from the everyday. As Reed puts it,

> For African Americans, however, the sacred/secular duality is relatively new. In the native culture of the first Africans transplanted to the New World, a 'non-religious' category of music didn't exist. The influence of Western culture led these Africans to incorporate the sacred/secular dichotomy into their thinking about music.
>
> In the West, music and the other arts are often approached as objects detached from human experience ... By Contrast, traditional West Africans fuse music with everyday life in much the same way that they fuse the divine with everyday life. (2003, pp. 1–2)

African religious worldviews can be described not in bipolar opposites or clear categories but, rather, in terms of blended or even fused dimensions. Pop cults have the advantage over mainstream Western religions, of being able to appeal to the whole person, to their body and spirit as well as their minds, of not being afraid of addressing physicality, sexuality or the body, and of being in tune with contemporary morality in relation to these issues. Pop sex cults have reached out to resacralize and explore sexuality.

Religions have historically explored a number of methods of achieving ecstatic states which were vital for exploring the self, connection with others, collective effervescence and communitas. As religions became increasingly out of touch with youth culture, and as agnosticism and atheism became more prevalent, and participation in traditional religions decreased, youth culture looked elsewhere for such experiences of physical and spiritual ecstasy, looking increasingly within cults of popular music, as was seen in the chapter on sex cults.

The achievement of altered states of consciousness, or achievement of ecstatic states, within cults of popular music and elsewhere, is regarded by some as a false form of consciousness, but the emotions and changes in perception associated with them are undoubtedly very real and powerful. One has in a liquid culture, an individual choice about how one approaches issues of ultimate or extensive concerns, how one deals with the most meaningful elements of individuals' lives. One can choose to see such elements as false or true, or to describe them as such. False and true have little functional meaning in a liquid postmodernity void of meta-narratives, they are often value judgements, essentially meaning 'I like or agree with this' or 'I don't like or agree with this'.

One can choose to take a culturally pessimistic approach, deconstruct and point out the difficulty of focusing on the experiences of the individual, as every individual is different. This has been an important cultural process, it has deconstructed culture, including a deconstruction of the modern experiment that has resulted in an atomized society where there are few opportunities for a deep spiritual form of connection, and where community and connection are systematically pulled apart in the name of modernity and progress.

One can instead of deconstructing or choosing reductionist arguments, choose to take a path of reconstruction and re-enchantment, to accept that the modern is now gone, and that the masses are now a controlling power in society, they have wrested control from the few. From this perspective, what is now needed is a period of rebuilding, involving creating a new sacred popular. Writers such as Suzi Gablik, with *Has Modernism Failed* (1984) and *The Reenchantment of Art* (1991), as well as Berman (1981) and Partridge (2005) have discussed this approach.

Many religions have a power structure that sees the few control the many. Not all religions are like this, or are seen as like this. Popular cults often do not operate in this way, as the specifics of belief are not dogmatically fixed, or the cult is based on practices rather than beliefs. This varies dependant on whether one chooses to perceive the person in charge as a dominant leader, or as an enabling servant. A pop cult ritual leader who co-ordinates activities is perhaps different than a Christian priest, who is regarded as having as his responsibility the cure of, or responsibility for, the souls of those he has within his parish. Within popular music culture the leader may be a DJ or musician, and is often preaching no dogma, although there are a whole set of meanings that participants can take part in if they choose.

Cults of the sacred popular are often based on practices and behaviours rather than beliefs. They involve mystical experiences, direct experience of the divine that are ecstatic, transcendental, meaningful, communal or sacred, rather than experiences that are mediated and controlled by another. For this reason writers such as Lynch and Badger (2006) and Heelas and Woodhead (2001) have described such popular cults as secondary institutions. Such a choice of language offers a second place to them, and putting them below the primacy of older religious traditions such as Christianity again prioritizes the institutions that are described as primary rather than secondary. Unmediated religion might be a more relevant description, or one might instead describe them as being part of the sacred popular, or as a directly experienced and therefore mystical tradition, or directly experienced religious practice. A number of texts have begun to explore the sacred popular by investigating postmodernity and the sacred, including Santana and Erickson (2008), Lynch (2007b) and McAvan (2007).

NRMs or cults are the result of culture changing quickly, rather than slowly, it is the place of cultural change that creates a need for NRMs or cults. Traditional religions are often based on written texts that cannot be changed or adapted quickly. This is something that is regarded as important, an antidote perhaps to the changing moods and whims of popular opinion, something that is important in a religion that aims to be sustained over hundreds of years. However the interpretation of these texts, and their translation, sacralization, selection and prioritization, is increasingly understood as a political choice made according to the changing moods and whims of the most powerful in society. At least changes made by or the opinions or attitudes of popular culture have to be agreed and approved in some way to achieve mass adoption. Moreover, pop cult texts are often not written, they are often cultural constructions, texts inscribed in local scenes such as hip hop, or texts contained in artworks, such as musical or visual texts. They are living traditions that move and flow along with or reflecting culture and history, rather than being set and attempting to control culture and history.

These kinds of texts can be explored, experienced and understood directly, using a range of practices or methods. Before the Christian reformation, the Catholic Church had increasingly centralized power, and access to the divine was carefully controlled. Forgiveness and salvation could be bought or granted, and understanding of both sacred texts such as the Bible and the liturgy of Church services, were restricted to those who could understand Latin. Religious leaders, rather than the deity they represented, had become the ultimate sources of spiritual power and authority in society.

This was the result of many years of accumulation of traditions and practices that had little to do with Christian biblical text. The reformation ended this absolute religious control, and began to democratize Christianity. However this process is incomplete in comparison to a Western culture where governments often follow popular opinion rather than leading it. The emergence of the sacred popular and of pop cults is the result of a grass roots revolution in religion and spirituality, is the result of young people in particular constructing their own NRMs, forming their own cults. This is as a result of a mixture of elements such as dissatisfaction with the other options available, the need for connection and meaning in a disenchanted and atomized world, and the careful manipulation of the music industry.

Pop cults are mostly youth cults. As we have seen, death cults worship those popular music icons who have died young, and who will always appear young in the popular memory. Extreme commitment to pop cults tends to come from young fans, or at least those under thirty. Some might consider this renders such cults inauthentic as religions, but in fact the most active membership of

traditional cults is often young people, and there have been a number of studies that have investigated how participation in religions tends to go through a
number of stages, which tend to occur at different stages of life, or ages.

Indeed, there are particular patterns of development of faith during human
lifetimes in many religions other than pop cults. James Fowler discusses stages
of religious development in his book *Stages of Faith* (1981). Fowler's theories are summarized usefully by John Mark (online 2009). Fowler's analysis indicates that faith develops and changes in a similar way in all religious
traditions, beginning in a naïve and immature fashion, passing through the
potential for extreme levels of unquestioning commitment, before maturing
into a more considered position with age. Fowler discusses faith, rather than
religion, which he regards as being concerned with the individual's relatedness
to that which is universal. It may be that the kind of teen pop cult that is often
built around individual pop stars or boy and girl bands is related to his second
stage, which he calls mythic-literal faith. Fowler describes this stage as being
characterized, among other things, by an inability to be critical of myth or
symbology, and in reciprocity. Thus when caught up in a teen pop cult, a child
may believe that the distant star cares about them, more than they actually do,
and may be characterized by an uncontrolled uncritical belief in the star. It is
often also an individualized relationship.

Fowler's third stage is called Synthetic-Conventional faith. Many people
do not move past this stage, which demands a high level of socialization and
integration into a group, something that can be facilitated by popular music
cults. This stage is characterized by a person aligning themselves with a group
and its ideology and conforming to it, often without realizing that an ideology
is present, as is the case with many popular music cults, where the participants
would not regard themselves as following an ideology, religion or cult. Those
who differ are regarded in this phase as other or different kinds of people.

Later stages include the fourth individuative-reflective stage, often experienced in the mid-thirties to late forties as a 'mid-life crisis', and characterized by
disillusionment, questioning and struggle. This leads to the fifth stage, conjunc-
tive faith, which involves the acknowledgement of paradox and transcendence,
and the understanding of the underlying nature and semiotics of differing religions. This leads to the final universalizing faith, in which a unifying vision of
religions is achieved. It is clear that most pop cults exist predominantly within
stages two and three.

Swidler and Modjes draw similar conclusions about stages of faith.

In popular religion, the degree of reflexive consciousness, or self-awareness,
is quite low. It is rather like that of children experiencing something. Children
are not very aware that they are experiencing something; rather they tend
to focus exclusively on the thing being experienced. We thus say that children are *naïve*—that is, their mentality is still close to the way it was when
they were born (*natus*). Children tend to experience things in a fashion that

is rather literal, straightforward, immediate—that is, with no intermediate element, with no mental distance between the thing experienced and the one experiencing. (2000, p. 10)

This naïve stage is a first stage of religious belief, which can be associated with fundamentalist approaches, and perhaps of some pop cults such as the possession cults of EDMC, in which the participants are not aware of their religious practice and adherence to an ideology or cult.

The text goes on to discuss how when children mature they develop a distance from themselves and the things they encounter, and are aware of experiencing things. This more reflective approach is considered more advanced than the initial naïve stage, and in it the simplistic beliefs of the first stage are condemned and disparaged. A second naïvete can be achieved at a further level of maturity, in which it is understood that the childlike understandings of the first stage are considered to have more validity than initially realized, and which synthesizes the first two stages (ibid., pp. 10–12).

The whole of Western culture could be described as having gone through these stages, with the first naïve stage consisting of prehistory through to the end of the medieval, the reflective stage covering the renaissance/enlightenment/reformation through to the modern, and the second naïvete represented by the postmodern or liquid age. A reflective approach to religion is given primacy by many religious traditions in the west, an intellectual distance being at the heart of Western concepts of modernity and rational understanding.

The separation of oneself from one's experiences has created a modernistic intellectual distance and disconnection that has created a homelessness that postmodern popular cults have acted upon by providing homes and cultures for young people in particular. Pop cults have provided for many a bridge across, or escape from, the crisis of Fowler's fourth stage, in which increasing numbers of those within Western culture have found themselves stuck, having no rituals or trusted religious traditions to guide them into the transcendence and through the paradoxes of twenty-first-century life. Pop cults have offered a reconnection with the body, and communal experiences of transcendence, that give a glimpse of a different world than the disenchanted modern existence. This has been seen in particular in the chapter on EDMC trance cults, but is also the case in other pop cults.

Swindler and Modjes (ibid.) further describe how the arts in particular are able to use metaphor, symbol and images (and indeed music) to engage directly with issues of spirituality, meaning, identity and existence in a way that words and distanced thought cannot, giving as an example the way that love can be expressed more readily in a poem or song than in prose. Thus it is perhaps not surprising that in an era when leaders of religious traditions are out of touch with contemporary culture, that pop cults should arise to take their place.

Religions are also described in this passage as often stuck in a religious level that is lower than that of contemporary culture. Indeed many within Western culture bypass the first stage very quickly, led by a modern education that encourages a reflective approach to existence. While fundamentalist religions are often characterized as being naïve, and liberal traditions as overly reflexive and distanced from the experiential, contemporary culture is full of well understood symbols, experiences, meanings and practices, and thus offers a more advanced approach to belief. This is because those who lead traditional religious groups are often conservative by nature, which keeps them within these first two levels, unwilling to go through the crisis necessary to advance further. Those that do advance beyond the first two stages experience in the crisis stage a disillusionment with mainstream religious traditions, and when moving on see traditional religions that are set in these first two stages, and have little of interest to offer. If they return to religious practice, they tend to do so within contexts such as NRMs, new age movements, or indeed pop cults.

These cults of popular music are not simply empty religion-like structures, that they are regarded as a secondary rather than primary religions does not mean they have any less impact or meaning to those participating. They are not simply some kind of opiates for young people. They do not quieten the populace, they do not act to simply subdue, to dull the pain of everyday life, in fact they are often signs of rebellion, of noise making in opposition to everyday life. Contemporary cults of the sacred popular offer social construction on the terms of the participant. They are constructed within popular culture, and therefore do not have enforced dogma, do not have literature that attempts to enforce behaviours. Instead they offer opportunities for connection, for interaction.

Sex is of course a fundamental form of human interaction, and a vital part of human culture. Sex leads to birth, is the ultimate act of creativity, as it can create life. The moment of sexual ecstasy is a moment of loss, of dissolution of self and joining with another. The neurochemicals released at the moment of orgasmic joy allows one to connect with the other and the self, and has much in common with moments of religious ecstasy or musical entrancement. Sex is addressed specifically in pop cults like that of Madonna; is an issue for boy and girl bands and teen stars; is part of the media personality construction of many pop icons; is referred to in rock and metal culture; is part of the ecstasy culture of electronic dance music; and is part of the pop cult holy trinity of sex, drugs and rock'n'roll. This phrase first appeared in this specific form in the Ian Dury and the Blockheads song 'Sex and Drugs and Rock and Roll', although sex, drugs and music had been discussed together many times before this in relation to pop and rock music. Shortened to 'sex, drugs and rock'n'roll', it provides an idealized shorthand view of the life of a popular musician.

Like sex, drugs are associated with many types of popular music cults. Pop drug cults have tried to establish cultures that are built around drug-induced mystical and transcendent ritualized music-based experiences. The ritualization of this drug taking attempts to place it in a social context, which restricts and contains it, and attempts to try to make these practices less dangerous and less potentially harmful. Pop drug cults are not simply a safe place for the dulling of pain, at least not all of them are, they are intended to be a safe place for drug-induced mystical experiences. Popular possession and electronic dance music cults have tried to reconnect with groups of people, to build collective effervescence and communitas. They have attempted to connect directly with other people, to join groups of people together mystically.

Electronic dance music has drug taking more significantly woven into the communal trance cult rituals at its core than other pop cults in which drugs enhance rather than embody the experience. Pop cults involving drugs are dangerous places full of illegality and risk, where many journeys and choices can, and do, lead to death. Death cults are not only a nihilistic self-destructive worship of a taboo subject, but also a way to address the mortality of humans. Pop death cults have tried to reconnect with the ancestors, and the past. They have also tried to connect with the shade, with the shadow, with the dark side of the human character. They are also often the likely result of pop icons living out their own mythologies. These mythologies are usually based on personality cults revolving around semi-fictional mediaphemes constructed from an exaggeration of the stars' real personality in order to achieve the level of pop icon within the sacred popular. Personality cults have tried to re-establish the roles of Gods and prophets as role models to direct our behaviour.

Pop teen idols, boy and girl bands and cartoon and virtual bands like S Club 7 and the Spice Girls, the Monkees and Gorrilaz take this personality cult system to its logical conclusion, inventing a band in some cases that is only present as a fictional media construction, blurring the boundaries between reality and fiction by appearing on television, in films and in concert. Virtual cults have attempted to create virtual worlds to connect into, in the context of an online world.

The local cult offers a sense of community, of locality. Local cults have tried to reconnect to the regional in a globalized world. The commercialism of many of these local cults is not necessarily a sign that such locality cannot be sustained, but an indicator of the need for, and success of, local cult popular music scenes. Hip hop, punk, Madchester, Merseybeat and the new Yorkshire have all become hugely successful musical scenes that have developed from a small localized beginning. Other scenes develop and have a strong local following but never expand into mainstream success.

That these areas such as sexuality, drug taking, death, locality and trance are at the core of cults of popular music, indicates their importance within human culture. In each of these cults it is connection that is often sought. The modern experiment begun with the enlightenment is over, and popular culture is reaching out to mend and replace the broken and lost rituals of community that have been allowed to fall into disrepair in the twenty-first century. Within a globalized world, music celebrates and expresses the local offering mediated pockets of locality that can be engaged with from any point.

Pop cults encourage individuality of expression within a globalized culture, yet also encourage connection with one's surrounding immediate environment, with place and the planet. In a western culture in which mind/body duality has treated the physical as secondary and surrounded sexuality with guilt and control, popular music cults have acted to offer broader and more liberal approaches to sexuality, where the individual is free to act as they choose and the meaningfulness of sex is not lost within a repressive mindset. Indeed in many ways pop cults of the sacred popular are about freedom from control, about expressing freedom from the traditional controls placed on popular culture by hegemonic society.

This does not mean that these cults are free from negative values, risks, dangers or problems. They have many of these. Many of these risky behaviours lead to death, and the valorization of those who have died in part from the pressures of their fans to serve them is a complex issue. Stars have been made to sacrifice themselves so that their fans can live vicariously through them. However these stars have often expressed their pleasure in this particular role, and again this underlines that the star does not control their audience any more than the audience control them, that there is a sense of hegemonic negotiation in this situation.

The role of the music industry in manipulating these relationships is also complex, as it often exaggerates, mythologizes or damages popular cults while seeking to commercialize and profit from them. As a result of this commercialization, local cults may become international movements, and then may lose their connection with their sources. Any religious tradition usually begins with a local cult, Christianity and Islam certainly did for example. Those that are considered to have merit grow, those that have something to offer, will become successful, and those that have no relevance fail.

We are in a transitional phase, where some religious traditions, more suited to a different era, are dying off rapidly, while other new religions are being born. Religions such as Christianity are trying to negotiate how much can be retained and how much must be given up if they are to survive, and whether it is possible to adapt to a liquid world without losing the essence of what the core of their faith means. In some cases, issues of control have so come to dominate a tradition that this has made the entire belief system unpalatable or lacking credibility.

Christianity, for example, has lost connection with the culture of contemporary society due to the conservative tastes of those in power within the organization. These conservative forces have not kept in touch with changes in culture and the changing ethical choices that have happened at the same time. With musical, dramatic and dance traditions that are largely out of touch with contemporary culture, Christianity is a good example of a religion that has lost its ability to offer opportunities for collective effervescence and communitas that the majority of the populace feels it can participate and engage in. Experiments in using elements of popular culture in Church services have failed to be adopted by an aging population of Christian leaders and members, who are fighting a losing battle to keep the status quo rather than moving forwards into the new reformation that is needed if Christianity is to remain a significant religion in the future. Theologian Matthew Fox (2006) has written of the need for a reawakening of the Christian spirit and a repudiation of the authoritarian, punitive tendencies that prevail in modern churches today. Greg Ogden (1991) has suggested that the priesthood of all believers is one of Luther's original reformations that was never fully addressed by the Christian church. Both call for a new reformation, and imply that Luther was calling for a sacred popular in which all participate equally in religious practice, attacking the hierarchies of religious traditions, much as Jesus Christ did.

This book indicates that religion is not merely the opium of the masses, some kind of delusion, but an important human communicative technology. It is not the reliance on some mysterious false other to make decisions in replacement of one's own responsibility, it is not looking for ghosts and spirits, at least not within the sacred popular. As culture has been individualized, our music experience has been individualized and atomized. The use of the iPod, the solitary experience of music with earphones plugged in, is the antithesis of the group bonding seen in so many pop cults. When one sees a subway train full of individuals tuned into their own soundworld, small white headphones in their ears, one realizes that this kind of music technology has the power to stop people communicating and interacting, rather than help them to do so.

Simon Frith (1996) defines three stages of the storage of music, the storage of music by memory in the body (the folk stage), the storage of music by notation (the art stage) and finally the storage of music via recordings (the pop stage). In 1985 in *File Under Popular*, Cutler describes musical history into three "modes" of production, 'The "folk" era/mode, based on memory and oral/aural transmission; the "art/classical" mode, based on music notation; and the "new", or popular mode, based on sound recording' (Horner and Swiss 1999, p. 212). In this new or popular mode, the text of the music is the recording, not the sheet music of the song.

In 1985, Jacques Attali discussed three similar stages of music in his book *Noise: The Political Economy of Music*. However Attali also describes a fourth stage, which he predicted would emerge in the future, where music would begin to be again made for pleasure, and is taken gradually away from commerce. This seems to be happening today, as computer music technology allows musicians to record music at little cost in their homes, the myspace revolution allows thousands of musicians to publish their music online for free, and i-tunes, downloads and file-sharing sites also are beginning to deregulate the music industry. In addition the pop cults studied show that popular music is not merely commerce, but integrated into a more complex nexus of belief and meaning.

The religion of pop cults is a vital ritual technology for connection. Modernity, enlightenment thinking, has been about individuation, or at least has led to a reductionist individualization. It focuses upon how the individual mind works. All must be provable in some way by the individual rational mind, this represents Fowler's fourth individuative/reflective stage, and Swindler and Modjes' reflexive middle stage, as already discussed. These stages of belief work as well for secular stages of development as those within religious traditions.

In post-enlightenment liquid culture, equivalent to the later stages under both systems of stages of faith, there is recognition of the need for reconnection, for that which is bodily, that comes from experience, and emotional and physical intelligence, rather than only a rational understanding. Physical intelligence, the understanding of being comfortable with one's body, comfortable in one's skin, is as important within liquidity as being intellectually rationally argued and correct. Popular culture has begun to create its own religions that address these dynamics, which are placed within a sacred popular as secularization is the dominant belief at present. As music is a key element, a key technology for ritual and for community construction, music has been a significant focus of this rebuilding of meaning, this reconnection, this re-enchantment, this reconstruction. Because popular music is at the centre of popular culture, especially youth culture, it has had an important role in this process.

These socially constructive elements of human culture have always existed within religion, and religion has existed in part to provide these social functions, because they are needed for society to operate effectively. Humans need agreed systems of ethics, philosophy and rituals, in order to bond societies together, to stop them from becoming atomized. Otherwise they can become self-obsessed, interested only in individual gain, and a ruthless capitalism can result, consumer culture run away with no controls. The global financial crisis that has developed at the end of the first decade of the twenty-first century has shown that uncontrolled capitalism based on endless growth is not an effective system. There needs to be some kind of counterbalance, some negotiation, in order to ensure a balance between the priorities of the individual and the group. Cults of popular music are one such counterbalance.

These cults even intervene in some cases in capitalist society, the most obvious example being the charity record phenomenon. Large-scale fundraising concerts activities such as Band Aid, Live Aid and Live Earth see pop stars intervening in the work of charities and politicians. Band Aid's record releases, and the associated Live Aid concerts, gathered the most celebrated popular icons of the 1980s together to raise money to support victims of a drought in Ethiopia. Charity is something often associated with religions, and it is again interesting to consider popular music's intervention into feeding the hungry. The enormous power and authority of popular icons brought together en masse, was able to raise huge amounts of money for charity.

Michael Jackson and Prince were involved in writing the USA for Africa song 'We are the World', but declined performing in the concert; Led Zeppelin reformed for a one-off performance; David Bowie and Mick Jagger released a version of the Motown song 'Dancing in the Streets'; a host of the leading pop stars of the UK, including Paul Young, Sting, George Michael, Boy George, Simon Le Bon, Bono and Tony Hadley took it in turns to sing lines on the UK

Band Aid single 'Do They Know It's Christmas?' and performed live in the UK along with rock bands Queen, Elton John and Status Quo. The Band Aid T-Shirt had 'this T-shirt saves lives' printed on it. The Live Aid concert was shown around the world, with simultaneous concerts in London and Philadelphia.

The concert was a powerful event. In the UK, after the final chorus of 'Do They Know It's Christmas', the audience carried on singing the last line, 'feed the world, let them know it's Christmas time again' for at least ten minutes as they left Wembley stadium. Pop star Bob Geldof of the Boomtown Rats managed to convince the world that pop stars were not just entertainers, but could reach out and save lives. Rather than governments or religions stepping in to provide aid in this situation, that pop stars used the cults of their personalities to successfully call upon huge numbers of people to give money, shows the enormous power they have the potential to wield. A follow up concert and single in 2004, Band Aid 20, was more ambitious, aiming to convince world leaders to write off the debt of African countries. Those who sang a lead line in Live Aid or performed at Band Aid were established within a canon of deified pop stars, whose fame and recordings careers were boosted enormously, and whose cults were established or enhanced.

It is clear that popular music has enormous power. If cults of popular music are not NRMs then what are they? They are clearly more important than 'just' entertainment. It is no longer normative in Western European societies in particular to grant authority to Christianity or any other religion to make moral and ethical decisions and decrees on the behalf of a person. In the past it was more normal for religions to be trusted to be specialists in this area. Many years of tradition and expertise were gathered, maintained and expressed by a priestly class who had the authority to wield such power and responsibility. From another perspective, this priestly class would take such power, and use it to control the people who are members of their religious organization. Both perspectives on these dynamics were operating to some extent simultaneously, and there was a negotiation between the two, between the audience and performer, between the congregation and priest.

As religious practice declined after World War II, members of popular culture in an increasingly postmodern culture looked less to mainstream religions to provide them with moral guidance on ethical decisions, and with advice on what to do in times of difficulty. The area that many people looked to instead was often music. Bob Dylan was often described as the voice of a generation in a 1960s of young Westerners who were looking for someone who understood their perspective, and who they could relate to. The world wars, the religious obedience, and the moral conservatism of a previous generation had been blown away by the permissive society associated with rock'n'roll, aided by the open passions of the popular music of the 1960s, along with the peace movement and left-wing politics of the growing counter-culture.

John Lennon became an important leader for young people. With its transcendental drug experiences caused by LSD, ecstatic mystical experiences triggered by all night dancing, and communal concert and festival experiences, 1960s and 1970s popular music was where youth culture looked to in order to construct meaning and identity, in order to feel part of something, to feel a sense of belonging, to understand a person's place within society and culture, to place themselves and relate to others, to feel less alone and more connected.

Whether one agrees that pop cults are religions, depends to some extent on one's definition of religion. This book aims to make an important point, which is not dependant on agreeing that pop cults are religions or religious. By discussing popular music as a series of cults, whether one considers this an accurate description or not, one points out the significance of popular music and the culture that surrounds it within liquid or postmodern culture. This book has aimed to identify that elements of popular musical culture are fulfilling some of the roles that were previously associated with religions. It has aimed to describe this in some detail, and to understand what is happening more fully. The study of religion has terminology and a historic perspective that is useful in this analysis, whether one believes or not that these pop cults are religions is perhaps not as important as an understanding of the significance that they hold for participants.

Perhaps more important still is a consideration of what it means for this to be the case, of what it means that it is within popular music culture that these functions are being fulfilled, rather than within mainstream religions. This has implications for our understanding of the definition of religion, community and meaning. It also has political implications for the control of moral and ethical decisions within our cultures. It is important that this process does not happen in a subconscious and little understood manner. If communal and ecstatic experiences are going to be contextualized within popular music culture rather than mainstream religions, then this is something that should be known, understood and considered.

Mainstream religions are in many ways out of touch with contemporary Western culture, and therefore their rituals, music and culture are such that they are often not effective in helping members of youth culture experience the divine or transcendental. In the West religions have traditionally been controlled by priests who were chosen from the educated classes, and who held religious knowledge in a world where few could read written religious texts. They therefore held a power to act as a negotiator between God and a congregation. The interpretation of these written texts, and the choices of which texts have been adopted canonically by a religion, are processes that are now more widely understood, in a culture where education has come to the masses. They are revealed as processes that are deeply political, and driven by the interests of those who have control or power.

Popular culture has turned away from these politically elitist systems of belief construction, cosmology and moral authority, and has chosen to look elsewhere for a sense of meaning, for feelings of well-being, belonging and self-construction. However, while religions were constructed in order to explore these issues, and their traditions have many years of expertise and consideration of these areas, the music industry has the generation of money at its centre, and shadowy figures such as managers and marketing teams lurk behind the scenes, trying to manipulate the way fans behave and spend.

The music industry has two overtly different faces, one that presents itself to the public as an art form, and another that exists as a behind-the-scenes business, to organize, market and promote its products. The music industry makes few attempts to present itself as morally or ethically just, and it does not hide that it is there to make money and not to enrich the lives of its customers. It does not claim to be a religion, and few in the music industry would suggest that it is what should replace religions as the centre of community and meaning. It does not hide particularly carefully that it is deceptive, and that it creates falsehood.

It is also the case however, that religious traditions are full of stories that are clearly myths or parables, and full of methods of raising money to provide religious services. The press is often full of the latest revelation about the behaviour of a priest, whether a sexual peccadillo or a financial impropriety. Perhaps the music industry is simply more open and honest about its failures, or perhaps by being presented as secular, its behaviour is not judged as a religion might. In any case this subject raises complex ethical issues.

There are few secular rituals that are carefully chosen and constructed for non-commercial purposes, and that aim to provide replacements for outdated religious rituals that are no longer relevant in contemporary culture. There are also few examples of religious cultures that have taken seriously the cultural needs and changes of contemporary culture. There are however some interesting examples that warrant discussion.

Buddhism has developments like the Friends of the Western Buddhist Order, which integrates contemporary music into its ritual culture. There is even a Buddhafields festival in the UK, which is part religious retreat or festival, and part music festival with bands, club events and a range of workshops exploring issues relating to a broad range of spiritual and religious beliefs and practices, including but not restricted to Buddhism. A particularly interesting practice called ecstatic dance takes place at this festival. Jewls Wingfield (http://www.heart-tantra.com) leads very ritualized participatory club events, with directive instructions. This has some similarities to the five rhythms dance techniques pioneered by Gabrielle Roth (http://www.gabrielleroth.com/). Roth states on her website that when dancing 'the body becomes our spiritual path'.

Wingfield's approach is somewhat different however, in being built around a DJ set. Participants are instructed to close their eyes; dance with a partner exploring touch with the ends of their fingertips; explore mirroring of movement with another person; and in general to build emotional bonds between participants through a number of dance-based exercises. Music is chosen which suits each section, and one climactic point at the event, for example, features women and then men separately dancing as a group in the centre of the space, surrounded by the other group. These ecstatic dance events are hugely popular, and massively oversubscribed, offering a mix of complimentary therapy, dance therapy, Tantra, personal development and a club event. It makes explicit many of the dynamics that are implicitly present in EDMC events, but carefully controls and structures them, rather than allowing complete freedom to participants.

Similar examples from within Christianity are the Nine O'Clock Service and the alternative worship movement, which have blended popular music culture and Christian worship (Till 2006) through services which used EDMC music, were held in nightclubs, or used rock band or ambient music. These have had a limited impact on Christianity as a whole however, although they show how much similarity there is between pop cults and organized religions. The use of arts technologies in this context is particularly interesting, and the focus on music and moving images on screens brought organized religion in contact with liquid culture, and had the potential to be very different from the text based worship events that are more common.

Written religious texts act as the foundation of many religions, and often provide the basis of ethical and moral codes, as well as being supposedly static and set foundations on which the religions are based. Deities personify goodness, all that that is aspired to, they personify the most positive or desired elements of human character and abilities. They personify the universe and allow connection to the ideal. Cosmology also helps us to understand our relationship to the universe, and the planet. Spirituality helps us to understand how we relate to other people. Religious practice helps people to establish, maintain and explore self-control, using prayer, chanting, fasting and other approaches. Mysticism helps people to explore being out of control, instinct and how to live in the moment. Different forms of prophesy help us to think about the future, to plan, explore and express hopes about what might happen. Priestly castes have professionalized, sustained and developed all of these processes.

Faith develops hope and optimism. The making divine of human figures, whether as manifestations of the deity as humans or human like-figures, or through ascribing various levels of holiness to individuals such as prophets or saints, has allowed role-models to be chosen and promoted. Rulers of countries have often been chosen from within religious organizations. Prayer has offered the opportunity for groups of individuals to cement their agreement about what they would like to happen, and to offer support for those in need of encouragement. Pastoral support and charity has cared for those in need, as well as providing simple versions of social care and psychotherapy. Healing has been offered by religious traditions in many cases. Education was often developed around religions, schools were part of the work of churches, and Universities often developed from study by religious orders. Thus, religion fulfils a variety of different tasks within society.

As the human technologies of culture and society have advanced, a number of these functions have been replaced as methods or practices within religions have been surpassed by more effective and reliable approaches. Belief in a supernatural god has been discredited as a scientific worldview has grown to become the dominant belief of human culture. The functions of religion have become increasingly discredited as some of the more superstitious or conservative traditions within religions have become widely disavowed. Religions have presented themselves as all or nothing, as a complete systematic approach to life, rather than a set of functions and practices developed as social technology, and selected as useful from a range of possibilities, and thus have largely ruled themselves out of postmodernity.

Religion is itself a form of technology. It is social technology, but this is as much a technology as any other. As certain parts of the technology that is religion became outdated, instead of it being updated, as one might expect, the entire technology has been abandoned en masse by large elements of the population. Religions served a number of functions within society. Ritual activities served to bond groups together by a shared experience in which the perception of the boundaries between individuals were softened, and the individual was able to merge into a group. This led to the loss of their self-hood to some extent, and their subsequent re-emerging having been reinserted into the group. This provided a way of exploring the relationships between self and the other. When connected to the divine at the same time as others, one could connect with an idealized version of oneself, and use the divinity as a common place to share such an experience. Personification of devils, demons and evil gods allowed people to explore their shades, the shadow elements of their characters, in a safe context that kept these elements under control.

As education and literacy has spread, the general public have come to understand that written religious texts are not as set in stone as religious authorities have claimed. It has become clear that the Christian bible for example has been shaped and formed by choices by political and other interests. The books that were put together to make the Bible were chosen for particular reasons, and others were left out, as has been discussed in the popular book *The Da Vinci Code* (Brown 2003) which was bought by millions of readers. There are numerous translations of the Bible that were created to satisfy the particular agendas of different theological opinions.

In 'From Work to Text' (1977) and in subsequent works, Roland Barthes has discussed the idea that instead of discussing a work by an author, which is set and defined, it is more relevant to discuss a text, which can have different meanings depending on how it is interpreted by an audience, thus we think of texts as being performed. In contemporary postmodern society, many things can be perceived as texts, including different kinds of performances, including popular music recordings. It is clear that there are many different ways to perceive these texts, and thus it is difficult for a religion (such as Christianity) that still claims that God is the author of a work like the Bible that is authoritative, to thrive within such a system.

Thus, the old technology of traditional religions has been abandoned by increasingly large sections of society. One might compare this with the move from vinyl records to digital recordings. Instead of using vinyl records, this old format has become discredited, and is seen as incompatible with contemporary approaches to playing recordings. Thus many music playback systems no longer have the capability to play such media, because they are discredited and old fashioned. Record players have been replaced by CD players and iPod docks. Some traditionalists still insist on using vinyl, but they are dying out year by year. Some people have a foot in both camps, able to use each where necessary. Many young people have either no experience or awareness of vinyl recordings, and many adults have simply moved on to more pragmatic solutions. Traditional religions are thus much like vinyl recordings, being replaced by new technologies.

It is no longer taken on faith that religions are able to offer the best answers in most cases, although they were seen as authoritative in the past. Scientific testing has offered evidence that other methods and sources of answers that have no connection to religions are preferable. Scientists are perhaps more often trusted to produce answers than those in control of religions. This has been driven in part by religions claiming certain things to be true, and proof subsequently showing that these things are incorrect, such as the world not being flat, or the Earth going around the Sun rather than vice versa. The reformation sought to remove the idea that any human religious authority, including the pope, was irrefutable and infallible. In our society, evidence is usually required that things are true, useful or would work, rather than religious authorities being trusted implicitly.

In Western culture, doctors rather than faith healers or witch doctors now usually control healing of the body, although some alternative therapists are still associated with spirituality. Psychologists and psychotherapists offer treatment for those with psychological problems, offering solutions based on documented evidence of their effectiveness. The needy are cared for by centrally funded social programmes rather than by charity, those who need to talk over their problems approach state funded or recognized counselling services rather than religious figures.

In the west, rulers are now chosen by popular vote; role-modes are chosen from popular culture and often reflect style as much as achievements or impeccable behaviour; faith and belief come from trust in evidence; prophecy is based on computer models or statistical likelihood; and priests have been replaced by politicians, philosophers and teachers. Mass education and both the distribution of information and open access to it have allowed individuals to make up their own minds rather than rely on the opinion of someone else. Whole industries have developed around replacing the functions served in the past by religions. This can be seen for example in the self-help and dieting books sold as a way of aiding self-control, and in the way that religious practices like yoga are often being presented as a secular practice.

Secular culture has not entirely managed to successfully replace all of the functions formally fulfilled by religions. It is still the case that a number of these supposedly secularized functions are not entirely so. Charitable giving is still dominated by organizations with religious traditions; counsellors are often part of religious organizations, even when working for secular organizations; the house of Lords of the UK parliament still has Christian bishops sitting in it; and in the USA the religious persuasion of political candidates, including the president, is an important factor.

In the main, Western cosmology is now largely governed by the religion-like dogmaticism of science, which claims a monopoly on truth. Like a traditional religion, science often presents itself as absolutely authoritative. However, the more fundamental the questions about the nature of the universe asked by science, the greater the amount revealed about the similarities between science and other religions or belief systems. Many scientific questions are considered proven on the basis that results achieve a level of statistical probability. This would mean that results are 80 percent, 90 percent or 95 percent probable, rather than absolutely true. Science rarely proves anything absolutely but only provides evidence that it is probable to a certain level, that the scientist themselves decide is acceptable. What is presented as scientific certainty is usually only actually a level of probability, often with numerous caveats. Often various other considerations have to be assumed to be correct, or not of relevance, in order for results to be accurate, numerous other variables have to be ignored, considered irrelevant or not discussed.

Science is particularly good at describing what is happening, and using that description in order to make things work. It is not very good at explaining in detail why it is happening, at fundamentally explaining things. For example, gravity is still a somewhat mysterious force that we still do not understand. Scientists have described how it behaves in such detail that humans are able to send rockets into space and back, but this does nothing to explain why it is like this. When one looks at the more complex operation of gravity across the universe, we understand less, and special relativity and general relativity are two theories that should link together but don't. Scientists believe (have faith) that one day a unified field theory will be possible, a theory of everything which will link the two theories together. Belief in this posited theory is a good example of religious belief within science.

Many other unproven theories are presented as facts. Einstein showed that time, previously thought of as constant, is in fact relative to how fast one is travelling, but time is still a complex and little understood phenomena. The big bang is an important part of contemporary cosmology. An educated guess of sorts, there is no actual proof that it is correct. It also often involves discussion of a prime mover, an initial force that caused the universe to come into existence. This is remarkably similar to the Christian idea that the Godhead created the universe out of nothing, the prime mover that caused the big bang is a linguistic construction that aims to take control of cosmology, our understanding of the universe, from the hands of the religious authorities and place it in the control of scientists. This is understandable, especially since religious authorities have often clung to outdated traditions despite evidence to the contrary, but scientists are often replacing one dogma with another.

Dark matter, the Higgs-Boson particle, superstrings at the centre of every particle, are all theoretical constructs. They do not exist in our reality, only in the imaginations of scientists, and since they cannot be proven to exist, they are surely more related to faith or religion than any kind of objective truth. This is also the case for the statistically possible multiple splintered universes said to exist according to another scientific theory, or the indeterminate statistical existence of Shroedinger's famous cat in its unopened box. Science is built on predictability, the idea that an experiment will have the same result every time, and that results are predictable and reproducible. Chaos theory has problematized this idea, as it tells us that many systems are not predictable, but chaotic, and that the universe may be far more chaotic and unpredictable than previously thought.

The big bang is still only one theory, and the more one discovers about it, the more problematic it seems. Rupert Sheldrake (1998) has pointed out that the first few seconds of the big bang are very complicated, and he is regarded as a heretical scientist. It seems that there was a time in the first seconds of the big bang, where there was no gravity, where atoms were not attracted to one another. He suggests that studying this moment implies that so called laws of physics all had to come into existence for the big bang theory to hold up. Gravity, it seems, may be more like a habit, so ingrained into probability and the universe that it seems like a law. Sheldrake expands his theories to discuss such habits as morphic fields, a theory that can be expanded to describe numerous other elements of the universe as fields. Even people can be described as fields, as they can interact and affect one another without contact, much like the effect of a magnetic field, which reaches out beyond the 'body' of a magnet. Sheldrake's theories go on to discuss human abilities that are much like extra-sensory perception or psychic abilities.

I have discussed these ideas to point out that simple, clear boundaries between extremes such as religion and science, the secular and sacred or the real and imaginary, are becoming less clear as we discover more about the universe. A religious metaphor like the music of the spheres has much in common with superstring theory. The big bang is not so different to the beginning of the Bible's creation story. Dark matter, black holes and anti-matter are unseen powers of great magnitude that are potentially dangerous or the antithesis of the light, much like religious 'dark powers'. Fields are conceptually much like souls.

Science is often increasingly like philosophy or religion. In addition the moral implications and repercussions of scientific discoveries such as genetic technology are complex and controversial, drawing science into discussion of ethics, meaning and belief. Much as some of the cosmological and ethical roles and fields of religion have been replaced by science in contemporary culture, some of the social and communal fields of religion have been replaced by cults of popular music. While fundamentalist religions have remained in the child-like naïve first stage of development of religious consciousness, modern science has often been rooted in the second reflective stage. A truly mature postmodern religion or science that has reached the third stage of maturity understands and embraces the links between the two. Pop cults exist in all three of these stages of religious consciousness, and interact with both secular scientifically driven reflective culture and the naïve but direct experiential world of the religious.

Popular music cults and culture have enormously enriched our lives, just as science has enriched our cosmological understanding of the universe. They have impacted upon the way we sustain relationships with one another, our spirituality, offering popular philosophy through its lyrics, and facilitating social interaction through dancing, concerts and mood and scene setting. Pop cults help disconnected postmodern individuals connect to one another and to their inner selves. They offer opportunities for self-loss, transcendental and mystical experiences. They allow communities to be developed and the individual to be reinserted into these communities. They re-enchant and reconstruct a disenchanted, deconstructed world.

They lack a coherent, consistent system, the purpose, direction, history, maturity and co-ordination that mainstream religions offer. They offer instead cults that do not demand a specific set of dogma, that do not need to be rigidly obeyed, instead offering fields that can be negotiated and navigated in a way that can be chosen by the individual. This means that the individual retains control of the power dynamics involved. They also retain responsibility for their own decisions, in a system where their transcendental, interpersonal, internal and/or individual interaction with the divine is directly experienced. Such experiences may be mediated by another person but usually remain within their own control.

Relationships with the body have been underdeveloped in both scientific and religious worldviews that are coloured by the body mind dialectic. This duality has coloured both the supposed objectivity of science and the spirituality and mysticism of religion. Pop cults involve powerfully embodied experiences, and explore many subjects related to physicality and considered taboo by mainstream religious traditions.

It is important to note that pop cults are far from perfect, and contain many negative attributes. Saints and religious figures have been replaced in pop cults by pop stars and celebrities who are found lacking as role models in many ways. It is perhaps their humanity and fallibility that makes them particularly attractive. Negative behaviours and dangerous practices are often presented as more acceptable than is normal in society by these popular icons. It is difficult to assess whether pop cults have encouraged a more positive and free, less guilt-ridden society, or a permissiveness in which crime, antisocial behaviour and misbehaviour are seen as more acceptable, whether we are more open and less repressive about our shadow sides, or if we no longer have adequate systems in place to discipline this side of our characters. It is probable that all these dynamics are active, rather than just one of each binary pair. In addition many long developed, powerful and useful practices of complex wisdom traditions have been abandoned and replaced by pop cults that are enmeshed in the music industry's commercial practices.

The definition of religion has been deregulated within postmodernity, just as most definitions have been deregulated. For some people this is negative, especially when cultural formations like religion and the arts are linked with commercial entities. For writers such as Adorno (1990) this is corporate commerce taking control of and abusing the power of cultural forms in order to have influence over a populace of consumers, in order to cynically sell more products. This perspective berates what Lyon (2000) might call the the disneyfication, or Ritzer (1993) might call the McDonaldization of culture, which will lead to a beaurocratized or rationalized control of the many by the few.

This is a culturally pessimistic perspective, assuming that consumers have no control and will blindly follow the lead of the multi-million dollar marketing departments of big business. For others, such as postmodern theorist Suzi Gablik (1991), postmodernity offers a culturally optimistic change in direction. As she puts it,

> a new paradigm of an engaged, participatory and socially relevant art is emerging ... bringing art back into a more vernacular, everyday world, and taking it out of the more rarefied sphere of professionalism. (Gablik 1998)

Brian Longhurst (1995, pp. 20–1) has discussed how Gramsci's concept of negotiation offers a middle ground between these two extremes. This perspective suggests that control resides within popular music, neither entirely in the hands of the music industry corporations who have to follow the wants and needs of their customers, nor in the musicians or audiences who have to work within the constraints of the music industry, but that control is negotiated in a complicated dance that involves many partners, and is different in the various sectors and subgenres of popular music cults and culture.

Again and again we have seen pop cults being based around deified individuals, who are associated with experiences of the divine or presented as superhuman. These leaders are often separated and treated differently than other participants, who seem to unquestioningly follow the lead of these popular icons. Cult membership has involved very high levels of commitments, and this has sometimes been isolationist, and created an 'us-verus-them' mentality. There have often been particular traditions of dress code, haircut, make-up and other elements of image involved. Entry into the cult may have been difficult, and may have involved a number of levels of participation and initiation, with practices often somewhat secretive.

Pop cults have often involved brainwashing-type activities, including strong peer pressure, the use of excessive repetition and drug taking. Drug taking and other practices have been used within pop cults to achieve altered states of consciousness or perception. Other practices, as well as drug taking, that are considered outside of 'normal' behaviour, have often been present. There have often been unusual sexual dynamics involved. Participation in the cult has often involved a substantial amount of money being spent, and the maximizing of the level of consumption by participants has been promoted by those involved. Cults have often been linked to a particular locality.

Pop cults have been associated with deaths, suicides and murders. Many pop cults have been characterized by reference to new forms of Paganism, such as Witchcraft, Druidry, Wicca, Satanism and the like. Pop cults have been described as cults in many situations and analyses, both by participants themselves in some cases, and also by anti-cult and religious fundamentalist groups. The pop cults that have been investigated seem to fulfil all the usual characteristics of cults, and the term cult is perhaps more suited to use in this context, than to describe many of the NRMs that are often described as cults.

It is perhaps the sense of control that is different between pop cults and the sacred popular, and traditional religions. Pop cults have power and control deregulated to a local level. They identify difference from, as well as similarity to, the rest of the world. Traditional religions often place control largely at the centre of their organization, believers are expected to behave as they are told, whether this is by a religious leader, a religious text or a deity external to themselves. As Bauman (1993) described in his discussion of *Postmodern Ethics*, in postmodernity individuals have the responsibility themselves to make ethical decisions framed by their surroundings and context. However a secularized world provides little context for these decisions, few rituals for dealing with the complexities of human lives, and little opportunity for exploring the important perspectives of human spirituality, relationships and cosmology. The sacred popular, in contrast to many organized religions, offers the opportunity for individuals to explore subjects related to religion such as community, meaning, identity and transcendental experiences, while not only maintaining control over choice, but suggesting through the example of the semi-mythical lives of popular icons that anything is possible.

It has been useful for the purposes of this book to use the term cult to describe these music-based cultures within the sacred popular. I hope that I have shown that these are really NRMs, new religious traditions in all but name that are replacing old religious movements in a new postmodern era that is a third era of consciousness. Western human culture has moved from the naiveté of the prehistoric, dark ages and middle-ages, through the dissociative disenchantment of the overly reflexive renaissance, enlightenment, reformation to the end point of modernism, and emerged into the re-enchantment and reconstruction of the postmodern and liquid, and what I would describe rather than as a second naiveté as the conscious experiential, or educated mystical. In this new era new ways of understanding and relating to one another are needed, and in the void left by the old religious movements largely refusing to move into a new cultural reality, NRMs formed around popular music cults and cultures have played a part in developing a new sacred popular. This is the beginning of an era, and it is unclear how this will develop in the future. It is clear however that popular music is a vital and significant social force that we must investigate further if we are to understand how meaning is developing in Western culture.

Bibliography

Adorno, T. (1990), 'On popular music', in S. Frith and A. Goodwin (eds), *On Record*. London: Routledge, pp. 301–14.

Aldridge, D. and Fachner, J. (2006), *Music and Altered States: Consciousness, Transcendence, Therapy and Addiction*. London: Jessica Kingsley.

Ant, A. (2006), *Adam Ant, Stand and Deliver: The Autobiography*. London: Sidgewick and Jackson.

Attali, J. (1985), *Noise: The Political Economy of Music*. Minneapolis: University of Minnesota Press.

Auslander, P. (2006), 'Watch that man. David Bowie: Hammersmith Odeon, London, July 3, 1973', in Ian Inglis (ed.), *Performance and Popular Music: History, Place and Time*. Aldershot: Ashgate.

Axelrod, M. (1999), *Beatletoons: The Real Story Behind the Cartoon Beatles*. Pickens: Wynn.

Azerrad, M. (2001), *Our Band Could Be Your Life*. New York: Little, Brown and Company.

Bailey, E. (1997), *Implicit Religion in Contemporary Society*. Kampen: Kok Pharos.

Bailey, E. (2001), *The Secular Faith Controversy: Religion in Three Dimensions*. London: Continuum.

Bailey, E. (ed.) (2002), 'The notion of implicit religion: What it means, and does not mean', in *The Secular Quest for Meaning in Life: Denton Papers in Implicit Religion*. New York: Edwin Mellen Press.

Barthes, R. (ed.) (1977), 'From work to text', in *Image, Music, Text*. New York: Hill and Wang.

Baty, S. Paige (1995), *American Monroe: The Making of a Body Politic*. Berkeley: University of California Press.

Bauman, Z. (1993), *Postmodern Ethics*. Oxford: Blackwell.

Beadle, J. J. (1993), *Will Pop Eat Itself? Pop Music in the Soundbite Era*. London: Faber and Faber.

Becker, J. (2004), *Deep Listeners: Music Emotions and Trancing*. Indiana: Indiana University Press.

Bennett, A. (2000), *Popular Music and Youth Culture: Music, Identity and Place*. London: Macmillan.

194   Bibliography

Berman, M. (1981), *The Reenchantment of the World*. Ithaca: Cornell University Press.

Besancon, A. (2001), *The Forbidden Image: An Intellectual History of Iconoclasm*. Trans. Jane Marie Todd. Chicago: University of Chicago Press.

Bey, H. (1985), *T.A.Z.: The Temporary Autonomous Zone, Ontological Anarchy, Poetic Terrorism*. Brooklyn: Autonomedia.

Boorstin, D. (1987), *The Image: A Guide to Pseudo-Events in America*. New York: Vintage.

Brown, D. (2003), *The Da Vinci Code*. New York: Anchor.

Brunet, R. (1997). 'Anti-Christ in a black G-string', *Alberta Reports*, 24, (7).

Buxton, D. (1985), 'Rock music, the star system and the rise of consumerism', in V. Mosko and J. Wasco (eds), *The Critical Communications Review, Vol. III: Popular Culture and Media Events*. Norwood, NJ: Ablex, pp. 187–9.

Catholic Truth Society (1986), *New Religious Movements: A Challenge to the Church*. London: Catholic Truth Society.

Chastagner, C. (1999), 'The parents' music resource center: From information to censorship', *Popular Music*, 18, (2), 179–92.

Chernoff, J. M. (1979), *African Rhythm and African Sensibility: Aesthetics and Social Action in African Musical Idioms*. Chicago: University of Chicago Press.

Chion, M. (1994), *Audio Vision*. Trans. Claudia Gorbman. New York: Columbia University Press.

Chryssides, G. D. and Wilkins, M. Z. (2006), *A Reader in New Religious Movements*. London: Continuum.

Clayton, M., Sager, R. and Will, U. (2005), 'In time with the music: The concept of entrainment and its significance for ethnomusicology', *European Meetings in Ethnomusicology*, 11, 3–142.

Cloonan, M. (2007), *Popular Music and the State in the UK: Culture, Trade or Industry?* Aldershot: Ashgate.

Collins, T. (1995), *Rock Mr. Blues: The Life and Music of Wnonie Harris*. Milford, NH: Big Nickel.

Cooper, C. (1983), 'Prince: Someday your prince will come', *The Face*, June 1983.

Cooper, K. and Smay, D. (eds) (2001), *Bubblegum Music is the Naked Truth: The Dark History of Prepubescent Pop, from the Banana Splits to Britney Spears*. Port Townsend, WA: Feral House.

Cowan, D. E. and Bromley, D. G. (2008), *Cults and New Religions: A Brief History*. Oxford: Blackwell.

Cross. C. R. (2002), *Heavier than Heaven: A Biography of Kurt Cobain*. New York: Hyperion Books.

Curry, R. (1990), 'Madonna from Marilyn to Marlene – Pastiche and/or parody', *Journal of Film and Video*, 42, (2), 15–30.

Cutler, I. (1985), *File Under Popular: Theoretical and Critical Writings on Music*. London: November Books.

Davidson, B. (1966), *African Kingdoms*. New York: Time-Life Books.

Davis, E. (1999), *Techgnosis: Myth, Magic and Mysticism in the Age of Information*. New York: Three Rivers Press.

Davis, S. (1985), *Hammer of the Gods: The Led Zeppelin Saga*. New York: Berkley Publishing Group.

De Chant, D. (2002), *The Sacred Santa: Religious Dimensions of Consumer Culture*. Cleveland: The Pilgrim Press.

Decker, C. (1995), *Deep Trance and Ritual Beats* [CD liner notes]. London: Return to the Source.

Deehan, A. and Saville, E. (2003), *Calculating the Risk: Recreational Drug Use Among Clubbers in the South East of England*. London: Home Office Research Development and Statistics Directorate.

Demerath III, N. J. (2002), 'The sacred as surrogate: Notes on implicit A-religion', in Edward Bailey (ed), *The Secular Quest for Meaning in Life: Denton Papers in Implicit Religion*. New York: Edwin Mellen Press.

Durkheim, E. (1965), *The Elementary Forms of the Religious Life*. Orig. 1912.

Dyer, R. (1979), *Stars*. London: British Film Institute.

Ehrenreich, B. (2006), *Dancing in the Streets: A History of Collective Joy*. New York: Metropolitan. English translation by Joseph Swain: 1915. New York: The Free Press.

Finlan, S. and Kharlamov, V. (2006), *Theosis: Definition in Christian Theology*. Eugene, OR: James Clarke and Co. Ltd.

Fiske, J. (1988), *Television Culture*. London: Methuen.

Fowler, J. (1981), *Stages of Faith*. Philadelphia: Harper & Row.

Fox, M. (2006), *A New Reformation: Creation Spirituality and the Transformation of Christianity*. Rochester: Inner Traditions.

Freeman, W. (2000), 'A neurobiological role of music in social bonding', in N. L. Wallin, B. Merker and S. Brown (eds), *The Origins of Music*. Cambridge, MA: MIT Press.

French, J. J. (1993), in Bruce Pollock, 'Rock Climbing: Baseball', Guitar for the Practicing Musician, March 1989, p. 12, quoted in Robert Walser. *Running with the Devil: Power, gender and madness in heavy metal music*. Middletown, CT: Wesleyan.

Frith, S. (1981), *Sound Effects; Youth, Leisure, and the Politics of Rock 'n' Roll*. Constable: London.

Frith, S. (1996), *Performing Rites – On the Value of Popular Music*. Oxford: Oxford University Press.

Frith, S. and MacRobbie, A. (1990), 'Rock and sexuality', in A. Goodwin (ed.), *On Record: Rock, Pop and the Written Word*. New York: Pantheon.

Gablik, S. (1984), *Has Modernism Failed?* New York: Thames and Hudson.

Gablik, S. (1991), *The Reenchantment of Art*. New York: Thames and Hudson.

Gablik, S. (1998), *New Renaissance magazine*, 8, (1), Renaissance Universal.

Garber, M. B. (1997), *Vested Interests: Cross-Dressing and Cultural Anxiety*. New York: Routledge.

Gauthier, F. (2004), 'Rapturous ruptures: The "instituant" religious experience of Rave', in Graham St. John (ed.), *Rave Culture and Religion*. Abingdon: Routledge, pp. 65–84.

Gauthier, F. (2005), 'Orpheus and the underground: Raves and implicit religion – From interpretation to critique', *Implicit Religion*, 8/3, 217–65.

Gettings, F. (1982), *Dictionary of Occult: Hermetic and Alchemical Sigils*. London: Routledge & Kegan Paul.

Goodwin, A. (1993), *Dancing in the Distraction Factory: Music Television and Popular Culture*. Minneapolis: University of Minnesota Press.

Gore, M. E. (1987), *Raising PG Kids in an X-Rated Society*. New York: Abingdon.

Gottdiener, M. (1999a), 'Dead Elvis as other Jesus', in Chadwick (ed.), *In Search of Elvis: Music, Race, Art, Religion*. Boulder: Westview Press.

Gottdiener, M. (1999b), 'Saint Elvis', in E. Doss (ed.), *Elvis Culture: Fans, Faith and Image*. Lawrence, KS: University of Kansas Press.

Grauer, V. A. (2006), 'Echoes of our forgotten ancestors', *The World of Music*, 48, (2).

Gray, A. (2001), *Transfigurations*. Rochester: Inner Traditions.

Gray, J. (1991), *African Music*. London: Greenwood.

Greil, A. L. and Bromley, D. G. (2003), *Defining Religion: Investigating the Boundaries between the Sacred and Secular*. Amsterdam and London: Jai Publishing.

Hallick, M. (2001), *The Story of Icons*. Brookline, MA: Holy Cross.

Hamilton, M. (1998), 'Sexual politics and African-American music; or, placing Little Richard in history', *History Workshop Journal*, 46: 161–76.

Hancock, G. (2006), *Supernatural*. London: Arrow Books.

Harris, J. (1993), 'A shite Sports car and a punk reincarnation', *NME magazine*, April 1993.

Harris, J. (2003), *The Last Party: Britpop, Blair and the Demise of English Rock*. London: Fourth Estate.

Harris, J. (2004), *Britpop!: Cool Britannia and the Spectacular Demise of English Rock*. Cambridge, MA: Da Capo Press.

Harris, K. (2000), 'Roots'?: the relationship between the global and the local within the Extreme Metal scene. *Popular Music*, 19, (1), 13–30.

Harrison, T. (1992), *Elvis People: The Cult of the King*. London: HarperCollins.

Haslam, D. (2000), *Manchester, England: The Story of the Pop Cult City*. London: Fourth Estate.

Hay, F. J. (1987), 'The Sacred/Profane Dialectic in Delta Blues: The Life and Lyrics of Sonny Boy Williamson' *Phylon (1960)*, 48, (4).

Hebdige, D. (1979), *Subculture: The Meaning of Style*. London: Routledge.

Heelas, P. and Woodhead, L. (2001), 'Homeless minds today?', in L. Woodhead, P. Heelas and D. Martin (eds). London: Routledge.

Heelas, P., Woodhead, L., Seel, B., Tusting, K. and Szerszynski, B. (2005), *The Spiritual Revolution: Why Religion Is Giving Way to Spirituality (Religion and Spirituality in the Modern World)*. Oxford: Wiley Blackwell.

Hill, D. (1989), *Prince: A Pop Life*. London: Harmony.

Hook, P. (2009), *The Hacienda: How Not To Run a Club*. New York: Simon and Schuster Ltd.

Horner, B. and Swiss, T. (1999), *Key Terms in Popular Music and Culture*. Oxford: Blackwell.

Huxley, A. (1954), *The Doors of Perception and Heaven and Hell*. London: Harper and Brothers.

Janata, P. and Grafton, S. T. (2003), 'Swinging in the brain: Shared neural substrates for behaviours related to sequencing and music', *Nature Neuroscience*, 6, (7).

Jarman-Ivans, F. (ed.) (2004), *Madonna's Drowned Worlds: New Approaches to Her Cultural Transformations*. Aldershot: Ashgate.

Johnson, F. (2004), 'U2, mythology and mass-mediated survival', *Popular Music and Society*, 27, (1), 79–99.

Khan, H. I. (1996), *The Mysticism of Sound and Music*. Boston, MA: Shambhala Publications.

King, N. (1986), *African Cosmos: An Introduction to Religion in Africa*. Belmont: Wadsworth Publishing.

Kleinman, A. (1988), *Rethinking Psychiatry*. New York and London: Free Press and Collier Macmillan.

Koch, R. (1930), *The Book of Signs*. London: The Limited Editions Club.

Lawrence, D. H. (1931), *Apocalypse*. London: Heinemann.

Lee, M. and Schlain, B. (1985), *Acid Dreams*. New York: Grove Press.

Lefcowitz, E. (1985), rev. 1989), *The Monkees Tale*. San Francisco: Last Gasp.

Leonard, M. (2007), *Gender in the Music Industry*. Aldershot: Ashgate.

Leventhall, G. (2007), 'What is Infrasound?', *Progress in Biophysics and Molecular Biology*, 93, 130–7.

Lewis-Williams, D. and Pearce, D. (2005), *Inside the Neolithic Mind: Consciousness, Cosmos and the Realm of the Gods*. London: Thames and Hudson.

Lewisohn, M. (1988), *The Beatles Recording Sessions*. New York: Harmony Books.

Lloyd, F. (ed.) (1994), *Deconstructing Madonna*. London: Trafalgar Square Publishing.

Lomax, A. (1968), *Folk Song Style and Culture*. Washington, DC: Transaction Publishers.

Longhurst, B. (1995), *Popular Music and Society*. Cambridge: Polity.

Lowenthal, L. (1984), 'The triumph of mass idols', in P. F. Lazarsfeld and F. Stanton (eds), *Radio Research 1942–1943*. (New York, 1944). Repr., *Literature and Mass Culture*. New Brunswick, NJ: Duell, Sloan and Pearce.

Lynch, G. (2002), *After Religion: 'Generation X' and the Search for Meaning*. London: Darton, Longman and Todd Ltd.

Lynch, G. (2005), *Understanding Theology and Popular Culture*. Oxford: Blackwell.

Lynch, G. (2007a), *New Spirituality: An Introduction to Belief Beyond Religion*. London: I. B. Taurus.

Lynch, G. (2007b), *Between Sacred and Profane: Researching Religion and Popular Culture*. London: I. B. Taurus.

Lynch, G. and Badger, E. (2006), 'The mainstream post-rave scene as a secondary institution: A British perspective', *Culture and Religion Journal*, 7, (1), 27–40.

Lyon, D. (2000), *Jesus in Disneyland: Religion in Postmodern Times*. Cambridge: Polity.

Magesa, L. (1997), *African Religion: The Moral Traditions of Abundant Life*. Maryknoll: Orbis Books.

Malbon, B. (1998), *Clubbing: Dancing, Ecstasy and Vitality*. London: Routledge.

Mallay, J. D. and Vaughn, W. (1993), *Elvis: The Messiah?* Chicago: TCB Publishing.

Marrou, H. (1957), *Saint Augustine and His Influence Through The Ages*. New York: Longman.

Marshall, P. D. (1997), *Celebrity and Power: Fame in Contemporary Culture*. Minneapolis: University of Minnesota Press.

Marx, K. (1975), 'Contribution to the Critique of Hegel's Philosophy of Right: Introduction', in *Early Writings*. Harmondsworth: Penguin.

Marx, K. (1977), 'The Communist Manifesto', in David McLellan (ed.), *Karl Marx: Selected Writings*. Oxford: Oxford University Press. Orig. 1848.

Maughon, R. M. (1997), *Elvis Is Alive*. Nashville: Vaughan.

McAvan, E. (2007), *The Postmodern Sacred: Popular Culture Spirituality in the Genres of Science Fiction, Fantasy and Fantastic Horror*, PhD thesis, Murdoch University, USA.

McKenna, T. (1993), *Food of the Gods: The Search for the Original Tree of Knowledge A Radical History of Plants, Drugs, and Human Evolution*. New York: Bantam.

Merker, B. (2000), 'Synchronous chorusing and human origins', in Nils L. Wallin, Bjorn Merker and Steven Brown (eds), *The Origins of Music*. Cambridge, MA: MIT Press.

Mintel International Group (1996), *Nightclubs and Discotheques*. London: Market Intelligence International Group.

Morin, E. (1960), *Les Etoiles*. New York: Grove Press.

Morley, D. and Robbins, K. (2001), *British Cultural Studies*. Oxford: Oxford University Press.

Moynihan, M. and Søderlind, D. (1998), *Lords of Chaos: The Bloody Rise of the Satanic Metal Underground*. Port Townsend, WA: Feral House.

Nettl, B. (2000), 'An ethnomusicologist contemplates musical universals in musical sound and musical culture', in N. L. Wallin, B. Merker and S. Brown (eds), *The Origins of Music*. Cambridge, MA: MIT/Bradford, pp. 462–72.

Ogden, G. (1991), *The New Reformation*. Michigan: Zondervan.

Olaveson, T. (2004), 'Connectedness and the rave experience: Rave as new religious movement', in Graham St. John (ed.), *Rave Culture and Religion*. Abingdon: Routledge.

Oliver, P. (1984), *Blues Off the Record: Thirty Years of Blues Commentary*. New York: Da Capo Press.

Paige, B. S. (1995), *American Monroe: The Making of a Body Politic*. Berkeley: University of California Press.

Palmer, Edwin H. et al. (1973), Deuteronomy, ch. 5, vv. 7–9, New Testament. *The Holy Bible: New International Version*. The New Testament. Grand Rapids: Zondervan. Revised 1978 and 1984.

Partridge, C. (2005), *The Re-enchantment of the West: Alternative Spiritualities, Sacralization, Popular Culture and Occulture*. Poole: T. and T. Clarke.

Plasketes, G. (1997), *Images of Elvis Presley in American Culture, 1977–1997: The Mystery Terrain*. Binghamton, NY: Hayworth Press.

Potter, R. (ed.) (1996), *The Madonna Reader: A Decade of Debate About the Diva*. New York: Continuum.

Raschke, C. (1990), *Painted Black: From Drug Killings to Heavy Metal – The Alarming True Story of How Heavy Metal Is Terrorizing Our Communities*. New York: Harper and Row.

Redfield, J. (1993), *The Celestine Prophecy*. New York: Warner Books.

Reece, G. L. (2006), *Elvis Religion: The Cult of the King*. London: I. B. Tauris.

Reed, T. (2003), *The Holy Profane: Religion in Black Popular Music*. Lexington: University Press of Kentucky.

Rein, Irving. Cotler, P. and Stoller, M. R. (1997), *High Visibility: The Making and Marketing of Professionals into Celebrities*. Chicago, IL: McGraw-Hill.

Reynolds, S. (1998), *Energy Flash: A Journey Through Rave Music and Dance Culture*. London: Picador.

Rietveld, H. (1998), *This Is Our House: House Music, Cultural Spaces and Technologies*. London: Ashgate.

Rietveld, H. (2004), 'Sacrificial cyborg and communal soul', in Graham St. John (ed.), *Rave Culture and Religion*. Abingdon: Routledge.

Ritzer, G. (1993), *The MacDonaldization of Society: An Investigation into the Changing Character of Contemporary Social Life*. Thousand Oaks: Pine Forge Press.

Robinson, J. and Martin, S. (2009), 'Of time and television', *Annals of the American Academy of Political and Social Science*, 625, (1), 74–86.

Robinson, M. G. and Winkle, T. K. (2004), 'The innocents abroad: S Club 7's America', *Popular Music and Society*, 27/3, 291–305.

Rothkopf, D. (1997), 'In praise of cultural imperialism,' *Foreign Affairs*, 107, 38–53.

Rouget, G. (1985), *Music and Trance: A Theory of the Relations Between Music and Possession*. Chicago: University of Chicago Press.

Salewicz, C. (1981), 'Prince: Strutting with the New Soul Monarch', *New Musical Express*, June 1981.

Sanders, B. (2006), 'Young people, clubs and drugs', in B. Sanders (ed.), *Drugs, Clubs and Young People*. Aldershot: Ashgate, pp. 1–12.

Sandoval, A. (2005), *The Monkees: The Day-By-Day Story of the '60s TV Pop Sensation*. San Diego: Thunder Bay Press.

Santana, R. and Erickson, G. (2008), *Religion and Popular Culture: Rescripting the Sacred*. Jefferson, NC: McFarland.

Saunders, N., Saunders, A. and Pauli, M. (2000), *In Search of the Ultimate High: Spiritual Experiences Through Psychoactives*. London: Random House.

Schwichtenberg, C. (ed.) (1993), *The Madonna Connection: Representational Politics, Subcultural Identities, and Cultural Theory*. San Francisco: Westfield.

Scott, R. B. (1993), 'Images of race and religion in Madonna's video "Like a Prayer: Prayer and Praise" ', in C. Schwichtenberg (ed.), *The Madonna Connection: Representational Politics, Subcultural Identities, and Cultural Theory*. San Francisco: Westfield, pp. 57–77.

Scruton, R. (2000), *An Intelligent Person's Guide to Modern Culture*. South Bend, IN: St. Augustine's Press.

Shaar Murry, C. (1989), *Crosstown Traffic: Jimi Hendrix and Post-war Pop*. London: St. Martin's Griffin.

Shapiro, H. (1999), *Waiting for the Man: The Story of Drugs and Popular Music*. London: Helter Skelter.

Sheldrake, R. (1988), *The Presence of the Past: Morphic Resonance and the Habits of Nature*. London: HarperCollins.

Small, C. (1987), *Music of the Common Tongue: Survival and Celebration in African American Music*. New York: Riverrun Press.

St. John, G. (2004), 'The difference engine: Liberation and the rave imaginary', in Graham St. John (ed.), *Rave Culture and Religion*. Abingdon: Routledge, pp. 19–45.

St. John, G. (2009), 'Neotrance and the psychedelic festival', *Dancecult: Journal of Electronic Dance Music Culture*, 1, (1), 35–64.

Stewart, A. (2000), 'Funky drummer: New Orleans, James Brown and the rhythmic transformation of American popular music', *Popular Music*, 19, (3), 293–318.

Sutcliffe, P. (1992), *Q magazine*, London, July 1992.

Swidler, L. and Modjes, P. (2000), *The Study of Religion in an Age of Global Dialogue*. Philadelphia: Temple University Press.

Sylvan, R. (2005), *Trance Formation: The Spiritual and Religious Dimensions of Dimensions of Global Rave Culture*. Abingdon: Routledge.

Thornton, S. (1995), *Club Cultures: Music, Meaning and Subcultural Capital*. Cambridge: Polity Press.

Till, R. (2006), 'The nine o'clock service: Mixing club culture and postmodern Christianity', *Culture and Religion Journal*, 7, (1).

Till, R. (2007), 'The blues blueprint: The blues in the music of the Beatles, the Rolling Stones, and Led Zeppelin', in N. Wynn (ed.), *Cross the Water Blues: African American Music in Europe*. Jackson, MS: University Press of Mississippi, pp. 183–202.

Till, R. (2009), 'Possession trance ritual in electronic dance music culture: A popular ritual technology for reenchantment, addressing the crisis of the homeless self, and reinserting the individual into the community', in *Exploring Religion and the Sacred in a Media Age*, Chris Deacy (Ed.), Ashgate: Aldershot, pp. 169–89.

Toledo, M. (1993), 'Roll Over Lugosi', *The Best of Metal Mania no. 2*, (1987). p. 84. in Robert Walser (1993), *Running with the Devil: Power, Gender and Madness in Heavy Metal Music*. Middletown, CT: Wesleyan.

Tompkins, P., and Bird, C. (1989), *Secret Life of Plants*, New York: Harper.

Tosches, N. (1999), *Unsung Heroes of Rock'n'Roll*, New York: Da Capo.

Tudor, A. (1975), *Image and Influence; Studies in the Sociology of Film*, New York: Allen and Unwin.

Turner, V. (1969), *The Ritual Process: Structure and Anti-Structure*, Chicago: Aldine.

Turow, G. and Berger, J. (Forthcoming), *Musical Time and Human Behavior: Perspectives on Rhythm in Ritual and Healing*.

Vincent, R. (1996), *Funk: The Music, the People, and the Rhythm of the One*. London: St. Martin's Press.

Von Appen, R. and Doehring, A. (2006), 'Nevermind The Beatles, here's Exile 61 and Nico: "The top 100 records of all time" – A canon of pop and rock albums from a sociological and an aesthetic perspective', *Popular Music*, 25, (1).

Vout, C. (1996), 'The myth of the toga: Understanding the history of Roman dress', *Greece & Rome*, 43, (2), 204–20.

Walser, R. (1993), *Running with the Devil: Power, Gender and Madness in Heavy Metal Music*. Middletown, CT: Wesleyan.

Watts, A. (1973), *Tao: The Watercourse Way*. New York: Pantheon.

Weber, M. (1992), *The Protestant Ethic and the Spirit of Capitalism*. London: Routledge. Orig. 1904.

Weinstein, D. (1991), *Heavy Metal: A Cultural Sociology*. New York: Lexington Books.

White, C. (2003), *The Life and Times of Little Richard: The Authorized Biography*. London: Omnibus.

Whiteley, S. (1997), *Women and Popular Music: Sexuality, Identity and Subjectivity*. New York: Routledge.

Wilson, R. A. (1995), *Cosmic Trigger*. Reno: New Falcon.

Wright, R. (2000), 'I'd sell you suicide: Pop music and moral panic in the age of Marilyn Manson', *Popular Music*, 19, (3).

Young, A. (1997), *Woke Me Up This Morning: Black Gospel Singers and the Gospel Life*. Jackson, MS: University of Mississippi Press.

Websites and Online References

All About Madonna. Available from: http://allaboutmadonna.com

Ashworth, J. and Farthing, I. (2007), *Churchgoing in the UK*. Available from: http://www.tearfund.org [Accessed October 2007].

Baitz, D., *Let's Go Crazy Analysis*. Available from: http://www.danabaitz.com/groove.php?s=2&t=l [Accessed 20 July 2007].

BBC, 'Eco-employee wins bid to appeal', 3 November 2009. Available from: http://news.bbc.co.uk/1/hi/england/oxfordshire/8339652.stm

BBC, Scots 'bucking funeral pop trend', Thursday, 16 April 2009. Available from http://news.bbc.co.uk/1/hi/8000652.stm [Accessed 5 January 2010].

Boom Festival, *Boom Festival 2006 Website*. Available from: http://www.boomfestival.org/afterboom06/index.html/ [Accessed 10 July 2007].

Budzynski, T. (2006), 'The clinical guide to sound and light', *Brainwave Entrainment to External Rhythmic Stimuli: Interdisciplinary Research and Clinical Perspectives*. Stanford: Stanford University's Centre for Computer Research in Music and Acoustics. Available from: http://www.stanford.edu/group/brainwaves/2006/theclinicalguidetosoundandlight.pdf [Accessed 10 April 2009].

Church of England (1978), *Alternative Services, Series One: The Form of Solemnization of Matrimony*. Available from: http://www.cofe.anglican.org/worship/liturgy/1928/texts/marriage.html [Accessed 7 December 2008].

De Chant, D. (2009), 'The economy as religion: The dynamics of consumer culture', in *The Civic Arts Review*, 16, (2). Available from: http://car.owu.edu/pdfs/2003-16-2.pdf [Accessed 9 June 2009].

Di Paolo, E. (1999), 'Chapter 9: Rhythm, entrainment and congruence in acoustically coupled agents', *On the Evolutionary and Behavioral Dynamics of Social Coordination: Models and Theoretical Aspects*, PhD thesis, School of Cognitive and Computing Sciences, University of Sussex. Available from; http://www.informatics.sussex.ac.uk/users/ezequiel/thesis/ch9.ps [Accessed 10 April 2009].

Horner, D. (2008). Heavy Metal Band Names. Available from www.comics-vsaudience.com [Accessed 20 January 2009].

Elvis-Themed Wedding in Las Vegas. Available from: http://www.youtube.com/watch?v=lKKMf_jfY0U [Accessed 18 November 2009].

Gabrielle Roth. Available from: http://www.gabrielleroth.com/

Gorillaz, http://www.gorillaz-unofficial.com/biography/realpeople.htm [Accessed 20 November 2009) provides a list of featured musicians.

Graceland Website. Available from: http://www.elvis.com/graceland/guardian. co.uk. *Karen McVeigh Judge Rules Activist's Beliefs on Climate Change Akin to Religion*, 3 November 2009. Available from: http://www.guardian. co.uk/environment/2009/nov/03/tim-nicholson-climate-change-belief

Hough, A., *Vicar Attacks 'Princess Diana Funeral Culture' for Pop Songs at Funerals*, 29 October 2009. Available from: Telegraph.co.uk

Jack Doyle, Madonna's Pepsi Ad, 1989. Available from: PopHistoryDig.com. Or go to http://www.pophistorydig.com/?tag—madonna-pepsi-controversy. [Accessed 25 April 2008].

John Mark, *James Fowler's Stages of Faith in Profile*. Available from: http:// jmm.aaa.net.au/articles/2219.htm [Accessed 11 November 2009].

Jewls Wingfield. Available from: http://www.heart-tantra.com

Lester, P. (2003), *Blur: Think Tank*. Available from: http://www.rocksback-pages.com/article.html?ArticleID=6096. [10 October 2009].

Letters to Elvis. Available from: http://www.letterstoelvis.com/

National Toxicology Programme, The National Institute of Environmental Health Sciences, U.S. Department of Health and Human Services (2001). *Infrasound: Brief Review of Toxicological Literature* (November 2001). Available from: http://ntp.niehs.nih.gov/ntp/htdocs/Chem_Background/ ExSumPdf/Infrasound.pdf [Accessed 15 April 2009].

Nicholas, S., Kershaw, C. and Walker, A. (eds) (2007), *Crime in England and Wales 2006/2007*. Available from: http://www.homeoffice.gov.uk/rds/ crimeew0607.html [Accessed 26 October 2007].

Obsession, *Obsession Website*. Available from: http://www.obsession.org.uk/ history/freedom.htm [Accessed 9 August 2007].

O'Hagan, S. (2004), 'Royal Blush', *The Observer*, 4 April 2004. Available from: http://www.guardian.co.uk/arts/features/story/0,11710,1186112,00. html [Accessed 8 January 2008).

Prince.Org. Available from: http://www.Prince.org

Purcell, A., 'The good the bad and the queen'. The Gorillaz/2006/Andrew Purcell/The Independent/Gorillaz/17/11/2009 08:19:57/http://www.rocks-backpages.com/article.html?ArticleID=10816

Reynolds, S. (2001), *Disco Double Take, New York Parties Like Its 1975*. Available from: http://www.villagevoice.com/news/0128,reynolds,26281,1. html [Accessed 2 August 2007].

Sanders, C. (2009), *The True Story of the Cocaine Blues: The History of Cocaine in American Folk and Blues Music*. Available from: http://tradi-tional-folk-music.suite101.com/article.cfm/the_true_story_of_the_cocaine_ blues#ixzz0VmeS0eLI

Sauvage, G. (1911), 'Mysticism', *The Catholic Encyclopedia*. Available from: http://www.newadvent.org/cathen/10663b.htm [Accessed 7 August 2009].

Sutton, D. (2003), 'King of kings', *Fortean Times*, February 2003. Available from: http://www.elvisinfonet.com/spotlight_religion_2008.html [Accessed 3 November 2009].

Synergy Project, *Mission Statement*. Available from: http://www.thesynergy-project.org/content/view/41/105/ [Accessed 2 March 2009].

The Elvis is Alive Museum. Available from: http://www.theelvisisalivemuseum.com/ [Accessed 18 November 2009].

The Synergy Project, *Mission Statement*. Available from: http://www.thesyner-gyproject.org/content/view/41/105/ [Accessed 2 March 2009].

The Truth About Elvis. Available from: http://www.truthaboutelvis.com

Thorne, J., 'Interview with Jamie Hewlett, co-creator of Gorillaz', *The Sound of Young America*, 9 January 2007. Available from http://www.maximumfun.org/jamiehewlett.htm (24 March 2007).

Turow, G. (2005), *Auditory Driving as a Ritual Technology: A Review and Analysis*, Religious Studies Honours Thesis, Stanford University, 20 May 2005. Available from: http://www.stanford.edu/group/brainwaves/2006/AuditoryDrivingRitualTech.pdf [Accessed 18 December 2008].

Williams, S., *dircon*. Available from: http://www.users.dircon.co.uk/~matrix/que/que_club.html/ [Accessed 9 August 2007].

Zoso – Jimmy Page's Symbol from the Led Zeppelin IV album, 17 September 2009. Available from: http://www.inthelight.co.nz/ledzep/zososymbol.htm [Accessed 4 2009].

Discography

'1999', Prince.
'A Day in the Life', The Beatles.
'Acquiesce', Oasis.
'Ain't Got Nobody to Grind My Coffee', Clara Smith.
'All You Need is Love', The Beatles.
'American Pie', Don McLean.
'Anarchy in the UK', The Sex Pistols.
'Are You Lonesome Tonight', Elvis Presley.
'Bodies', Robbie Williams.
'Brown Sugar', The Rolling Stones.
'Cigarettes and Alcohol', Oasis.
'Come and Get it', Whitesnake.
'Come Together', The Beatles.
'Common People', Pulp.
'Crossroads Blues', Robert Johnson.
'Crosstown Traffic', The Jimi Hendrix Experience.
'Dancing Girls', Whitesnake.
'Dancing in the Streets', David Bowie and Mick Jagger.
'Darling Nikki', Prince and the Revolution, *Purple Rain*.
'Day Tripper', The Beatles.
'Dedicated Follower of Fashion', The Kinks.
'Die Young, Stay Pretty', Blondie.
'Disco 2000', Pulp.
'Do They Know It's Christmas', Band Aid.
'Don't Fear the Reaper', Blue Öyster Cult.
'Don't Look Back in Anger', Oasis.
'Everybody Needs Somebody To Love', Solomon Burke.
'Fake Tales of San Francisco', The Arctic Monkeys.
'Fire', The Jimi Hendrix Experience, *Are You Experienced?*
'Get it On', T. Rex.
'Girls, Girls, Girls', Mötley Crüe.
'God Is a DJ', Faithless.
'God Is a DJ', Pink.

'God Save the Queen', The Sex Pistols.
'Good Rockin' Tonight', Wynonie Harris.
'Guns of Brixton', The Clash.
'Hanky Panky', Madonna.
'Heaven Knows I'm Miserable Now', The Smiths.
'Hellhound on My Trail', Robert Johnson.
'Hello', Oasis.
'Hello, Hello, I'm Back Again', Gary Glitter.
'Help!', The Beatles.
'Heroin', Velvet Underground.
'Hersham Boys', Sham 69.
'Hey Baby', Bruce Chanel.
'Honky Tonk Woman', The Rolling Stones.
'How Soon is Now', The Smiths.
'How Sweet to Be an Idiot', Neil Innes.
'Hurry Up Harry', Sham 69.
'I Feel Fine', The Beatles.
'I Feel Love', Donna Summer.
'I Feel Love', Donna Summer and Giorgio Moroder.
'I Only Want To Be With You', Dusty Springfield.
'I Saw Her Standing There', The Beatles.
'I'd Like to Teach the World to Sing', The New Seekers.
'I'll Take You There', The Staples Singers.
'I'm So Bored With the USA', The Clash.
'Imagine', John Lennon.
'Kitchen Man', Bessie Smith.
'Last Train to Clarkesville', The Monkees.
'Lazy Sunday Afternoon', The Kinks.
'Let's Go Crazy', Prince and the Revolution, *Purple Rain*.
'Like a Virgin', Madonna.
'Live Forever', Oasis.
'London Calling', The Clash.
'London Lady', The Stranglers.
'London's Burning', The Clash.
'Loose Fit', Happy Mondays.
'Louis, Louis', The Kingsmen.
'Love Me Do', The Beatles.
'Love to Love You Baby', Donna Summer.
'Lucy in the Sky With Diamonds', The Beatles.
'Lyla', Oasis.
'Manteca', Dizzy Gillespie.
'Me and He Devil Blues', Robert Johnson.
'Morning Glory', Oasis.
'Mr. Clean', The Jam.

'Mr Soft', Cockney Rebel.
'My Generation', The Who.
'My Way', Frank Sinatra.
'My Way', The Sex Pistols.
'Parklife', Blur.
'Penny Lane', The Beatles.
'Pig Meat Papa', Lead Belly.
'Pinball Wizard', The Who.
'Proud Mary', Creedence Clearwater Revival.
'Purple Haze', The Jimi Hendrix Experience, *Are You Experienced?*
'Ready an' Willing', Whitesnake.
'Rock Around the Clock', Bill Haley and the Comets.
'Rock'n'roll Star', Oasis.
'Rosalie', Thin Lizzy.
'Sex and Drugs and Rock and Roll', Ian Dury and the Blockheads.
'Shake, Rattle and Roll', Big Joe Turner.
'Shakermaker', Oasis.
'Shakespeare's Sister', The Smiths.
'Shave 'Em Dry', Lucille Bogan.
'She Loves You', The Beatles.
'She Sells Sanctuary', The Cult.
'Slide It In', Whitesnake.
'Slow an' Easy', Whitesnake.
'Slow Poke Music', Whitesnake.
'Soft and Wet', Prince with Chris Moon, *For You.*
'Some Might Say', Oasis.
'Something Else', Eddie Cochran.
'Something Else', The Sex Pistols.
'Sorted for Es and Whizz', Pulp.
'Spit It Out', Whitesnake.
'Stairway to Heaven', Led Zeppelin.
'Stand by Me', Ben E. King.
'Stop Out', Oasis.
'Strawberry Fields', The Beatles.
'Street Fighting Man', The Rolling Stones.
'Sugar Sugar', The Archies.
'Suicide Solution', Ozzy Osbourne.
'Tainted Love', Gloria Jones.
'Tainted Love', Soft Cell.
'That Black Snake Moan', Blind Lemon Jefferson.
'The One I Love', REM.
'There's No Other Way', Blur.
'Things Can Only Get Better', D:Ream.
'Tutti Frutti', Little Richard.

'Twist And Shout', The Beatles.
'Two Pints of Lager and a Packet of Crisps Please', Splodgenessabounds.
'Uptight', Stevie Wonder.
'Video Killed the Radio Star', The Buggles.
'Waiting for the Man', Velvet Underground.
'Watch Your Step', Bobby Parker.
'Waterloo Sunset', The Kinks.
'We are the World', USA for Africa.
'What Difference Does it Make', The Smiths.
'What'd I Say', Ray Charles.
'Whatever', Oasis.
'Whip in My Valise', Adam and the Ants.
'Wine, Women and Song', Whitesnake.
'With a Little Help From My Friends', The Beatles.
'You Can't Catch Me', Chuck Berry.

Albums

Abbey Road, The Beatles.
Deep Trance and Ritual Beats, Return to the Source.
Definitely Maybe, Oasis.
Demon Days, Gorillaz.
Different Class, Pulp.
Kaya, Bob Marley.
Let It Be, The Beatles.
Like a Prayer, Madonna.
Madchester EP, Happy Mondays.
Never Mind the Bollocks, The Sex Pistols.
Nevermind, Nirvana.
Parklife, Blur.
Praise God I'm Satisfied, Blind Willie Johnson.
Purple Rain, Prince and the Revolution.
Quadrophenia, The Who.
Rock'n'Roll, John Lennon.
Sticky Fingers, The Rolling Stones.
The Kinks are The Village Green Preservation Society, The Kinks.
This is Hardcore, Pulp.

Films, Television, DVDs and Videos

Benedek, L. (dir.) (1953), *The Wild One*.
Browne, C. (dir.) (2001), *Charts of Darkness*.
Cliton, P. and Massot, J. (dirs.) (1976), *The Song Remains the Same*.
Dunning, G. (dir.) (1968), *Yellow Submarine*.
Frawley, J. (dir.), (1966–1968), *The Monkees*.
Gallagher, Noel (2008), gonzo, mtv 2 london.
Hamri, S. (dir.) (2003), *Prince – Live at the Aladdin Las Vegas*.
Hughes, K. (dir.) (1968), *Chitty Chitty Bang Bang*.
Keshishian, A. (dir.) (1991), *In Bed with Madonna*.
Kubrick, S. (1968), *2001: A Space Odyssey*.
Kubrick, S. (1971), *A Clockwork Orange*.
Lambert, M. (dir.) (1989), *Like a Prayer*.
Landis, J. (dir.) (1980), *The Blues Brothers*.
Lester, Richard, (dir.) (1964), *A Hard Day's Night*.
Lester, Richard, (dir.) (1964), *Help!*
Levy, C. (dir.) (2008), *Bananaz*.
Magnoli, A. (dir.) (1984), *Purple Rain*.
Pennebaker, D. A. (dir.) (2002), *Ziggy Stardust and the Spiders from Mars: The Motion Picture*.
Ray, N. (dir.) (1955), *Rebel Without a Cause*.
The Smiths (1987), *Stop Me If You Think You've Heard This One Before*.
U2 interview, *The Culture Show*, BBC Television, Tuesday 24 February 2009
Walker, C. (prod.) (2004), shown 14 March 2004, 'John Lennon's Jukebox' on *The South Bank Show* (documentary) by Initial, Endemol UK, for ITV television, UK.
Winkler, D. (dir.) (1998), *Finding Graceland*.

Index